Dear Reader:

The book you are about to re
St. Martin's True Crime Lib
Times calls "the leader in true c...... Each month, we offer you
a fascinating account of the latest, most sensational crime that
has captured the national attention. St. Martin's is the publisher
of bestselling true crime author and crime journalist Kieran
Crowley, who explores the dark, deadly links between a promi-
nent Manhattan surgeon and the disappearance of his wife fifteen years earlier in THE SURGEON'S WIFE. Suzy Spencer's
BREAKING POINT guides readers through the tortuous twists
and turns in the case of Andrea Yates, the Houston mother who
drowned her five young children in the family's bathtub. In Ed-
gar Award-nominated DARK DREAMS, legendary FBI profiler
Roy Hazelwood and bestselling crime author Stephen G. Michaud
shine light on the inner workings of America's most violent and
depraved murderers. In the book you now hold, SIGNED IN BLOOD,
Jeanne King looks at an unusual case involving two older women
and a plot involving murder.

St. Martin's True Crime Library gives you the stories behind the
headlines. Our authors take you right to the scene of the crime
and into the minds of the most notorious murderers to show you
what really makes them tick. St. Martin's True Crime Library
paperbacks are better than the most terrifying thriller, because
it's all true! The next time you want a crackling good read, make
sure it's got the St. Martin's True Crime Library logo on the
spine—you'll be up all night!

Charles E. Spicer

Charles E. Spicer, Jr.
Executive Editor, St. Martin's True Crime Library

Titles by

JEANNE KING

Never Seen Again

Signed in Blood

from the True Crime Library of St. Martin's Paperbacks

Signed in Blood

The True Story of Two Women,

a Sinister Plot, and Cold-Blooded Murder

Jeanne King

St. Martin's Paperbacks

SIGNED IN BLOOD

Copyright © 2009 by Jeanne King.

For information address St. Martin's Press, 175 Fifth Avenue, New York, NY 10010.

ISBN: 0-312-94900-6
EAN: 978-0-312-94900-6

Printed in the United States of America

St. Martin's Paperbacks edition / July 2009

St. Martin's Paperbacks are published by St. Martin's Press, 175 Fifth Avenue, New York, NY 10010.

10 9 8 7 6 5 4 3 2 1

*For Chris, who is always there with
wise suggestions.*

Acknowledgments

First and foremost, I would like to thank the two detectives, Lee Willmon and Nelson Hernandez, who compared notes about their current and old cases and put the dots together. The case was going nowhere until these two detectives got a phone call from Ed Webster, a MONY insurance investigator who had uncovered a bizarre insurance scheme. From this point on, the case took on a life of its own.

I am also deeply indebted to lead detective Dennis Kilcoyne, who with detective Rosemary Sanchez put together a fantastic investigative team that included special FBI agent Samuel Mayrose and Robert Brockway of the California Department of Insurance.

I am forever grateful to deputy district attorney Shellie Samuels for outlining the case for me and to lead prosecutor Truc Do and Bobby Grace for sharing their thoughts about the case.

A special heartfelt thanks goes to Sandee Gibbons, the spokeswoman for the Los Angeles District Attorney's office, and to her dedicated public information staff, including Jane Robinson for assisting me whenever I needed help. And a really big thanks to Patricia Kelly and her boss, Allen Parachini in the clerk's office, for even checking out the buzzer systems for jurors.

Kudos also go to Superior Court Judge David Wesley

and his clerk, Gloria Armenta, for smoothing out the legalities during the trial.

I want to thank Sandra Salman, the sister of Kenneth McDavid and to Stella Vados, the daughter of Paul Vados, for sharing their heartwarming stories about their loved ones. And to Los Angeles lawyer Gloria Allred for assisting these families.

Thanks are extended to Charles Suhayda, the pastor of the Hollywood Presbyterian Church, who feeds the homeless and assists them with their everyday living.

I would like to thank Michael Sklar, the deputy public defender and Roger Jon Diamond, the lawyers for Helen Golay and Olga Rutterschmidt, for their assistance in filling in the details of their lives together. Thanks also to Dr. Vernon Golay for spending time with me in sharing his memories of Helen Golay.

A special thank you to Linda Deutsch of the Associated Press, my buddy and friend for many years. It was fun seeing and working alongside you on the Granny case. Thank you to my friend, Yvonne Adler, for joining me in locating Helen and Olga's homes. And to Steve Somerstein whose love of the law always provided me with 24/7 legal explanations whenever I called with a question.

I also owe a deep debt of gratitude and thanks to my friend of many years, Lilly Lawrence, for putting me up in her home while researching the book, and to Sue Pollock who put me on to this incredible story.

This book would never have been done were it not for the inspiring assistance and enthusiasm of Charles Spicer, Executive Editor of the St. Martin's True Crime Library, and my editor, Yaniv Soha, for his support, confidence and involvement for the book.

And finally, a huge thanks to my agent, Jane Dystel of Dystel & Goderich Literary Management, who is absolutely incredible as she watched over the project 24/7. You are truly amazing. Thank you. Thank you. Thank you.

Chapter 1

"Bingo! We Hit Pay Dirt!"

Tuesday, June 21, 2005. The summer solstice. June 21 marks the longest day of the year and is officially the first day of summer in the Northern Hemisphere. For most people, the day represents the occasion when the bountiful harvest yields its abundant fruit. This day, in 2005, was also that of June's full moon, sometimes called the Honey Moon, because it's the best time to gather honey from hives.

That night in 2005 started out beautifully with the bright full moon lighting up the city of Los Angeles, California, shining overhead on the well-known HOLLYWOOD sign as the solstice officially made its debut just fourteen minutes before midnight. It was a warm, pleasant evening with the night temperature hovering in the sixties, and patchy low clouds and fog near the Pacific coastline.

But for Detective Nelson Hernandez of the West Traffic Division of the Wilshire police precinct in Los Angeles, who was assigned to investigate traffic accidents, Tuesday, June 21, 2005, was just another night. It was his turn to be on call in the 24/7 business of being a cop.

Nelson was at home, some forty miles from the station when the phone rang in his bedroom, awakening him. It was around one in the morning.

"We have what appears to be a hit-and-run accident. We don't have a license plate of the hit-and-run vehicle. But we have a dead body in the alley, and it appears that a car ran over this person," said the matter-of-fact voice of the dispatcher on the other end of the phone.

As he got dressed, Hernandez called to tell his partner, Officer Brent Johnson, to meet him at the Wilshire police precinct on Venice and La Brea. Just before leaving home, he placed another call to speak with the watch commander to see if there was any update on the incident. There being none, Hernandez proceeded to the station house.

The 51-year-old Hernandez had wanted to be a pilot as a young boy, but he'd chosen instead to become a uniformed officer nearly a quarter of a century ago when he'd joined the Los Angeles Police Department, working his way up the ranks, first as a sergeant and now as a detective.

With hundreds of arrests under his belt, Hernandez was the kind of cop who, if something didn't look right, had to delve further. As he was driving to his office, Hernandez learned that he had his work cut out for him: There were no witnesses and no license plate numbers for him to check out. He didn't know what else to expect as he headed to the scene in an unmarked detectives' vehicle.

"This being Hollywood, we've been involved with many movie star cases concerning traffic accidents. They run the gamut from A to Z, so I was prepared for anything," he recalled.

Hernandez made the eight-mile trip from the station house to the approach of the alleyway off of Ohio Avenue and Westwood Boulevard behind Bristol Farms, the upscale gourmet emporium, in twelve minutes.

The Westwood area, in the western section of Los Angeles, is best known as the site of the University of California (UCLA). The district is often referred to as Westwood Village because of its cozy small-town atmosphere. It is also home to the Westwood Village Memorial Park cemetery, the final resting place of many of Hollywood's biggest stars. Nearby, located on Santa Monica Boulevard, is the Los Angeles California Temple, the second-largest temple operated by the Church of Latter-day Saints. Major thoroughfares such as Santa Monica and Wilshire Boulevards and the San Diego Freeway (I-405) service the Westwood area.

A little more than a quarter of a mile from the center of the affluent and bustling Westwood Village, an innocent bystander, Karen Toshima, a 27-year-old graphic artist, was murdered on January 30, 1988, during a gun battle between rival gangs. It took more than a decade for the perception that the area was riddled with crime to fade. Today, Westwood is again regarded as one of the safest neighborhoods in the city. Or it was, until now.

"One of the first things I observed as I approached the area was that the scene didn't appear to make any sense. We had this guy dead in the alley, and it was dark. There was a bicycle laying there near the victim with the wheels up to the side of the man's body from the edge of the alley. One of the tires had been removed and was on the side of the bike.

"On the surface, it appeared that maybe the victim had been working on the flat tire. That maybe he was riding the bike when he got a flat tire, took the tire off, and was about to repair the tire, when this happened—and he was run over."

One of the first things Hernandez checked was the tire that had been removed, and it was not flat.

"That was another thing that didn't make any sense. Why would the victim take the tire off if it wasn't flat? The other thing that didn't make sense was that if he was going to repair a flat tire, you are not going to do it in the dark alley when, if he went just a few feet away to the front of the grocery store, he would have had the use of the street lights."

Hernandez took a closer look at the guy in the alley. He didn't look like he had been living on the dark side of Los Angeles, on skid row, domain of thousands of homeless. "Those that hang out in the alleys for the most part are transients—they're homeless—but this guy was clean. I'm talking about, other than grease from the undercarriage of the car, he appeared to have clean clothes. His socks were clean, his shoes were clean, and his hands were clean. The part of his pants that didn't have grease from the under-carriage were clean. Transients' hair usually hasn't been washed for months, but this guy's hair didn't appear dirty.

"Here was a clean-looking guy, but he was in the alley, the victim of a hit-and-run."

Hernandez suspected the victim wasn't homeless—the profile didn't fit. Besides, the detective theorized, if the guy had been riding his bike for the exercise—and a lot of people do that in Los Angeles—why would he be doing it in the alley? "So that didn't jibe either."

When the coroner got to the scene, he went through the man's pockets. Other than a California ID, with his name, address, and picture, and a credit card, there was nothing else on him.

"The victim's name was Kenneth McDavid, and I can't remember whether he had a Visa or MasterCard. But he had no money, no coins, no wallet, and no piece of paper. It was as if someone had just planted those two ID docu-ments on this guy, and wanted him to be identified, so we would know who he was.

"We knew the scene didn't look right, that something was wrong, but we couldn't get a handle on it. This guy is clean, but he's in the alley. This guy appears to be working on this bike, but the tires aren't flat. And if you have a flat tire, you're not going to be fixing it in the dark. You are go-ing to be working on it in the main street where there is light. So there was just a series of things that just didn't add up, and made the situation suspicious."

To compound this scenario, Hernandez now had the job of making the notification of death to McDavid's next of kin. "My partner and I followed the coroner to the 1843 North Cherokee Avenue address we had found on his ID card to see if he had any family.

"When we pulled up to the four-story beige building, it was rather nondescript. The building was probably built in the 'twenties and had never been restored. It had obviously sustained some serious damage from earlier earthquakes, because of the many visible plugs that could be seen on the outside throughout the building that was used to reinforce the damaged brick."

As he walked into the Palm Court Apartments, Hernandez noticed that the landlord had spruced up the place by adding a water fountain, and planting some palm trees and yellow daffodils to give the building some charm.

"We knocked on the door of resident manager Danielli Cosgrove and asked whether there was an individual in the building by the name of Kenneth McDavid," Hernandez said.

"Yeah, I know who you are talking about. He lived upstairs in apartment four-ten," she replied.

According to her, McDavid had appeared to be homeless. "The apartment was rented for him on September first, 2002, by a Helen Golay," she said.

"This lady appeared to be well-to-do. She didn't seem to be the same type of person that he was, not in the same economic class as him, you know what I mean?"

Cosgrove described the unit Helen was renting for McDavid as a 550-square-foot studio apartment. Aside from the living area, there were no separate bedrooms, although there was a kitchen and bathroom facility. Initially the apartment had rented for $875 a month, but that was later raised to $900, and rent was paid monthly, on time, by Helen, who mailed the check to the building owner.

"But then, in November or December 2004, Kenny apparently had a problem in that he began to bring other people into the apartment, and that's the first time I actually met up with Olga." She said she did not know Olga's last name, as Cosgrove had never been formally introduced to her by Helen.

Cosgrove went on to tell the detective and coroner a bizarre story about McDavid. "The only issue was, as I started to tell you . . . that at some point Kenny started bringing these friends to the apartment. There were several people living there, and I don't know their names. I only knew one person's name was Patrick. There were probably, at some point, maybe five individuals were living in this studio apartment.

"It was around that time that I saw some people coming and going. I didn't go into the apartment until Olga came by one day and said to me that I need to get rid of them. That was around November or December of 2004. I believe Olga came to me first, because Olga always spoke for Helen.

"And she said to me, 'You need to get rid of those people.'

"Olga was very aggressive with me, just like, *You need to do this. You need to get rid of them. You need to call the police. You need to do something.*

"And I said, 'Well, there is nothing I can do.'

"I told Olga that it was not in my power, unless—I would have to evict Helen to get them out, because they were her subtenants.

"Olga just went ballistic. She demanded that I get them out of the apartment, and I said, 'I'm not the police. I'm not, you know . . . I can't get them out. Try the police.' So I believe she called the police. The police came to me, and it became a back-and-forth thing.

"And I said to Olga, 'Well, the only solution I have is to evict Helen. And I don't think you want that.'"

In the beginning, Cosgrove said, she'd dealt with the eviction problem only with Olga, but then Helen got involved. Eventually, the two women kicked out McDavid's friends, and they changed the locks to the apartment.

It didn't make any sense to Hernandez. "Why would this lady, who didn't live in the apartment and who didn't seem to be in the same economic class as McDavid, why would she allow him to stay in her apartment?"

What was really bizarre was, why would this lady pay McDavid's rent for nearly two years, and then throw him out?

Cosgrove said that the last time she'd seen McDavid was in December 2004 at a fast-food place, a Jack in the Box on Cahuenga and Sunset, less than a mile from the apartment.

"He wasn't riding a bike, but was using a bike as a carrier for his homeless stuff," she said.

As Hernandez left the Cherokee address, he had to admit that he still didn't know what he had.

"After we talked to the house manager, that same day we went back to the scene where we found the body, and waited until daybreak . . . before we started knocking on doors and canvassing the area for witnesses," he recalled.

"We started by talking to the businesses around the alley. There's a Ross discount dress shop and a Bristol Farms convenience store on Westwood Boulevard. In the alleyway, behind these stores, we had found a security camera at one of the businesses. The problem was that they had not adjusted the lenses of their camera, so what we saw was out of focus and we couldn't see very much. The photos were too dark to distinguish anything clearly. It shows the alley in the southbound direction. But we could make out the lights of cars going through.

"We backed up the videotape from the security camera to the time when this accident had occurred and we could see taillights of a vehicle that goes right through the alley. So we knew that that particular car was not involved in the accident.

"All we could see is two red lights, the taillights of a car. But then we see another pair of lights a few minutes later, going southbound down the alley, and you could see the brake lights come on as the lights get brighter, and then the car lights go off.

"There is a counter on the security camera so you can see the time that is elapsing. Five minutes go by with the lights out on the car. After five minutes, the lights came back on again and the car disappears."

It was at that point that Hernandez realized that something had happened with that car.

"I couldn't see it because it was dark. The whole picture is dark except for those taillights. To my mind, that didn't make any sense. Why would this car drive down an alley and stop for almost five minutes?"

The detective said it was interesting to see what the next pair of taillights did as it went down the alley. "They stopped midway, you could see the brake lights come on, and then you can see the reverse lights come on when you put the car in reverse, and you can see this particular car going back north on the alley—in other words, backing up. The next set of lights after that that came down the alley was the ambulance."

Even though the detective and his team couldn't actually see what was going on, they were able to figure out what the vehicular traffic was doing.

Hernandez was confident that when the first car had gone by in the alley, there was no obstruction, because there was nothing there—there was no body. When the second car went by, the detective was sure that "Something happened. That car stopped for five minutes. Why? Yet when the third car came by, something blocked the roadway in the alley, because that car did not, or could not go through. Obviously because there was a guy apparently lying in the middle of the alley. That driver wasn't going to run him over, so he put the car in reverse and backed up his car to the street and took another route in a different direction. The third vehicle to come down the alley was when the paramedics arrived.

"That means that the second car that stopped for five minutes is the killing machine, the murder weapon. It's the car that ran over Kenneth McDavid," Hernandez explained. "And if you were to accidentally run over someone, there's no reason for you to turn the lights off. Any way I looked at it, there were more questions than answers to solving the case of who killed McDavid."

Hernandez and Brent Johnson spent the next several weeks investigating the case. McDavid's body was taken to the coroner's office, where an autopsy was conducted. A few days later, a woman named Helen Golay showed up at the coroner's office, claimed she was a relative, identified the body, and had it cremated.

Meanwhile, it was futile attempting to locate the mysterious Olga without a last name, but the detective did try to find any relatives of McDavid by consulting and checking missing persons files and other state records.

The case remained inactive for almost three months because Hernandez and the others on his team were still thinking McDavid's death was the result of a hit-and-run traffic accident—until mid-September when Hernandez got a phone call from Ed Webster, an investigator with MONY (Mutual of New York) Life Insurance.

"I just want you to know that there are a couple of ladies in your jurisdiction that took out some insurance on a Kenneth McDavid that adds up to a million dollars or more," Webster informed him.

That news was like a jolt of strong black coffee.

By Monday morning, the two men were busy talking and exchanging notes for the first time. Hernandez realized, as he later put it, that "something really doesn't add up. The kind of policy that these women took out on McDavid's life indicated he was, like, the brains of a business, and that if he had died, the whole business would have collapsed. It's called *keyman insurance*. It's when a business takes out insurance to compensate that business for financial losses that would result from the death or extended incapacity of that person of the business."

In a nutshell, a keyman can be anyone associated with that business whose loss can cause financial strain.

Webster had already run a background check, he said, and learned that at some point in his life, McDavid had been a custodian or janitor at Universal Studios. So he didn't appear to be the brains of any operation.

Webster shared with Hernandez a mother lode of other investigatory information, including addresses and telephone numbers of both Helen Golay and Olga Rutterschmidt, the women named on the policies.

After talking with Webster, Hernandez went back to his desk and began poring over the new information. "[Detective] Lee Willmon sits in front of me in the office, and I was just talking out loud to myself and he's listening to me rambling on about the McDavid case I had caught that was frustrating me."

Willmon had wanted to be a Coast Guard officer, but because he was planning to get married, instead took the test and became a police officer twenty years ago. At 45, he had worked as a detective for the last ten years, investigating "important people around Tinsel Town—you know, actors, actresses, and those in the political arena." Ever the gentleman, he declined outing those he has arrested. "Be assured, you know the names. This town is juicy even on a dull day," he said with a smile.

Both detectives like talking about their cases, and Hernandez started to unload to Willmon about the McDavid hit-and-run. "You know, Lee, this just doesn't make any sense. There has got to be more than this. I'm going over everything I observed and noted during the preliminary investigation at the scene."

As Hernandez spoke, Willmon thought back to a case he'd had in 1999—that of Paul Vados—"because I got soaking wet investigating the case, and his death didn't make sense to me," Willmon said.

It wasn't until Hernandez started talking about his case that Willmon learned about McDavid's life insurance policy.

"And Lee just looked at me with a puzzled look on his face as I rambled on and on. I'm talking about the incident, and the name Olga, and Helen, and now I've got this insurance policy guy calling me, and I find out about these women in their seventies who are taking out insurance policies on this man. And I came to the conclusion, 'This is not a traffic accident.' A pattern began to emerge. 'This looks like a homicide.'"

"Boy," Willmon interrupted Hernandez, "you know, I had something like that a few years ago, something similar. Wait a minute. I have these two old ladies . . .

"It was a guy in the alley, and there were a couple of old ladies who had insurance policies on this old guy that appeared to be homeless . . ."

And with that, Willmon got up from behind his desk and went over to the unsolved case files and grabbed the Murder Book, a thick black binder, and began flipping through it, and just put two and two together and that was it.

"What was the name of the old lady who took out the insurance policy in your case?" Willmon asked.

"Well, the only name I have is *Olga*," Hernandez replied.

"That's the same as in my case," Willmon said.

"What was the name of the other one?" Hernandez asked.

"Helen," Willmon shot back, referring to Helen Golay.

"Same as my case."

"And then Lee adds for good measure . . . 'and her phone number in Santa Monica is . . .' and rattles off the numbers for not only Helen, but for Olga Rutterschmidt in Hollywood."

"Why, those are the same phone numbers I've got for my two old ladies!" an exuberant Hernandez blurted out.

The two detectives looked at each other and at the same time, shouted, "Bingo! We hit pay dirt!"

"What time of day was your accident? What year?" Hernandez queried Willmon.

"Finally, the dots began to come together," Hernandez said.

Like the Kenneth McDavid case, the case of Paul Vados also didn't initially add up for him. "I got the call on November eighth, 1999, that there was a dead body in the alley west of La Brea Boulevard and south of Oakwood Street in Hollywood," recalls Willmon. "It was four-fifty in the morning. The local weather forecasters had predicted it would be a nice sunny day, but it rained. In fact, I never got so wet in my life. The weather kind of stuck in my mind for all these years."

Willmon found Vados lying perpendicular in an east–west position right in the middle of the alley, which runs north and south. Vados had grease on his hands and he didn't look like a transient. He had on clean clothes. The person who had discovered the body was a man on a bicycle, and he went down to La Brea and Beverly Boulevard until he found a gas station to call for help.

"He told the gas attendant what he had discovered, and the call went out to 911. When I got to the scene, Vados had no ID on him, nothing whatsoever. The only thing we found at the scene was a baseball cap, which may or may not have belonged to him. . . .

"We did a door-knob check of businesses in the area, but no one knew who the dead man was, and we couldn't put it together, so we tagged our hit-and-run victim as John Doe and sent him off to the coroner's office," Willmon recalled.

"No one had ever seen him in the neighborhood, including the man on the bicycle who initially came forward and discovered the body.

"That was pretty much it. We had no name for the victim and we didn't know who to notify."

From an investigative point of view, there wasn't much that could be done. "We posted flyers in the area with no results. Later, we learned that the victim, Vados, lived six miles away from the fatality scene . . . at eight-sixty-one Fedora Street, and that he liked to walk.

"There was no evidence that Vados was intoxicated. Toxicology tests came back negative for everything, and it just didn't make sense as to why he would be taking a nap in the middle of the alley.

"The only thing I had was that he had grease on his hands. He had no broken legs, which was surprising, because usually when people are hit with a vehicle standing up, their legs are broken. It just seemed that this guy was lying in the alley as if he were on a magic carpet and was run over like a roll of carpeting. It just didn't make sense. All of this was in my mind when I kept going over the crime scene and getting soaking wet in the process.

"I was getting nowhere in my investigation," Willmon recalled.

"Then nine days later, on November seventeenth, 1999,

Olga and Helen made a missing persons report at the Wilshire station, where our office is located.

"Every criminal usually trips up in what they think is the perfect crime, and our little old ladies, Olga and Helen, goofed."

In order to collect on the insurance, the ladies needed a death certificate on Vados. They had obviously been careful to strip him of all identity when he was killed. But when they went to cash in on the life insurance policies that they had been paying for two or more years, they suddenly realized they were missing the one vital document they needed: proof that Vados was actually dead. Because without a death certificate, there was no way they could file for the proceeds.

"That didn't stop these two brazen ladies. What they did was to file a missing person report in another section of our office, and eventually I got a phone call from Helen Golay," Willmon said.

Nothing seemed to faze these women. It didn't scare them one bit. It took a lot of nerve on their part. The late-night comedy circuit would call it *chutzpah*.

"Without batting an eyelid, she wanted a copy of the accident report, and seemed annoyed that I wasn't jumping at her command. I explained to her that as a courtesy, what we do when we have fatalities is that we offer a copy of the report to the next of kin. But Helen had identified herself to me by saying she was a friend of Olga Rutterschmidt and that she just wanted to get the report.

"I informed Golay that . . . I could provide a copy of the report, but that because of our privacy laws, I had to give it to Olga, since she claims to be Vados' cousin.

"A few days later, Olga marches into my office for a copy of the report. She basically just walked in, demanded the report, took it without even looking at it, and walked out the door, never asking me one question about the investigation—which raised suspicions in my mind.

"Her whole attitude, her demeanor just didn't make any

sense to me. Most people, whether you are a distant relative, a neighbor, or acquaintance, the curiosity factor enters in, wanting the report and asking us questions. Usually, the person picking up the report asks, 'How did this happen?' And that's one thing we'll do is to explain our investigation process to the next of kin.

"But Olga had no interest in finding out anything about how Paul Vados died. It was like she was in a big hurry. The feeling she conveyed in her attitude with me was that her only interest in being at the station house was 'I need that paper and I got to go and get out of here,' " Willmon said.

Nothing else happened on the McDavid case until about two or three weeks later, when it was learned that Vados had a bunch of insurance policies out on his life. "That piqued my curiosity as to why a person like that would have multiple life insurance policies. I could see maybe one, but not multiple policies. But that was it," Willmon said.

"The Vados case was filed away in 'unsolved fatals'—the Cold Case files—and that's where it remained until Hernandez began muttering about his case.

"It's just ironic that it all came together. If we weren't working the same day, the same time, we might never have put it together. It's amazing," Willmon said.

Chapter 2

The Good Guys Go After the Girls

After hearing what Ed Webster had to tell him, Nelson Hernandez notified his superiors, who in turn handed the investigation over to the Robbery-Homicide Division of the Los Angeles Police Department.

By September 15, 2005, Detectives Dennis Kilcoyne and Rosemary Sanchez had caught the case and begun checking out "the girls," as Golay and Rutterschmidt were referred to throughout the investigation.

A thirty-one-year veteran of the LAPD, Kilcoyne has been a detective for over a quarter of a century. Born in Boston, he moved to Los Angeles in his junior year of high school, after his father, an aeronautical engineer at Rockwell, was transferred. His older brother had been with the department even before that. "I was a young married man with a house payment, and I needed a job," is the way six-foot-four no-nonsense Kilcoyne likes to tell about why he became a cop.

Kilcoyne has seen a lot of rough stuff. He has worked Homicide for about twenty-three years, with about ten years assigned to the Hollywood Homicide Division. His most memorable high-profile case? O. J. Simpson's. He quickly lost his Bostonian accent to become a native Californian.

Several of his cases have been profiled on A&E with Bill Curtis, including the murder of a Los Angeles sheriff sergeant in 1985 that went unsolved for fourteen years. "But in 1999, it turned out that another deputy sheriff had murdered him—and when we approached the deputy in Spokane, Washington, he committed suicide."

When he isn't playing basketball with his two young sons, or visiting his two older children, one son owns a restaurant; his daughter is a school teacher. Kilcoyne also finds time to head up the California Homicide Investigators Association, which is made up of detectives throughout the Western United States.

As for Rosemary Sanchez, she's been a cop since 1981, and has been assigned to the Robbery-Homicide Division since October 1998. Ask her why she became a police officer and she chuckles. "I remember I was in seventh grade in junior high. We had a career day at school and the local police came, and I became interested in what they were telling us, and I thought, 'You know, I want to be a cop, and I want to go to L.A.'"

Santa Maria, California, her home town, is a small agricultural community sixty-seven miles north of Los Angeles. Sanchez says she couldn't wait to leave the wine country area for the big city. "When I finally got to L.A., I loved it so much that I became a police officer and have never looked back. I was truly exposed to the big city."

Sanchez went from investigating gang murders in Los Angeles but found investigating Helen and Olga far more interesting.

Kilcoyne and Sanchez initially theorized that "the girls" were involved in these capers for financial gain, and would leave the actual dirty work of killing to someone else. But that wasn't the way it turned out, the detectives soon learned. "They were pure evil," Kilcoyne said.

For more than six years, Helen Golay and Olga Rutterschmidt pretended to be like real-life *Arsenic and Old Lace* angels, befriending homeless men they picked up at the Hollywood Presbyterian Church by feeding, clothing, and housing them, then taking out huge life insurance policies on them, and bumping them off.

What particularly raised a red flag at Ed Webster's home office in Syracuse, New York, and what led MONY to launch the initial investigation, was that one of the two policies that the women wanted to collect on had only been in force less than two years—which meant that the company had the right to challenge its validity.

Most state insurance codes, including California's, require that a statement be placed in every insurance contract that makes the policy incontestable after two years, except for non-payment of premiums. During that two-year "contestability period," the company is protected from fraudulent and misleading statements made by applicants.

The first application that Helen and Olga filed on Kenneth McDavid was policy number 2LTA013075, which he signed on November 21, 2002, and was issued by MONY on January 16, 2003. It listed his annual income as $65,000, and gave 1776 North Sycamore, Apartment 314, in Los Angeles as his address. That was Olga's home address. Both Olga and Helen were listed as beneficiaries of the policy.

Technically, when McDavid died on June 21, 2005, that policy was already enforced and could be paid out, with no questions to be asked by the carrier.

But it was the second policy, 2LTA021348, issued on August 6, 2003, and based on an application signed by McDavid on July 4, 2003, naming Helen and Olga as the beneficiaries, that tripped up the old ladies. The "problem" was that when Helen and Olga filed a notice of claim, that policy was forty-six days shy of the two years, which opened the door for the company to question and challenge the validity of the policy.

The woman who called MONY's Syracuse headquarters on Thursday, July 28, 2005, identified herself as "Helen McDavid" and claimed to be Kenneth's cousin. She said that he had died, and requested that a claim package be sent to 424 Ocean Park Boulevard in Santa Monica, which was the home of Helen Golay.

Sixteen days later, on Saturday, August 13, Helen and

Olga signed a written claim to MONY for payment of death benefits under the two policies. In the application, they indicated that McDavid had died on June 22, 2005 (the investigation showed it was actually June 21), and listed the cause of death as "accident."

Both Helen's Ocean Park Boulevard address and Olga's Sycamore Avenue address were listed on the claim forms. Both policies revealed that McDavid's employer was "HKO Associates," and that his occupation was "investor." Further, the application also indicated that McDavid was married.

Ed Webster was about to travel to Los Angeles on another assignment regarding an unrelated claim when an e-mail landed on his computer from his home office indicating that MONY had received a notice of claim from Helen and Olga.

By the time Webster left New York for Los Angeles, the main office had not as yet received the document to report the claim, or the certificate of proof of death that typically accompanies it.

The home office told him that it was a contestable claim, since the insured person had died within the initial two-year period.

"They told me it was a hit-and-run, and they forwarded me the paperwork that they had thus far, and asked me, while I was in Los Angeles, if I would look into it," Webster said.

But before he left for Los Angeles, Webster inquired of the Social Security Administration regarding McDavid's prior income. According to his FICA payments, McDavid had had earnings of $42 in the year 2003, $889.72 in 2002, $2,603.13 in 2001, and $11,364 in 2000.

On his first visit to Los Angeles, Webster said, he attempted to contact Helen Golay. "I telephoned her, and left a message on her answering machine at home." There was no reply.

"I visited Olga Rutterschmidt on that visit at her home, but she wasn't there. I thought it was actually Kenneth McDavid's business address, since it had been listed on the policy as his business address, and it was the same address as her home address," Webster said.

"There was no business conducted at that address," he said.

While unsuccessful in speaking to either of the two women, Webster did not return to New York empty-handed. Before heading back home, he stopped by the coroner's office and picked up a copy of the medical examiner's report, had his first conversation with Nelson Hernandez, the responding traffic detective assigned to the case, canvassed the alley where McDavid had been killed, and searched the area for witnesses.

Before going back to Los Angeles, Webster again tried to telephone Helen Golay at her home. "I called her on September sixth and left a message advising her that I was returning to L.A., and tried to arrange a meeting. I called again on September twelfth, thirteenth, fourteenth, and fifteenth from L.A. while I was there." Again, there was no response.

His efforts to reach Olga at the same time were also futile. But on October 3, 2005, she may have been getting nervous. When MONY life-claim specialist Randy Collins contacted Olga by telephone, she blurted out that HKO Associates—the entity listed in the life insurance applications as McDavid's employer—had never been formed.

That was all Olga had to say before hanging up.

Prior to leaving New York for his second Los Angeles trip, Webster received a phone call from Detective Dennis Kilcoyne. The conversation they had caused Webster to take his investigation in a different direction.

"I was then told about the [Paul] Vados accident, and that Ms. Golay and Ms. Rutterschmidt had claimed that they were the Hungarian native's only living relatives, and that there may have been other insurance contracts involved covering Mr. Vados," Webster said.

It was at that point that police learned that Vados actually had two children living in the United States: a daughter, Stella, in Northern California, and a son serving time in a Washington jail, Stella Vados' boyfriend informed authorities.

"As a result of the call about Vados, I requested a meeting with the Traffic Division and whatever investigators might have been involved in his case."

Two applications for MONY policies had been made on Vados, but were never completed and never issued.

Helen stonewalled Webster on his third attempt to contact her in November 2005, despite his leaving messages on her answering machine. Webster then attempted to visit with both women at their homes unannounced.

The women played cat-and-mouse with the investigator. It was a futile exercise. Webster soon became convinced that they had something to hide. Finally, in November 2005, after much persistence, he got lucky. Olga Rutterschmidt answered the door.

"She was very cagey and wouldn't open her door even after I identified myself," Webster said. "She insisted she was taking a shower. When I offered to wait in the hallway, she began screaming at me to leave, and began making all kinds of threats. Finally she told me to go see her lawyer or call for an appointment."

It was rather difficult for Webster to try to carry on a conversation with her in the hallway from behind a closed door, but when he asked for the lawyer's name and how to contact him, Olga flat-out refused to give him the information, and essentially told him to leave.

Webster's next stop was Santa Monica, to drop in and have a chat with Helen Golay. However, Helen didn't answer the door. Olga had no doubt alerted her partner in crime—Webster observed that Helen's car was parked outside of her garage, so he deduced that she must have been at home.

Webster didn't give up easily. He knew the tactics used by subjects who were trying to avoid him. He simply retreated to an old stand-by, the telephone, and began calling the women from the streets of their respective homes.

"I knew exactly when Ms. Rutterschmidt was home, and I was hoping to engage her in a telephone call and then perhaps see her. But again, by listening at her door, I could hear the answering machines, and so I again left a message, but she never replied," Webster summed up.

Webster did learn during that third Los Angeles trip that McDavid had been an employee of Universal Studios in Burbank for a period. Further investigation at the studio revealed his address at the time, who his family was, his next of kin, and emergency contacts.

One thing was for sure: Neither Helen Golay nor Olga Rutterschmidt was McDavid's next of kin.

When Webster returned to Los Angeles a fourth time, in January 2006, he finally managed to speak with Helen. A meeting was set up at her favorite eatery, Izzy's, a 24/7 celebrity diner on Wilshire Boulevard in Santa Monica, where Helen would hold court daily at table 22.

"I had a letter and a check to deliver to her, representing the company's decision on her two claims, and a refund of the premiums that had been paid," Webster said.

"The letter was to tell her that MONY had no intention in paying off on the policy."

The letter actually explained in detail to both Helen and Olga that the company was going to rescind both contracts and return their premium to them in full.

"I gave Helen the letter and she became very agitated. She threw it back across the table. She said it was unacceptable, that she was going to sue us. She got up and she started to storm out of the restaurant, but only got to the front of the diner, pulled out her cell phone, and made an animated call to someone, before storming out the front door."

Webster never had a chance to give her the check for her premium. "I gave her that with the letter, but she tossed them both back to me. She was in a rage, fuming that we couldn't do that to her . . ."

What Helen was not aware of was that undercover surveillance was recording her encounter with Webster in the restaurant. In fact, both Rosemary Sanchez and Dennis

Kilcoyne were in the booth right next to Helen, eating breakfast, not only overhearing her outburst with Webster, but also witnessing her throwing the letter and premium check back at him. For posterity, the detectives had even filmed the entire scene.

The next item on Webster's agenda was to meet up with Olga Rutterschmidt. About two hours later, as he was approaching the bank where the appointment was scheduled, he got a call from his Syracuse office saying that Olga had called and was canceling her appointment with him.

"Since Olga wasn't at the bank, I proceeded to her residence, and to my surprise, when I got there, she opened the door a bit. I did pass the letter in to her. She threw it back out, and she became irate. She began cursing and screaming and yelling, threatening to throw hot water on me, and demanding that I leave the premises."

As Webster would soon find out, Olga had a mean streak, and he was not about to be her latest target, so he took off. That was his last visit to Los Angeles to check in on "the girls," and the last contact he had with them on this case.

Helen and Olga may have thought they had been clever in their hide-and-seek dealings with Webster, but their off-the-wall behavior would haunt them as detectives built a case against them. Ultimately it would give a trial judge a clear picture of just how manipulative and deceptive they were in their dealings with insurance companies.

Chapter 3

Meet the Girls

Any murder investigation amounts to lots of leg work. As Dennis Kilcoyne described it, "At first what we did was to canvass the neighborhood where McDavid's body was found. We spoke with witnesses who either work at the stores in the Westwood area or who lived nearby in the area of the alley where McDavid met his death, and took photos of the crime scene."

In October 2005, a month after being assigned to the Golay–Rutterschmidt case, Kilcoyne put together a core of super-specialist detectives to form the investigation team. He first contacted Samuel Mayrose, a special agent with the Federal Bureau of Investigation. Kilcoyne had heard that he was considered an expert in the field of wire and mail fraud. A twenty-four-year veteran with the bureau, Sam, as he is affectionately called by colleagues, had received specific training at the FBI Academy at the United States Marine Corps Base in Quantico, Virginia.

A month later, in November 2005, Sam in turn brought in Robert Brockway, a retired Los Angeles County Sheriff's Department officer, who worked as an investigator for the California Department of Insurance. Rob had vast knowledge about insurance matters, having conducted extensive investigations involving and analyzing different policies.

Kilcoyne, Sanchez, Mayrose, and Brockway became key figures of the fifty-member task force that crisscrossed the state and, in some instances, the nation, gathering evidence that would ultimately lead to the conviction of the girls.

At times, investigators from nearly two dozen insurance companies, the Los Angeles Police Department, the Federal Bureau of Investigation, and even the United States Postal Inspection Service fanned out, probing who these two grandmotherly women were, and what made them tick.

"The girls" were in their forties when they decided to join forces and take the insurance business for everything they could get. Fitness nuts, Helen and Olga found each other in the early 1980s, at a place in Santa Monica called Sports Connection, an athletic club whose roots trace back to the 1970s when it changed its name and became the spectacularly landscaped Spectrum Water Garden complex. The pair would hang out at the Spectrum Athletic Club, with its majestic fountains and duck pond, which they found was the ideal spot to relax and unwind as they entered into a greedy alliance that began with small-time scams, spurious swindles, and sham lawsuits.

Helen Louise Salisbury was born in Eastland County, Texas, on February 3, 1931. Her mother abandoned her shortly after her birth and went off with an itinerant farm worker to pick fruit and have babies. After her father's death, her maternal grandfather raised her for a brief time until his death, and then she moved in with a cousin in Hoquiam, Washington. It was there, according to Kilcoyne, that Bonnie Williams' family took Helen in, and cared and nurtured her for two years before she was placed in a foster home.

But it was while Helen lived in Hoquiam, 150 miles north of Portland, Oregon, that she excelled and was an honor student at the local high school, and it was there, friends say, that she spent some of her happiest days.

"We didn't smoke or drink or anything like that. She was as normal as we were," Williams said, referring to the group Helen hung out with.

In a rare interview Williams gave with the *Los Angeles Times* after Helen's May 2006 arrest, she said that it "has really bothered me bad. I really haven't slept."

With her diploma in hand, Helen headed to Oakland, California, after graduation. By age 20, she'd met a young Navy aviator, Vernon Golay, at a nightclub, and married him in 1951. Under the GI Bill, he went on to become a dentist. The couple moved to Salem, Oregon, had two daughters, Pamela, now a chiropractor in Cape Cod, and Lisa, considered the black sheep in the family who, according to the police, has been in and out of trouble most of her life and has had some drug problems.

The Golays divorced after nine years in 1960. By April 1962, Helen, still single, was pregnant by an unknown man with her third daughter, Kecia, and left Salem for California.

"Let me make one thing perfectly clear. Kecia may have been raised by Helen using the name *Golay*, but she is definitely not my daughter," Vernon emphasized. "She is not a Golay . . . and Helen knew that." Dr. Golay was quite emphatic, insisting that after divorcing Helen, he only paid her $400 in child support for Pam and Lisa, but never a dime for Kecia.

"From what I've heard, and they are only rumors, Kecia's father still lives in the Salem area, but no one knows his name," the retired dentist says. Los Angeles investigators have learned that Kecia's father turned out to be homosexual and ran away from Helen.

"I haven't spoken with Helen in over a quarter of a century," Golay said, but added he was stunned when he'd learned that his ex-wife had been accused of killing people for money. "My last dealing with her was when she left Salem, and she said she wanted a car, which I got for her, just to get rid of her. She is not an easy person to talk to," Golay said.

By 1970, Helen had married David J. Wells, but that union only lasted about a year, the *Los Angeles Times* said.

A retired Orange County engineer, Wells has not spoken

to Helen since about 1980, and had no idea the depth of her problems with the law. "Oh, gee whiz, that sounds so unlike her. It's so opposite her true nature, which was gentle, with a zest for life," he told the paper.

Dumping Wells was a snap for Helen. She simply switched gears and, with her good looks, wearing miniskirts that highlighted her slim thighs, and six-inch stiletto heels and soaring bouffant hair-dos, Helen set her sights on the glitzy Hollywood scene and began hobnobbing with the upper crust.

It didn't take long for Helen and Olga to find each other, and they began hanging out at the Beverly Hills Hotel and the Hollywood Roosevelt, Kilcoyne said.

While the women did not make friends easily, nevertheless they struck up this unholy friendship, an implausible, Mutt-and-Jeff alliance. Whether it was a mystical bond that drew them close together or the need to make a fast buck, it didn't take these two women long, Detectives Kilcoyne and Sanchez theorized, to figure out that stealing purses and credit cards from gyms and hotel patrons was easier than robbing banks.

"For money, what these two would do is dress up like brassy Dolly Sisters and drop by these upscale hotels, slip into a bathroom, change clothes, and then waltz around lounging at poolside, pretending they were registered hotel guests in their sexy swimsuits, while keeping an evil eye open for easy 'marks,'" said Kilcoyne.

"It was mostly petty stuff," he says. They were a sight to be seen. "We had a couple of young, handsome undercover surveillance detectives keeping an eye on these two exercise devotees. Helen always wore those short skirts that showed a lot of what she had above the knee. She made sure to visit her hairdresser almost daily to make sure her blonde hair was styled and teased enough to form an enormous bouffant."

"I am evil" is what Helen liked to say, her hairdresser for the last eight years told Kilcoyne. She complained about everything from "stupid men, tenants who were pigs, and the high cost of being mortgaged to the hilt."

One thing is for sure: Helen never wore a wig, despite reports after her arrest that her blonde bouffant tresses were fake. She was, however, a once-a-week—at least—regular with her hairdresser.

In August 2002, Helen had a face uplift and complained bitterly of the pain she encountered from the plastic surgery.

In one letter to Olga from Helen that was found at Olga's apartment after federal agents executed a search warrant, she wrote:

> I better look good after this hell and live long enough
> to enjoy this "face job." If only I could get a new
> 21-year-old body for this brain I've been working on
> for 70 years.

It was after the surgery that Helen began drinking hot coffee from a cup with a straw, presumably not to ruin the facelift. Waitresses at both Izzy's and Fromin's, another Wilshire Boulevard restaurant frequented by Helen, all remember her bizarre coffee routine.

Helen was so narcissistic and full of herself that even after the feds arrested her the first time, she challenged her jailer by demanding that she be supplied with an eyebrow tweezer and makeup. At the same time, she complained bitterly that she needed her beauty sleep, and didn't want to be disturbed and awakened at the horrid hour of three in the morning to get ready for a court appearance. Needless to say, her self-absorbed requests landed on deaf ears.

In the beginning, it didn't take detectives long to find out that Helen had amassed her vast real estate holdings, owning millions of dollars' worth of properties in the Santa Monica and Playa del Rey areas, when she went to work for Artie Aaron, a real estate mogul in Santa Monica, Kilcoyne said.

"Helen worked for him about fifteen or sixteen years as

his girl Friday. It is believed that Aaron died mysteriously in 1999, although some people in the area say that it was cancer that did him in, at the age of 73. Helen used a power-of-attorney agreement she had with Aaron and took ownership of the real estate holdings, and was able to swindle his family out of the houses, apartment buildings, and parcels of land that he owned," Kilcoyne said.

Always looking for a quick payout, the detective said, Helen cheated Aaron's daughter, Diana Aaron Olson, out of her inheritance by deeding her father's Playa del Rey land, and property in the Antelope Valley and Madera County with an assessed value of about $1.2 million, as well as eleven other properties, to herself.

Olson took Helen to court, but was unsuccessful in suing her over her aggressive behavior. "She was stealing something that wasn't hers," Olson told the *Los Angeles Times*.

Helen also began suing people around this time, and bragged how she was able to buy an apartment after "getting a man's property," the detectives discovered during their investigation.

Those in the Santa Monica area who had any dealings with Helen thought that as a landlady, she was "mean-spirited." David Rodwin, a film writer and producer who lived at her Third Street rental property, said that Helen had put up a fence across his patio so he would be unable to have barbecues. She, in unreasonable fashion, held her tenants in such disdain that she would call the police to report them over minor parking violations. She had painted the curb surrounding the property red, making it legally off-limits and thus preventing any car, including Rodwin's, from parking near the house.

"I felt she was spying on us. I would honestly hide from her whenever I saw her prowling around the grounds. I didn't want to talk to her," Rodwin told a *Los Angeles Times* reporter.

One of Helen's tenants at her Third Street building in Santa Monica, Emily Meyers, labeled her "a bully." According to the *Santa Monica Daily Press*, Meyers claimed that Helen would repeatedly drive by the six-unit apartment complex and eerily peek in her windows.

"She showed us the property one way, and then when we moved into it, it would be another way," said Meyers, a documentary filmmaker. And if any tenants had a problem with an apartment, she'd yell at them to call her lawyer.

Helen, the detectives said, relied on Olga to be her lookout, her scout, and to do the dirty work. She was Helen's right hand. She was the one to size up strangers, the "marks" they were about to hit. She would talk in her friendly, cutesy Zsa Zsa Gabor accent, disarming them.

So how did Helen learn about insurance fraud? "We don't know," admitted Kilcoyne. "However, during our search warrants of her Santa Monica home, we found books on insurance, so it was apparent to us that she was schooling herself," he said.

The detective said that Helen "was meticulous about her bookkeeping, which was a godsend for us in our search warrants, because she had files on everybody—the payments, the schedules, canceled checks. All kinds of good stuff, which, in the end, did her in at trial."

Helen also had an extensive file of newspaper clippings and magazine articles on various ways of permanently doing away with a person using a variety of exotic poisons and other methods, such as: the use of antifreeze or combining vodka and rat poison. "She had files on all kinds of wild ways to kill . . . showing different ways of people dying. She was obviously researching," the detective said.

The detective also recalled being told that Helen had once boasted about insuring an older man, naming herself as beneficiary, of course, and then plying him with Viagra until it caused a heart attack. "After I found out about Helen, it was sure something I knew she could do," Kilcoyne mused.

Law enforcement was baffled as to what had triggered Helen's entry into a life of crime. To this day, investigators delving into her early life are at a loss to figure it out. Was it that Helen Golay felt cheated by her childhood after her father was killed when she was 9 years old, and that she'd spent her formative years shunted from foster home to foster home as a youngster, always envious of her friends, who seemed to have more of the little things that young girls yearn for? Or was it her two failed marriages and having to raise three daughters on her own, never knowing if there would be enough for their next meal that caused her obsessive need to hoard money?

Or did Helen come up with the brazen idea after reading the massive pre-trial publicity about sweet-faced grandmotherly Dorothea Puente, back in the 1990s, who opened up a boarding house in Sacramento, tending to the elderly and homeless, and then murdered the lodgers she had befriended in order to steal their government checks? Puente had systematically drugged her nine known victims with flurazepam, also sold as Dalmane, used to treat sleep disorders, before killing them and burying them in her garden.

There are many similarities between Helen Golay and Dorothed Puente. Both women are around the same age. Puente's father died when she was 4 years old, and she was sent off to an orphanage after her mother died. Relatives adopted her when she was 6 and, like Helen, Puente married for the first time at a very young age.

And, like Puente, who had a handyman dig out the concrete in her garage, presumably to bury her victims, Helen, at one point before McDavid was killed, had asked a Santa Monica construction contractor to remove the concrete in her garage. Why she wanted this done will never be known. But it sure would have been convenient for her to simply drop one or more dead bodies into the hole and cover it up with a fresh concrete slab.

Helen was known for being a little on the cheap side, and ultimately she nixed having the contractor dig up the garage when she was told she would have to buy a city license in order for him to do the job.

Although she was the owner of some of the most valuable property in the Santa Monica area, Helen liked passing herself off as being stone-broke. Often, while dining at

Fromin's, she would come in at night with daughter Kecia, grandchild Sophia, and 40-something boyfriend Gary Hilaiel.

It was Helen, according to the waiters at both Fromin's and Izzy's, who, wanting to make sure that Kecia met the right man, introduced her to Hilaiel—but when her daughter lost interest in him, Helen took him on as her boyfriend, despite the vast age difference.

And yet it was also Helen who paid a generous $50,000 for Kecia to have a boob job, her friends said.

Helen liked sitting by the front window of Fromin's, and would "act up" in front of Kecia and her granddaughter, according to Javier, the waiter. "One day," said Javier, "she was upset when another patron was seated in her favorite booth. She started screaming at the host and at the other waiter, who was defending the host to the manager. And when Helen's boyfriend came into the restaurant, he began yelling at the waiter who had defended the host, shouting, 'You're a liar! You're a liar!' And then Helen started screaming at the waiter, saying, 'You're a liar! You're a liar!' But she was really very picky," Javier said.

Most of the waiters at Fromin's remember Helen as being very cheap, Javier recalled. "Helen and the boyfriend would order the Brisket Special for ten-ninety-five, and then split the dinner, which was for one person, between themselves—and then complain that they had not been served enough food."

Margie, a waitress at Fromin's, recalls that Helen was on welfare when they'd first met some thirty years ago, and that this may account for her being so frugal.

Yet there are those who remember Helen's business skills as a real estate agent. "One tough cookie, a fantastic negotiator," said Peter Mullins, who sold her four properties, two of them the apartment buildings that made up a substantial part of her vast realty holdings. "Helen knew the business inside out. Sure, she was frugal, but that's the way she ran her business," he said.

* * *

Hungarian-born Olga Rutterschmidt was born March 5, 1933, in Budapest. By the time she was six, World War II had broken out in Europe and she and her mother were forced to search for places to hide because of the German occupation of Hungry. Because the Allied forces were bombing Budapest, they spent most of the time taking up shelter in the basement of the apartment building where they were living. They would go upstairs when there wasn't any bombing and when the bombings would begin again, they'd all go downstairs and live for periods of time in the basement.

At one point, Olga, who was not supposed to go upstairs, went anyway to play her piano, and it was at that moment that her building was bombed, causing her right hand to be severely hurt.

After her arrest on federal mail fraud charges in May, Dennis Kilcoyne and Sam Mayrose interviewed Olga and noticed she had a slight deformity to her right hand. "When we tried talking to her, she got very vile with us about the American bombing raids in Hungary during the war, and became very anti-Semitic in speaking with us, by the way. Her hand was injured severely during one of the bombing raids, and as we tried talking to her, she kept referring to us saying, 'You Americans! It was *your bombs* that did this to me.' It was a flashback about American bombs that did this to her hand. 'Your bombs did this to me.' She kept on saying to us, 'Your bombs did this to me.' It was pretty wild."

It is believed that Olga's father started her with music, and to this day she is very talented in playing the piano, despite the injured right hand. Olga's parents eventually divorced and he remarried and had another child with his second wife, a daughter, leaving Olga's mother to fend for herself and raise her alone on meager assets.

Olga's early life was traumatized by the bombing raids at night, and the brutal killing by day of hundreds of Jews who were rounded up and transported to the Auschwitz–Birkenau extermination camp or shot before her eyes in the streets.

Once the war ended, Olga, by then a young teenager, began having psychological problems, and so her mother had her hospitalized, and it was then that Olga started receiving a series of eight electroshock treatments.

After the war, a new government took over in Budapest and it became a communist country. For whatever reason, Olga's mother remained there. She died not long ago in Hungary, but Olga, for whatever reason, has never discussed her mother with either her attorney, Michael Sklar, or with others at the jail, for that matter.

Olga eventually made it to the United States, by first walking to another country in Europe, which she never revealed to anyone, and then settling in New York City after she was sponsored by a family there. She moved on to Los Angeles, where she met and married her husband Endre. Among the documents found in her apartment, where she had lived from 1975 until her arrest, was an expired electrolysis license—yet her bank activity showed very little visible means of support. At some point the couple had opened a coffee shop in Hollywood, but in 1978 Endre took off.

"Endre is believed to have died in 2005 in Hungary," Mayrose said. And it was around the time Endre left that Olga felt the need to sow her middle-age oats.

Some investigators believe that Olga and Helen had first met at an adult writing class. If that is true, Helen did not have too much in the way of money except what she got working with Artie Aaron.

But one fact was clear. During the years Helen was with Aaron, she built her real estate empire, while Olga was living off of government assistance. Olga always perceived Helen as making it big because she had her finger in a lot of pies, acquiring more and more real estate.

While Olga would see Helen on a regular basis, at a minimum she was envious, and wanted to be on the gravy train, instead of living on subsidies from Section Eight Housing and Social Security.

Olga's style was poles apart from Helen's, even though

she was a 50-percent partner. "It was different," Kilcoyne observed. "She was the muscle. . . . She did the dirty work while Helen did the investing, the thinking, and the finances."

Olga did not appear to have any close friends, and rarely entertained guests. Neighbors at her apartment building say she would often lay claim to the fact that she knew how to rip off companies by using thirty to forty credit cards and not paying them, Kilcoyne said.

She not only ran credit card scams, but also bragged about not paying income taxes.

Detectives found Olga was "crazy as a fox, explosive, loud, and hard to deal with in public."

"Olga was a piece of work," Kevin Rea, a neighbor, said of her shortly after her arrest. "She's alternatively reclusive and then was really in your face. She has this bombastic manner about her, this operatic presence," he told the *Los Angeles Times*.

"She kind of intimated that there were avenues to extra money," said Rea, a probation officer. "But I never [delved] into the details," he said.

Another resident in her building, Dwight Emile, a composer, said Olga often would play the piano in his apartment, or borrow his CDs.

For the most part, Olga, although a loner with no family in this country, ruled the roost in the building, and was often referred to as the "enforcer," because she would yell at residents if they played music too loud or talked in the hallways late at night. But that didn't stop her from blasting her record player in her apartment as she listened to jazz and classical music.

"By the time these two girls were arrested, they had begun calling each other vulgar names and the situation between the pair had become explosive," Kilcoyne said. "They were definitely quarrelling about money."

It would appear that what Olga enjoyed doing most, aside from listening to classical music, was taking her daily hikes in Runyon Canyon, or getting in her Honda Civic and taking it down to Santa Monica so she could go running on the beach, the detective said.

"Olga was pretty athletic, and we had a lot of young guys working undercover following the girls before we moved in and arrested them. Olga would go hiking, either up in the Hollywood hills or on the beach, almost daily. She was like a little bulldog.

"One time we had these guys who were following her. They were fit. These were young officers and yet they were having trouble keeping up with her, she was in such good shape.

"One day they were up in the hills of Hollywood and they were following her down this trail and trying not to be obvious. All of a sudden she disappeared from their sight, and they lost her. The undercovers kept radioing each other: 'Where did she go?' They couldn't figure out where in hell she was, and then all of a sudden they realized what had happened.

"Olga had jumped behind the bushes and she was taking a crap."

Chapter 4

The Investigation Gets Underway

By December 2005, the investigation into the deaths of Paul Vados and Kenneth McDavid was in full swing. Almost immediately after getting the case, a surveillance team was placed on both Helen Golay and Olga Rutterschmidt, and undercover detectives began following the girls virtually 24/7, keeping tabs on their every move.

"Rosemary and I took a few days off and went up to the Sacramento area searching for relatives of Vados and McDavid," Kilcoyne said.

The detectives found Stella Vados living with her longtime boyfriend, Randy Hansen, in Grass Valley, California. And of course, they gave her the bad news about her father.

Stella had told Kilcoyne and Sanchez that she had looked long and hard for her father, even writing to the Social Security Administration seeking a current address for him, though the agency was not helpful in reuniting her with him.

What surprised the couple was when the detectives informed them that her father's Social Security checks had been sent to an address in Santa Monica owned by Helen Golay.

When told that Helen had claimed to be her father's fiancée, and Olga his cousin, Stella and her other relatives said they'd never heard of the women.

Stella said that the last time she'd seen her father was in

1996, shortly before she'd moved up north to Grass Valley.

She went on to say that she'd tried sending correspondence to her father at the 1776 Sycamore address—which, as it turned out, was Olga's—but never got a response.

"Were Helen Golay or Olga Rutterschmidt cousins of your father's?" Kilcoyne asked.

"No," was Stella's terse response.

Stella said that her dad had been a retired foreman and had worked at Apple Computers before she moved to Grass Valley. She acknowledged that he was an alcoholic, but added, "We were very close before he disappeared." She said that her mother had died in 1983 or 1984, before her parents could divorce.

"I found out where he was living after he had passed on . . . that he was living somewhere different from where he had been living. When I came down to Southern California to see where he was living, it was not on Sycamore, and the Social Security offices could not find him."

To her horror, Stella said she had later learned that the two women had claimed the body from the coroner and buried it in an unmarked grave. Over the years, Stella and her family fought unsuccessfully with Helen and Olga to move Vados' body to the family plot at Forest Lawn Memorial Park.

It wasn't until July 18, 2006, after Helen and Olga were arrested, that Stella was able to rebury her father in a small ceremony attended only by Stella and her attorney. Vados was laid to rest next to the grave of his wife, Judith, at Forest Lawn in the Hollywood Hills. Stella sobbed, but said little, as the casket was lowered into the grave.

"Paul Vados was a perfect candidate for this scam," Hansen said. "But we had no money to fight this. We had no clues. Until the detectives found us, we didn't know what had happened."

As for McDavid, the detectives didn't have any family addresses on him when they got to Sacramento, so they started with some old addresses that he had used fifteen, twenty years earlier, and began knocking on doors. "Ulti-mately we found his brother, Robert, and he was in a group home for men. And from him, he had another address for his sister, Sandra, who is a nurse," Kilcoyne said.

"It turned out she hadn't seen or heard from her brother Robert in six or seven years, and yet he was living about two miles away from her. The good part of our trip is that they are all together now, and Robert lives with Sandra and her husband, and her mother is living in a home across the street from her."

Once back in Los Angeles, the detectives began the te-dious job of attempting to unravel the unusual entangle-ments between Helen and Olga. For starters, the detectives focused on a number of people who had crossed paths with the girls. They soon learned about the death of Fred Downie, a 97-year-old man whose eyesight was not exactly good, who had been struck by a car on November 18, 2000, while crossing the street, almost one year after Vados was killed.

Downie died of his head injuries a month after he was struck. When detectives checked into the circumstances, it raised a red flag, because not only did he live in an apart-ment owned by Helen Golay, but the accident had occurred very close to her Ocean Park Boulevard home.

The car that had hit Downie was a Honda Civic driven by a woman named Cheryl Clark who, law enforcement de-termined, was not at fault. In fact, detectives made a point of emphasizing that Clark had no connection whatsoever with either Helen Golay or Olga Rutterschmidt.

A widower, Downie was a West Harwich, Massachu-setts, retiree who was the former owner of a private kinder-garten school who had lived alone since his wife's death in 1978.

Kecia had met Downie the summer of 1999 while visit-ing her half-sister, Pamela Golay Latimer, a chiropractor who had introduced the two, and lived near his West Har-wich home. Pam was estranged from her mother and has refused to talk about the case.

Kecia was in her thirties when she met Downie, who was some 60-plus years older. He called her "Bubbles," and she called him "Grandpa." The May–December romance took off, and Kecia convinced him to leave his home, and before anyone realized what was happening, Kecia had the old man packed and moved to Santa Monica, where, she said, Helen would put him up in one of her vacant apartments.

While they were never able to pin Downie's death on either Helen or Olga, detectives did suspect them of being behind it. It was theorized that someone could have signaled the old man that it was safe to cross the busy street, knowing that he couldn't see all that clearly, just as the car, driven by an unsuspecting Cheryl Clark, was approaching. The spot where Downie was killed does not have a crosswalk, Santa Monica Police Lieutenant Frank Fabrega observed.

One of the first things Kecia did before moving Downie to California was to take title to his Massachusetts home—for one dollar. Then she borrowed money on it, taking out an $81,900 loan and then selling it for $200,000, according to property records. She also became executor of his will, and had complete control of his assets, none of which was ever shared with Downie's elderly surviving relatives.

But what really raised eyebrows during the Downie probe was that a third-party witness to the traffic incident also happened to avail himself of the kitchen services on Sunday at the church where Helen and Olga plied their so-called good deeds. Kecia also frequented the soup kitchen with her mother and Olga, always on the lookout for prospective victims. Detectives were about to move in to speak with the witness, when he turned up dead from a drug overdose. Detectives were never able to determine whether his death was in any way connected with their investigation of Downie or those who might have been familiar with him during his Santa Monica stay, and no one was ever charged with Downie's death or accused of causing the potential witness's death.

Mildred Holman, Downie's 85-year-old niece, told a

Los Angeles Times reporter "that there are a lot of things, looking back, that looked very, very shady." She never offered any details about what she suspected, but she did say she thought Kecia had taken advantage of Downie.

Downie's move to California had come as a big surprise to his friends and family, Holman said. "He lived alone, and he told me, 'I'm getting older and if I live with Kecia, there would be somebody around all the time for me,'" Holman said.

Downie at first seemed to be enjoying himself in his new home. He said he was living in this great apartment with Oriental rugs and antique furniture, and he loved the California weather. Then, a few months later, he wrote that he was lonesome and wanted to come back. He told his niece that "California was a mistake, and that he was very unhappy." But before he could return, he was fatally struck by the car, Holman said.

"He trusted them so much," she said. "He really thought they would care for him."

William Fillebrown, pastor of the Chiltonville Congregational Church in Plymouth, presided over Downie's memorial service, and called him a "swamp Yankee," meaning that some of the folks in town considered him to be "crusty." "He was very set in his ways," the minister told the *Los Angeles Times.*

The townsfolk, he said, were surprised that Downie had taken up with a young woman, because it was "so out of character for him."

Another bizarre aspect to the Kecia affair is that Downie had bought headstones and plots for Helen Golay and her daughter so that they would be buried in a Plymouth cemetery next to Downie and his late wife.

According to Holman, that's where Helen and Kecia wanted to be buried.

The logs kept by surveillance officers assigned to follow Helen indicated that, for the most part, she either went from her Ocean Park home to Izzy's in the morning, or to Fromin's at night. At no time did she visit Olga's Hollywood apartment. And Olga never stepped foot in Helen's Ocean Park property.

Kecia was often seen at Helen's home, but it appeared to detectives that she was merely visiting. They often followed Kecia on numerous occasions to 609 Marine Street in Santa Monica, but that just turned out to be another property owned by Helen that Kecia used as her residence.

As for Olga, she was observed on numerous occasions, beginning in November 2005, leaving in the greenish-blue Honda Civic that was parked in the garage underneath her building.

On November 17, 2005, the surveillance team saw that Olga drove her car to the Hollywood Station Post Office at Wilcox and Selma, less than a mile from her apartment. There, she picked up an $8^{1}/_{2} \times 11$ envelope and brought it back to the car. She then drove another three miles and parked at the corner of Lorraine and Eighth Streets.

About ten minutes later, a frail-looking man, five-foot, six-inches tall, 75 to 80 years of age, walked up to her. Olga directed him to sit in her car. Then she got back in and drove about one block, and parked again.

The surveillance log indicates that Olga and the man had sat in her car for about five minutes and then Olga got out with a manila envelope similar to the one she'd picked up at the post office. She placed the envelopes on the trunk, and opened the passenger door. The man continued to sit in the car.

According to the log:

Rutterschmidt removed numerous forms from the envelopes and appeared to direct the elderly male where to sign the documents. Rutterschmidt made about five to seven trips from her trunk to the elderly man with paperwork. The elderly man would sign a form and she would place copies of the paperwork back into the envelope on the trunk. Rutterschmidt then took the envelope with her into the driver's side.

With the man in her car, Olga next drove one block north to the Washington Mutual bank at 4333 Wilshire Boulevard. There, she assisted the man into the bank. Once inside, Olga sat with the man at a desk that was not occupied by bank employees. Olga was seen by the surveillance team taking envelopes out of the plastic bag that the man was carrying.

The log continues:

Rutterschmidt and the elderly man then approached a teller window. The elderly male signed for several traveler's checks. A few minutes later, Rutterschmidt and the elderly male returned to the same desk and she went through numerous envelopes from the white plastic bag he was carrying. Rutterschmidt separated the paperwork from the envelopes, took some paperwork, and placed other paperwork back in the white plastic bag. Rutterschmidt tore and tossed envelopes into the waste basket under the desk. A short time later, they both approached another bank teller window, but no transaction apparently was completed.

No sooner were Olga and the man out of the bank when the LAPD surveillance officer contacted bank employees. The bank manager indicated that the man was known as "Josef Gabor" and that he resided at 751 Crenshaw Boulevard, apartment 8.

The undercover officer also looked into the trash can that Olga had used, and saw torn envelopes with insignia letterheads of Bank of America, Washington Mutual, and Mercury Insurance Group, with Gabor's name.

Olga and Gabor separated after they left the bank. Olga got into her car and drove off, the surveillance officer who was following them noted, while Gabor walked east on Wilshire Boulevard with the white plastic bag. Gabor was then spotted by another surveillance officer, who observed him walking two blocks to 751 Crenshaw Boulevard, where Gabor's name was on the directory for apartment 8. Gabor used a key to open the front door to his apartment and went in.

In checking out the property, the detectives found that the building was owned by the Hungarian Reformed Church.

The surveillance team logged Olga making stops at a coffee shop and another bank. Then she drove to the Fed-Ex Kinko's at 7630 Sunset Boulevard and entered the parking lot. After sitting in her car for about ten minutes, she went into the retail store and bought time to use Internet service, but ran into problems signing on to the computer.

Unaware that the gentleman seated at the next booth to her was an undercover LAPD surveillance officer, she struck up a conversation with him and asked for his help with the computer. She was attempting to open a platinum credit card with HSBC (Hongkong and Shanghai Banking Corporation).

The officer saw that Olga opened an account as Carol Vane, at 751 Crenshaw—the same address as Gabor, but a different apartment number. The officer was also able to tell that Olga had used a Social Security number beginning with "603-78," but he could not see the last four digits.

Olga obviously didn't suspect that the man she was speaking to for assistance was an undercover officer. She spontaneously stated to him that she was from Hungary and had made her money from a coffee shop she had inherited. She then attempted to log into "Providence" or "Provident Bank's" website, but had trouble accessing it.

For whatever reason, she also told the officer that she never gave out her true e-mail address.

When officers interviewed Gabor, he said that he had first met Olga in 1988 when a mutual friend who worked at a swap meet introduced them.

The 74-year-old Gabor was a retired chiropractor who had moved to the United States in 1980. The virtually blind

Gabor later told detectives that as he'd left his apartment building to go to his bank, Olga offered to drive him there and to assist him in any way that she could.

It was fairly obvious to the detectives that Olga had already picked out Gabor as a possible victim in their insurance fraud scam.

At first, Gabor wasn't suspicious of Olga's gracious offer. After all, he frequently sought assistance from strangers, so he'd gone along with whatever she told him.

It wasn't until Gabor made it home on his own after detectives followed Olga to the copy shop that he learned that his supposedly helpful friend was trying to open a platinum credit card under someone else's name.

"I was shocked when a detective came to my door and told me I was Olga's next victim," a stunned and shaken Gabor said. "Olga and her partner wanted to kill me."

Day by day, the detectives learned more and more about Olga and Helen, but they still did not have enough evidence to arrest the pair on state charges for murder.

Digging further, the team soon learned that Olga had made arrangements at a local establishment to use rubber signature stamps to sign the insurance forms with the men's names.

It didn't take detectives long before they were able to identify about a dozen names garnered from the Hollywood Rubber Stamp Co. at 6564 Santa Monica Boulevard.

Rutterschmidt, using the name Olga Smith, purchased rubber stamps for dozens of men, Lieutenant Paul Vernon of the Los Angeles Police Department said. "We know they're using those rubber stamps to take out other life insurance policies," he said.

And Rick Constantinescu, owner of the stamp company, confirmed that Olga was a long-time customer, and had used the name *Olga Smith* in doing business with his firm.

Almost immediately, police began looking for Nicolas Koos, 67, Jimmy Allen Covington, 46, and Scott Gones, whose age was not immediately known. "These two ladies fattened these people up like Christmas turkeys—it's beyond bizarre," chief investigator Kilcoyne said, shaking his head in disbelief.

The three newly identified men were all described by Kilcoyne as transients who were being sought by police as a result of insurance applications and rubber stamps found with their signatures.

Olga and Helen were obviously obsessed with identity fraud. The rubber signature stamps were not only made for the two known victims and the dozen other unknown men, but Olga had also had signature stamps made for her deceased husband. In fact, until she was arrested, her dead husband still had a checking account—"he" continued cashing checks and "he" still voted.

And on October 19, 2005, Olga even arranged to have a signature made for Helen.

A paper trail showed clearly that Helen had provided rent on apartments for McDavid and Vados—that she had paid for food and utilities, and also paid the insurance premiums in their names.

There was no doubt in the minds of the detectives that Olga and Helen had intended to murder Josof Gabor just as they'd done with Paul Vados and Kenneth McDavid.

For the most part, it was Olga who did the scouting for new victims. At times, Helen would also join in the hunt. The two looked just like any charity-minded social butterflies as they scanned the church soup kitchen looking to pick up new prospects.

If anything, the septuagenarian odd couple seemed to fit right in. They would chat with the other church-goers—all volunteers—and eventually, they introduced themselves to the minister, Pastor Charles Suhayda of the Hollywood Presbyterian Church, who ran the community programs to feed the homeless and destitute.

"They seemed like such nice ladies. They were like grandmothers," he said.

"While we were continuing to investigate the deaths of McDavid and Vados," lead LAPD investigator Kilcoyne said, "we felt that we had to put a stop to the women's activities. We had watched them make contact with other men, we believe for the purposes of setting up more life insurance policies."

To buy the LAPD time to develop a state murder case against the girls, agents from the FBI immediately froze Helen's and Olga's assets. That meant that all the property Helen owned—bank accounts, stocks, bonds, furniture, cars, you name it—was frozen and was the property of the United States government. While Olga did not own property, she did have her share of bank accounts, to say nothing about the Honda Civic she owned.

Investigators had already estimated that the women had collected over $2.2 million in life insurance payouts. Eighteen policies had been taken out on Kenneth McDavid and six on Paul Vados.

"These two women appeared to be preying and profiting on the most vulnerable persons in our society," said State Insurance Commissioner John Garamendi. "The residents of California are also victims in these kinds of schemes through the higher premiums they pay. I am committed to prosecuting this type of fraud, and others like it, to the fullest extent."

J. Stephen Tidwell, the assistant director of the FBI in Los Angeles at the time, agreed. "Given the scope of this fraud and the fact that it may be more extensive, the FBI will continue to provide the necessary resources, either in Los Angeles or around the country, to this joint investigation," he said.

The pink two-story building that Helen called home until her May 18, 2006 federal arrest is located at 424 Ocean Park Boulevard in Santa Monica. Located on the south side of the street, the three-unit, 2,500-square-foot structure has a terra-cotta roof trimmed with a dark green awning. The upstairs windows have gray shutters. There is an eight- to ten-foot wall of thick ficus hedging that runs across the property, giving the building an eerie, ghost-like feeling. At the far side of the hedging, there is a gray wooden gate with the gold numbers *424* attached. The gate has one unmarked mail slot in it. In the alley behind the building, there are gates into the property.

After Helen's arrest, the house was put up for sale with an asking price of $1.575 million, according to Multiple Listing Service.

It was in this building that Dennis Kilcoyne, Rosemary Sanchez, and other members of the Los Angeles Police Department, accompanied by investigators from the FBI, armed with a federal search warrant, arrested Helen shortly after 3 a.m. on May 18, 2006. Olga was arrested at her Hollywood address a few hours later.

"Who would do this to me? Who would do this to me?" Helen protested, her voice dripping with disdain as Sam Mayrose cuffed her hands behind her back.

"Helen was a well-rounded sociopath, and I wanted to tell her that she did this to herself, but I kept quiet and said nothing," Mayrose said. "It was hard to believe that this sweet, angelic-faced woman even had the strength to do what she was being charged with."

Over and over again, Helen kept repeating that she had done nothing wrong and had not committed "no mail fraud.

"You know, I'm not a spring chicken, I'm a seventy-five-year-old woman, and I'm not going to go out of the way to harm anyone.

"The insurance company is behind my arrest. The insurance companies did not want to pay on a very tragic accident, so they made a federal case out of it," Helen kept repeating.

Among the items seized at her house were prescription medications, keys to her cars, documents referring to a 1999 Mercury Sable, her driver's licenses, identification, passport, Social Security card, and bank and credit cards.

When the FBI impounded Helen's new Mercedes SUV, which was parked in the alley behind her building, they found a ratty-looking ticket stub, dated the night before Paul Vados had been killed on November 8, 1999. The stub showed that someone had attended the 10:45 p.m. showing of the movie *The Bone Collector*, which dealt with quadriplegic detective Lincoln Rhyme (Denzel Washington) and rookie cop Amelia Donaghy (Angelina Jolie), who team up to solve a string of serial murders in which a shard of bone is removed from every victim.

The ticket stub was attached to a yellow Post-it and had Vados' name on it, with his date of birth and Social Security number. Whether Vados was actually taken to watch the film is not known.

What impressed Kilcoyne and the other investigators when they entered Helen's house was how immaculate the place was kept. "There was nice expensive antique furniture in the house. There was a small love seat in the living room with a coffee table next to it with a lamp. And on the love seat was a blanket. She had obviously been sitting there or sleeping on it before we came a-knocking on her door."

As Kilcoyne was taking in the surreal scene, his eyes focused on a hardcover book that was turned open on an end table near where Helen had been sitting in her living room. "It was obvious she had been up half the night reading the book when we knocked on the door. I even had our photographer take a picture of the book. It appeared she had just put the book down. The cover of the book was just a pair of eyes, just staring at you. And the title of the book was *The Sociopath Next Door*, by Harvard psychologist Martha Stout.

"It was pretty eerie to see that she had been up half the night reading this stuff just the morning of her arrest, in that the author points out in the book that the 'foremost indicator of a sociopath is that the person has no scruples, has no ability to feel shame, guilt or remorse.'"

The search warrant also revealed another eye-opener about Helen's reading habits. One of the books found on the night stand in her bedroom was a copy of *The Modern Identity Changer: How to Create and Use a New Identity for Privacy and Personal Freedom* by Sheldon Charrett, which was published in 2004. According to a synopsis of the book, it offers readers instructions on how to obtain a new identity, including how to produce supporting documents and get Social Security numbers and drivers' licenses.

Another tidbit turned up in the search warrant was a condolence letter that Mutual of Omaha had written to Helen one month after Vados had died. "We are very sorry to learn of your fiance's death," they wrote, and attached a pamphlet called "Grief and Healing." When Mutual of Omaha had balked at paying Helen, she threatened a lawsuit over their "outrageous delays," and within a week, she got a $25,000 check in the mail.

Helen wasn't the only person to save letters. FBI investigators found a treasure trove of items when they searched Olga's one-bedroom Hollywood apartment at 1776 N. Sycamore Avenue on May 18. Olga lived alone in a pre-war building on the third floor. According to court documents, the apartment was partially subsidized by the government's Section Eight Housing program, which provides assistance to low-income tenants in helping them pay their rent. Olga also received a monthly pension from Social Security.

Olga had thousands of handwritten pages in the small apartment. FBI investigators reported finding notebook upon notebook of her writings everywhere. It was obvious she wrote all the time, whatever was in her head. Every scrap of paper that was found had writing on it. It wasn't diary writing, but mostly dealt with calculations on how much money was due her from insurance policies.

In a 2000 letter found by investigators, Olga wrote:

Dear Helen,
I have a few very interesting and good life insurance
company listings. They pay regardless of illness, or
accidental cause. (No hassle, no investigations)

Among the more interesting items found were computer print-outs on how to beat traffic tickets, details about Ponzi and pyramid schemes, hundreds of news articles on unusual ways that people die, lots of names of people with their Social Security numbers, and how to rip off and sue insurance companies. "And she also had stashed away calendars from the early nineties showing the dates when she and Helen would meet," Mayrose related.

But perhaps one of the biggest surprises that Sam Mayrose found during the search of Olga's apartment was an M26 Taser electroshock weapon in her dresser drawer, with a $400 receipt for it.

"The other eye-opener for me," Mayrose said, "was that Olga had Kenneth McDavid's original death certificate."

When word trickled out about their arrests, it shocked even hardened law enforcement veterans, as well as those in the media. As the news spread that Olga and Helen were locked up in a federal facility, the hit-and-run grandmas took on a new name: Newspapers began calling them "the Black Widows."

In their book *Murder Most Rare*, Michael D. and C. L. Kelleher identify the essential traits of the Black Widow as:

Typically they are intelligent, manipulative, highly organized and patient. She plans her activities with great care. Her crimes are usually carried out over a relatively long period of time. In many cases, the Black Widow begins to murder relatively late in life (often after the age of thirty) and therefore brings a good deal of maturity and patience to the planning and commission of her crime. She relies on her ability to win the confidence or trust of her victims as a precursor to any attack.

As for Helen and Olga, Michael Kelleher had this to say: "Female killers operating for profit by taking out insurance policies on their victims are working one of the oldest scams in the book. What makes this situation unique is that they rarely operate in pairs. And a hit-and-run? I've looked at over three hundred female serial killers and this is the first time I've heard of this method. Now that's pretty brutal."

Chapter 5

The Hidden Tape

The federal arrest gave Dennis Kilcoyne and the LAPD some breathing room to gather evidence to make a murder case against the two women.

"The investigation brought us to this point today," Kilcoyne announced to the media in a sidewalk press conference outside police headquarters. "While we continue to investigate the deaths of these two men, Paul Vados and Kenneth McDavid, we had to put a stop to the women's activity. We've watched them make contact with other men, for the purposes of setting up more life insurance policies."

Kilcoyne asked anyone with information in this case to either call him or Rosemary Sanchez, and gave the media their twenty-four-hour toll-free number—1-877-LAWFULL (529-3855)—and FBI hotline number 1-310-477-6565.

While the two women would eventually be walked across the street to the federal courthouse to be arraigned before a federal judge, they made an unusual stop at Parker Center, the headquarters for the Los Angeles Police Department, named after former LAPD Chief William H. Parker, who died after a fatal heart attack. Most readers will remember seeing Parker Center featured in the television drama *Dragnet*.

Initially charged only with mail fraud, everyone involved with the investigation from the get-go knew that the federal government was never going to prosecute the Black Widows for that. Kilcoyne freely admitted that the sole purpose of the arrest was to give the special team of detectives he'd amassed more time in their investigation so that the Los Angeles District Attorney could put together a solid case and actually file murder charges against them. But Kilcoyne's team knew that was going to take some more time.

Olga and Helen, after their federal arrest, were placed in a rather antiseptic white-walled room at police headquarters, where they spent about thirty minutes of downtime while the legal niceties of court paperwork were being prepared. What they didn't know was that Criminal Rule Number One if arrested is: Don't talk. Their conversation was surreptitiously recorded and videotaped. They also didn't know that the room they were in was wired. Every word they were saying to each other was being recorded, and the video system was photographing them as they spoke.

In the videotaped conversation, which runs about thirty minutes, the two women engage in chit-chat conversation, although for the most part, Olga does most of the talking.

On the tape, they clearly incriminate themselves on the mail fraud charges. More pertinently, it clearly shows how cold-blooded these women are: Vados and McDavid are dead, and all Olga and Helen talk about is money.

The tape is an absolute bombshell. For thirty minutes, Olga blabbers on in her delicious Hungarian accent, very animated, gesturing always with her hands, stiffening them up or wringing them in a grotesque, twisted manner, practically non-stop. She is irate as she keeps telling Helen off in her paprika-seasoned English. In demonstrating her anger, she not only displays her avarice, but shows she has no conscience for human life.

"You can't have that many insurances . . . you were greedy," she accuses Helen. "It's your fault. That's the problem." At times, Olga becomes so explosive that even her brown doe-like eyes seem to pop out in anger. She spews her venomous diatribe at Helen while trying to suppress the rage she has stored up against her.

Even before being taken to the interview room, Olga blasts Helen, telling Kilcoyne and Mayrose that "Helen had a whole bunch of insurance companies with her name as a beneficiary, only Helen Golay, not me, so better interrogate her. I don't know nothing about those companies. I'm not named. She knows more about this than I do.

"Helen Golay is named with all these insurance companies, but I'm not part of it. I don't even know nothing about it. How can I take . . . ? Why don't detectives ask her? It's on her name, not mine. They have to interrogate her. I don't know nothing about this . . ."

Helen, on the other hand, sits throughout Olga's non-stop tirade against her as if she is milquetoast. Very composed, very self-confident—yet very defiant. Like a rebellious kid being scolded by her mom for the umpteenth time for coming home late from a date—but so what!

Then, for some unexplained reason, Helen confides to Mayrose that she had been a body-builder, and taken gymnastics and performed acrobatics for years, but that she has a rotator cuff that was permanently damaged. "I spent too many years body-building and weight-lifting," she says.

Otherwise, aside from these bizarre remarks and constantly complaining about insurance companies, she is absolutely calm, cool and collected, as though she doesn't have a care in the world. *There was no fraud*, she keeps reminding Olga in a rather condescending monotone. *Why, McDavid loved us. He wanted to be part of our family.*

Relax, Helen urges as Olga keeps up her rant. While Helen may be facing a lifetime of uncertainty, she certainly doesn't sound the least bit concerned or worried. The fact that she is under arrest and in handcuffs doesn't seem to faze her, because in her mind, she already has it figured out. There was no fraud, let *alone* murder. If anything, Helen just sits on that hard folding chair in that lockup room like a high and mighty grande dame, waiting to be served by a waiter in a tux who will plop down some tea and crumpets on fine Rosenberg china.

In excerpts of their conversation, Olga is heard constantly scolding her partner in crime:

"Helen, this is your fault. You cannot make that many insurances," Olga says. "It's on your name only. Three, four different extra insurances."

"All right," Helen replies, trying to get Olga to stop talking about insurance policies. Helen, suspecting they are being recorded, orders Olga to shut up. "I want to ask for a different location if you're going to talk. I don't want to talk. Don't talk to me."

"Well, you have to [talk to me], because you did all these extra insurances. That's what raised the suspicion. You can't do that. Stupidity. You should have a good relationship with me, that would not have happened."

The detectives who had been following the women were of the opinion that Helen was the brains of the operation and Olga was the gofer.

No matter how many times Helen tries steering Olga away from the case, saying that she doesn't want to talk to her anymore, it doesn't stop Olga from incriminating the pair and digging a deeper hole.

Helen tries to convey to Olga that all the police are after them for is mail fraud, not murder, which is a half-truth.

"They will confiscate the money they paid you and me," whines Olga.

"Be quiet. Who cares? They could be listening. The only thing they're after is mail fraud. All the insurance companies have gotten together collectively. They don't want to pay anything."

Olga, still not "reading" Helen's lips to stop talking about their legal problems, begins to question Helen about her legal defense. Again, Helen asks Olga to "Be quiet."

Olga finally changes the subject and begins to complain about the treatment she suffered when federal agents banged on her apartment door at six in the morning.

"Yeah, I couldn't believe this morning, they broke into my place. I was in my nightgown, barefeet on the street. They dragged me out [of] the whole building," Olga says.

"What do you think about me?" Helen says.

"And they made pictures and twenty-five years I lived in this building," says Olga. "It was like a scene out of a nightmare.

"I've never seen anything like it. There were ten cars in front of my house. They went into overkill. I was in my nightgown, Helen. They broke down my gate.

"Helen, I was in my bare feet. I was on the street."

"Me too. Bare feet."

Having discussed the trauma of their arrest, Olga reverts back to attacking MONY and Helen's greed, reminding her that her attorney said, "You fucked up the case."

"There's a limit. You can't do that. You were greedy. That's the problem. That's why I get angry. We had no problem with the relationship. You pay me and be nice. I was doing everything for you."

"You are talking, and you must be quiet," Helen reminds her.

"I know, but it's your fault that our relationship ended up like this. Admit that it was your fault," Olga insists. "No, you're going to go to jail, honey. They're going to lock you up."

"I don't think so," replies Helen. "This is mail fraud. I paid for them," Helen says, referring to the policies.

"You have to pay back," says Olga. "They will lock you up."

"I will sue them to the gills," Helen promises. "Besides, Kenneth [McDavid] loved us. He wanted to be part of our family."

And when gently reminded that on the insurance applications, Helen posed as McDavid's fiancée and misstated that Olga was his cousin, Olga gets sarcastic.

"Yeah, I was the cousin, you were the fiancée. Baloney."

"He signed for these policies, and we happen to be punished because of what he wanted us to do. That's not right.

Now remember the bottom line," Helen says. "Whatever Kenneth wanted, he did. Kenneth wanted all of this. Why? I don't know . . . what his philosophy was, if he planned to keep these policies enforced. I have no idea. I don't know where all of Kenneth's money came from, and neither do you."

At this point Helen is "writing" a script for the two women to follow when questioned by authorities.

"But we supported him," Olga agrees.

"Yes, we gave him money. Our money was intermixed," says Helen, who has now come up with a new scenario to explain to authorities why they are named as beneficiaries on so many of McDavid's insurance policies.

"When he needed money, I gave him money. You gave him money. Whatever. But you have to remember, I don't know where Kenneth got his money from. As far as I know, he always seemed to have money in his pockets, and . . ."

"No, he was a writer," Olga interrupts to add to the new storyline. "You know what . . ."

"I think he was paid under the table," Helen says.

Picking up on the latest reason on why Helen paid McDavid's bills, Olga further enlightens her that McDavid had money because she had typed up a $32-million movie script called *Checking Out* for him.

"But we supported him financially, very heavily," Olga divulges.

"Yes, and he let me to pay his bills, and he reimbursed me when he could," Helen lets Olga know.

"But in appreciation, why did he make the life insurance, why?" Olga asks. Before she can get an answer, Olga drops a bombshell of her own. Hearing from Helen that she might have to pay a defense lawyer "millions" to defend herself, she confides that she had planned to split.

"I should have taken the plane last month and get the fuck out of here and go back to Europe. I just wanted to open up another business."

Olga explains that she and her friends were going to

open a new business similar to the operation she and Helen
ran in California, but in Canada.

"I wanted a new business for two million dollars. But
it's all fucked up now," Olga says.

Olga may have offered more details about her new
scam, but Kilcoyne interrupted the exchange because the
two women had a date with the federal magistrate who was
to arraign them.

Chapter 6

Nailing the Coffin Shut

When detectives initially started investigating the case, it reminded them of the classic movie *Arsenic and Old Lace*, about a pair of dingbat elderly sisters who have an unusual proclivity for dispatching "lonely old bachelors"—who, they were convinced, were suffering—by kindheartedly giving them elderberry wine laced with arsenic, a dash of cyanide, and "just a pinch" of strychnine, and burying the bodies in the cellar.

Of course, Hollywood pulled out all the stops with this farcical black comedy, which starred Cary Grant as the bewildered nephew trying to cover up the dastardly deeds of his deadly duo of aunts.

But there wasn't anything comical or humorous about the murders of Paul Vados or Kenneth McDavid and possibly dozens of other homeless men whom Helen and Olga had reached out to in the guise of helping them.

With Helen and Olga tucked away temporarily in federal detention lockups, charged only with mail fraud, it gave the Los Angeles Police Department breathing room to gather evidence against "the girls" as to their involvement in the deaths.

Lead Detective Dennis Kilcoyne had started to put together a crack investigative team shortly after their federal arrest. The decision he made was that he and LAPD Detective Rosemary Sanchez would concentrate on seeking evidence involving the murders of the two men. FBI Special Agent Samuel Mayrose would probe all of Helen and Olga's bank records to determine where they'd hidden money, and also examine and check into all of their cell phone calls. This left Robert Brockway of the California Department of Insurance with one of the most difficult jobs of all: finding all of the policies the women had taken out, not only on McDavid and Vados, but on any other potential victims. "It was like finding a needle in a haystack," he said.

Trying to gather enough evidence to charge Helen and Olga with murder was not going to be easy. Kilcoyne had already learned early on in his investigation that one reason the girls had been able to get away with their crimes was that insurance companies are so secretive. There is no clearing house where these firms can check each other's policies to see if the person is overinsured. And these companies certainly don't share information. As a result, one company doesn't know what the others are doing.

At their first meeting, it was agreed that Brockway would handle the insurance aspect of the case with the assistance of Mayrose, who would handle the banking issues.

"We met every Thursday at the L.A. Homicide Division on the third floor at the Parker Center. Dennis explained the two murders, and I remember at the conclusion of that first meeting, I felt, from the information I heard, that Helen and Olga were done . . . cooked. I knew that even though they were in a federal facility, we were going to get them for murder. I remember telling Sam, 'These two ladies are done. They are good to go.'

"Why did I say that? Because having worked as a sheriff's deputy, handling the insurance aspect of cases, I knew from my experience that whenever anyone commits white-collar paper crimes, they keep their records. They always do," the optimistic Brockway said.

Brockway explained that when dealing with insurance policies, people must make the monthly premium, and at the same time, keep track of and know the value of the policy.

"Even though the feds had already locked them up for mail fraud, I knew we were going to get these ladies on insurance fraud," Brockway said. "We knew if there was one insurance case, there would be a lot more. After that first meeting, when I walked out of that room, there was no doubt in my mind that we were going to get them, because if there was one case of insurance fraud, there would be a lot more, and that there would be a paper trail. And in that paper trail would be the motive and evidence for the murder.

"Obviously the motive was greed. I knew that the evidence for the murders would come up through the paper trail. I just knew that we just had to be patient and we'd get them," he said.

When Brockway got back to his office, he started to randomly fax about fifty insurance companies around the country and made inquiries about possible fraudulent claims. He checked and ran the names not only of Helen Golay and Olga Rutterschmidt, but also that of Helen's daughter, Kecia, through the systems of dozens of insurance companies, to determine where they had applied for policies.

"Eventually I got reports back from the NICB—the National Insurance Crime Bureau, one of my contacts. The NICB tracks . . . claims of possible fraud," explained Brockway.

Initially, he received reports of what is called "slip and falls" and a lot of traffic accidents to see if there was a pattern to an incident. Brockway checked on every involved party in the case—Helen, Olga, Vados, McDavid, Jimmy Covington. He ran their dates of birth, Social Security numbers, drivers' licenses and any known addresses they had ever used through the database.

The NICB was able to show Brockway possible claims, including any "near misses regarding the names" he had submitted.

After getting the NICB report and reviewing it,

Brockway's next task was to start making phone calls. "I must have made over five hundred calls. I sent out faxes and e-mails, and soon realized it was just the tip of the iceberg. It was like going through the Yellow Pages," Brockway recalls. "I then began to connect different insurance carriers, and requested insurance policies."

Brockway fanned out across the state and country searching for insurance policies, finding over two dozen that had been issued naming Helen and Olga as beneficiaries. The team began meeting daily.

"What was helpful is that sometimes Helen and Olga would list other insurance companies on a policy that they applied for. And then I would make additional inquiries to those insurance companies, and that's how the evidence in the case began to mount and mushroom," Brockway said.

Despite the complexity of finding these policies, Brockway was considered a miracle man by the team, and eventually he learned that Helen and Olga had taken out eighteen policies on McDavid and six on Vados, from some of the largest insurance companies in the country.

Among them were Transamerica, First Penn-Pacific, MONY, North American, AAA Life, Garden State, Empire General, Mutual of Omaha, Globe Life, United Investors, Great-West, AARP (New York Life), American Life, John Hancock, Interstate Assurance, Guarantee Trust, Monumental Life, CNA/Continental, American Bankers, and Guarantee Reserve.

When the team added up the total coverage on the life of Kenneth McDavid that the girls had applied for, it totaled $5,700,090. On Paul Vados, it added up to $879,500.

The detectives suspected that Helen and Olga had lined up another victim by the name of Jimmy Lee Covington, but they had no idea where to search for him. While they felt that the girls had already taken out a policy in his name, they had no way of finding what company had issued it.

Sam and Rob worked hand-in-hand on this case. "Do you know how we located Covington?" Brockway asks.

"When I made my inquiries to the insurance companies, Triple A got back to me, because we were checking on Vados and McDavid. That's when I learned that a policy application had also been made on Covington.

"I was given a date of birth, but that's all. I started checking with Motor Vehicles to determine if Covington had ever applied for a license or had any reason to register a car. We next checked with the Social Security Administration to see if he was collecting disability or SSI checks. You name the agency, we're running it through the system," Brockway remembers.

"Well, we got a hit and it showed that he was getting a Social Security SSI check at the Hollywood branch of Social Security at Sunset and Vine. We learned that Covington was to pick up his check at this office, but Sam and I decided to put a hold on him. Which meant Covington had to come in to the office and speak to a certain person in order to pick up his check.

"When Covington came in for his check, Sam and I were waiting for him, and that's how we found him the first time," Brockway said.

Covington was so frightened on learning that these women really could have had him killed, that after meeting with Sam and Rob, he went into hiding. It took law enforcement several months to locate him again.

"As for Helen and Olga, if they had just stopped with the six policies on Vados, they never would have gotten caught. They just did it too many times when it came to McDavid," observed Shellie Samuels, the deputy district attorney who was originally assigned to the case by the state during the investigation phase.

Along with their arrest on May 18, 2006, the federal government was able to trace the insurance proceeds Helen and Olga had received. Mayrose found that all Helen had left in her bank accounts was $1,181,008.71, while Olga had a mere $628,589.98 in hers. As a result, the government seized a total of $1,809,598.69 of their funds.

The forfeiture cleaned out Helen's and Olga's bank accounts, but it didn't stop Olga from filing a lawsuit seeking additional funds that she claimed were owed her as McDavid's beneficiary. The judge tossed out her bizarre request without even holding a hearing. But it also meant that since both women were without funds to pay an attorney, a public defender would have to be assigned to defend Olga, while Helen's private lawyer needed to apply to the court to determine whether the state would pay him.

On many of the policies, McDavid is listed as an "investor," "business associate," "real estate investor," or "retired real estate investor," with an annual income of anywhere from $100,000 to $150,000, and a net worth of $3 to $4 million. His home address is listed on all the policies as that of 424 Ocean Park Blvd., Santa Monica, California—which, of course, was Helen's residence.

On the personal financial statements, before being issued a $500,000 insurance policy, the girls would indicate that McDavid had $700,000 in assets, earned $72,000, and had earnings the year prior to the application of $65,000.

Olga's Hollywood address was on the policies where she was a beneficiary. In most cases, Helen listed herself as McDavid's fiancée, with Olga always listed as his cousin on policies that they shared.

On one $500,000 application, Helen and Olga falsely claimed that McDavid had written a $2 million screenplay called *Checking Out* to prove that he was an insurable interest and to show that they were investment partners.

In another policy Brockway found on Vados' life, Helen had submitted a letter to Mutual of Omaha in which she wrote that

> *he took this* [sic] *policies through the mail and paid by check or direct. Sometimes he'd give me money (cash) and ask me to pay the premiums. I believe he took out insurance for Olga and I* [sic] *to show his appreciation and to let us know he cared.*

As a result of Brockway working the case, perhaps one of the first big breaks in nailing the murderous matrons happened when he received some mind-blowing information while speaking with Ganae Smith, a supervisor with AAA.

Although probably best known for its emergency road services and maps, AAA provides its members with other services such as travel, financial, auto sales, and yes, insurance, including life insurance, in which the two enthusiastic spinsters had acquired a good deal of astounding expertise.

Smith, a twelve-year veteran with AAA, supervised a dozen agents and was responsible for overseeing the term life policy Helen Golay had taken out on Kenneth McDavid for $800,000. Initially, there was a contingent on the policy, stating that Helen's daughter, Kecia, and her granddaughter, Sophie, were entitled to share the benefits 50–50, if the primary beneficiary died.

The policy in question was actually entered into the AAA data system on January 17, 2003. At the time it was issued, Helen Golay was listed as the fiancée of Kenneth McDavid.

Helen sought a change of beneficiary on September 15, 2003, some time after the policy had been issued, and requested that the named contingent beneficiaries, Kecia and Sophie, be removed, which made Helen the full beneficiary of the $800,000 policy.

Brockway initially had called Smith seeking information as to whether AAA had any policies taken out by Helen Golay on a Jimmy Covington, whom the investigative team suspected might be a new prospective victim in her scam.

Smith began reviewing Helen's database files. They showed that an $800,000 policy had been applied for in Covington's name, but that there had been no further follow-up on it.

It was at that point in Brockway's conversation with Smith that she decided to check Helen's history with AAA.

"Oh, I also have a call for road service," Smith told Brockway. "Let me check another screen."

After a few minutes, Smith gave Brockway the news

that, in the end, would lead to the downfall of the girls. "Yes, Helen had a roadside service call on June twenty-second, 2005," Smith said.

"Where? Where abouts?" asked Brockway, his voice getting excited.

"On June twenty-first, 2005, at eleven-fifty-four p.m., a Helen Golay called the auto club requesting that a vehicle be towed. She called from a Chevron gas station at the corner of Westwood and Santa Monica Boulevards in Los Angeles."

The vehicle to be towed was a 1999 silver Mercury Sable. The tow ticket request indicated that the license plate number was "unknown," but that the car did have California tags.

Smith informed Brockway that a closer examination of Helen's database file also showed that she had submitted an order to AAA to claim payments of benefits, dated September 16, 2005, and it listed McDavid's date of death as June 22, 2005.

"That's odd," Smith observed.

Because the submission dates from Helen were unusual, Smith's suspicions were aroused. An immediate review of Helen's entire file with the auto club was next on the agenda. "It was kind of spaced out," Smith said, referring to the dates on the claim forms. "As a rule, when we see someone has passed away, they usually file the claim right away. This one just kind of struck me, in that they waited almost three months before they filed the claim."

Another oddity that stood out to Smith as she delved further into the file was that Helen Golay had not only used her roadside service membership to call for a tow around the same date and time of Kenneth McDavid's death, but had requested that the disabled vehicle be towed to the alley behind her Santa Monica triplex.

It was one of the best clues in the case, Brockway said, in that it came from Helen Golay herself. It directly linked her and her partner in crime, Olga Rutterschmidt, to the murder of Kenneth McDavid.

With the information Smith provided to Brockway, he and the investigative team began tracking down the history of the Mercury Sable.

Another surprise for investigators was that the car had never been registered to or owned by either Helen or Olga. What saved the day was that, after the feds issued their search warrants on Helen's home and on her personal car, a Mercedes-Benz ML500 sports utility vehicle with dealer plates, they found her daily planner notebook.

On one of the pages of the planner, a Post-it note was found that read:

lic FYR482 Hilary Adler 99 Merc Sable wagon VIN # 604946

Information from the Post-it was run through the Department of Motor Vehicles databases, and it revealed that the current registered owner of the Sable was the same person listed on the note. The registration had expired in 2004.

By May 26, 2006, Dennis Kilcoyne and Sam Mayrose had interviewed Hilary Adler. It turned out that the Encino woman had been a victim of identity theft, and that she had never purchased or owned a 1999 Mercury Sable. She did say, however, that her purse had been stolen in April 2003 from the Spectrum Athletic Club, where both Kecia and Helen were also members.

Further, when investigators executed the search warrant at Olga's residence on May 18, 2006, they found an envelope indicating that "Helen Sent Pictures," of Hilary Adler's name and address and cell phone number. The envelope also contained several photocopies of Adler's driver's license.

By then, the same car had been cited by the Santa Monica Police Department in June 2005 for being illegally parked in an alley, directly behind where Helen lived. But when the detectives arrested her, the vehicle was no longer near her home.

A few weeks later, according to documents found by

Brockway, the car mysteriously showed up in the 1700 block of Vista Street in Hollywood, which was less than a mile from Olga's apartment on Sycamore Avenue.

A check of the vehicle showed that it had been ticketed three times between July 15 and 20, and that it was then impounded and determined to have been abandoned.

By tracking the Mercury through DMV databases, investigators found out that it had been sold to Olga Rutterschmidt on January 20, 2004, more than two years before it had been used as the murder weapon to kill Kenneth McDavid. The vehicle had been kept in the alley behind Helen's apartment until June 21, 2005.

Auto salesman Mario Medina of Mexicar Auto Sales said he had sold the car to Olga, who'd claimed she was buying it for her friend when she'd falsely used the name of Hilary Adler to execute the transaction.

The impound records indicated that the Sable, which had front-end damage, was eventually sold by Hollywood Tow to another person who was unaware of its past, said Detective Rosemary Sanchez.

The vehicle was ultimately purchased by the LAPD for $4,000. Kilcoyne had it towed to their Scientific Investigation Division, where it was taken apart and checked for past damage and analyzed for DNA.

An inspection of the right rear of the car found what looked like blood, and also discovered wiping marks and a repaired fuel line. This indicated to the expert examining the vehicle that the fuel lines had been broken. When a vehicle has had a sharp impact or collision with another object, the fuel line usually breaks, making it impossible to drive the car.

McDavid's autopsy report showed no bruising or broken bones in his legs, which are typically found in collisions in which pedestrians are struck by vehicles while upright.

Based on the autopsy report and photographs of McDavid's body, it appeared that he had been wearing his eyeglasses when he was run over. This led investigators to believe that the vehicle's impact with him had been at a fairly low speed, as higher-speed vehicle collisions tend to result in the pedestrians' eyeglasses being thrown away from their bodies by the force of impact.

A closer examination of the undercarriage of the Mercury was conducted, revealing what appeared to be blood and organic matter, which DNA tests confirmed was McDavid's.

Autopsy reports and preliminary forensic analysis indicated that both Vados and McDavid likely had been lying flat, horizontally, face up on the ground when they were initially hit and run over. A toxicology analysis of McDavid conducted during the autopsy indicated that he'd had three substances in his blood at the time of his death, including two prescription drugs that, taken together, could have rendered him unconscious.

The toxicology analysis of Vados run during his initial autopsy did not test for prescription drugs. The autopsy reports for Vados and the photos of his body did not indicate any bruising or broken bones in his legs.

Based on their preliminary findings, the detectives concluded that neither Vados nor McDavid had been standing when hit by the vehicles that killed them.

What grabbed the detectives' attention was that the autopsy report contained a toxicology screening of McDavid's blood that showed that it contained chemicals found in alcohol (ethanol), prescription sleep aids such as Ambien (zolpidem), and prescription painkillers such as Vicodin (hydrocodone).

Based on the medications discovered during execution of the search warrant, Kilcoyne was convinced that McDavid had been drugged with pills or alcohol first, and then run over.

"If they were awake, it would be a slow, painful death," Deputy District Attorney Shellie Samuels said of the report.

"Such chemicals, in the amounts described in the autopsy report as being found in McDavid's blood, could render a person of his size and weight unconscious," concluded Sam Mayrose, who had a second search warrant issued on

June 9, 2006, by U.S. Magistrate Judge Marganel A. Nagle. This was done so that detectives could search Helen's and Olga's residences to look for similar medications.

Four bottles of hydrocodone were found at Helen's home, each of which had initially contained fifty pills. Three were prescribed to Helen. The fourth bottle was in Kecia's name.

Of the bottles prescribed to Helen, one was prescribed on September 15, 2003, and contained twenty-nine pills. Another bottle prescribed on September 17, 2003, contained forty pills. The third bottle, dated September 29, 2003, contained thirty-eight pills.

The bottle prescribed to Kecia had been prescribed after McDavid's June 21, 2005, death.

A bottle of Ambien, which contains zolpidem, found in McDavid's body during his autopsy, had been prescribed to Helen on June 24, 2002, and consisted of 10-milligram tablets.

By June 2006, Mayrose had had a judge sign an order to exhume and examine the remains of Paul Vados, who was buried in Plot RE-363, Section F of the Evergreen Cemetery in Los Angeles. The purpose was to determine whether Helen and Olga had drugged him before running him over in November 1999.

Vados' body was immediately transported by a staff member from the Los Angeles County Coroner's office on North Mission Road.

It was at that point that Kilcoyne met with Joseph Muto, chief of the LAPD forensic laboratory, who explained that standard toxicology procedures at the time of Vados' death in 1999 did not include testing for the existence of prescription medications. And, unless there was a special request for a more complete screening, Muto's division only tested for the presence of alcohol, marijuana, and cocaine. There was no evidence that those substances had been found in Vados' body, and there was no check for the presence of prescription medications.

Detective Rosemary Sanchez went back to North Cherokee Avenue, where McDavid had lived, to again touch base with building manager Danielli Cosgrove to see if she could recall any details about Patrick, the elusive roommate who had stayed in the apartment with him for a brief period of time.

From information she gathered from Cosgrove and others in her search, Sanchez learned that his full name was Patrick Lamay, and tracked him down in Michigan. Lamay told her he had met McDavid in 2001 in Los Angeles. In 2004, McDavid told Lamay that Helen Golay had approached him at the Hollywood Presbyterian Church on North Gower Street, and offered to get him off the streets if he would sign an application for a $500,000 life insurance policy.

Lamay said that it was his understanding that McDavid had then moved into apartment 410 at the North Cherokee Avenue address, where Lamay lived with him for about four or five months.

He said that Helen had paid the rent, and did not want anyone other than McDavid living in the apartment. But at some point, Olga, who had a key, showed up. When she saw that Lamay, his girlfriend, and two others had also taken up residence there, Olga left, to return later with an unknown man carrying a revolver.

Olga began yelling at Lamay and told him that he and his friends could not live there. At that point, he gathered his belongings and left.

Sometime after this incident, Lamay ran into McDavid at Sunset and Las Palmas in Los Angeles. McDavid told him that he was no longer staying at the apartment and that Helen was putting him up at a number of different motels in downtown Los Angeles.

During the course of the early investigation, court records were found showing that both Helen and Olga were litigious ladies; they had filed over forty civil lawsuits between them over the last twenty years. Most had been filed by Helen, naming tenants, real estate partners, banks, health clubs, restaurants, and neighbors.

She was not even above suing her own daughter. In 2003, she was bold enough to accuse Kecia and Steve Taracevicz, her boyfriend at the time, of assault and trespassing, and demanded $275,000. In turn, Kecia and Taracevicz denied the allegations and pointed the finger right back at Mommy Dearest. "My mother has exhibited thirty years of psychopathic behavior," was Kecia's response, charging that Helen had threatened to kill Taracevicz, scratched his automobile with a key, and hired a security guard to prevent him from visiting Kecia.

Over the years, however, the mother and daughter appeared to have reconciled.

In 2005, Kecia served a 200-day jail sentence on charges of stalking her former boyfriend, according to the district attorney's office.

And when Helen was arrested, Kecia showed she was a chip off the old block, at least with respect to her treatment of her mother's tenants. She took to living at one of her mother's properties—a four-unit structure at 609 Marine Avenue in Santa Monica with white picket fencing. And she sent handwritten notes to all of Helen's tenants, including her mother's property at 2817 Third Street, a rent-controlled complex with a number of single apartments, instructing them that they were now required to make out their rent payments to her.

"I mean, look at this. She wants us to pay her quick before heading off to jail too," an unidentified tenant told the *Santa Monica Daily Press*.

Not to be outdone in suing people, albeit on a much smaller scale, the investigators found that Olga had also gotten into the act. She'd filed several lawsuits naming the Ralphs supermarket chain, claiming a stack of boxes had fallen on her. She sued a Hollywood coffee shop as well, alleging that a diner had shocked her with a stun gun. It was unclear from documents filed in civil court whether she ever collected on either lawsuit.

Helen and Olga were arraigned on June 5, 2006, before

U.S. Magistrate Judge Paul L. Abrams. Both were asked whether they understood the charges against them, and then entered their not guilty pleas.

At the arraignment, the judge denied her lawyer's request that Helen be moved from a San Bernardino federal lockup to the Metropolitan Detention Center in downtown Los Angeles to be closer to where Olga was being held, saying that another judge had ordered that the women be kept separate.

Watching the proceedings in the spectator section of the courtroom were Stella Vados and Kecia Golay.

"I just wanted to see them," Stella said when asked why she'd made the journey from her Northern California home.

Kecia refused to comment about her mother, but Helen's new attorney, Roger Jon Diamond, described the hit-and-run grannies as "two nice ladies who did nothing wrong."

The lawyer's response to the traffic death of Fred Downie, the 97-year-old struck dead a year after Vados, was merely to shrug off the suspicions that his client had anything to do with the death. "It's a titillating issue for some lawyers. But it is not a criminal case, there was no wrongdoing, she's not a suspect. She fully cooperated. That should be the end of the matter," Diamond said.

Outside of court, Diamond insisted that Helen had done nothing wrong and that she and Olga were merely friends. "Helen is eager to have a trial and get this thing resolved. She has an explanation, and what has happened now is that she has become a victim of innuendo," Diamond said.

The lawyer attributed the deaths of Vados and McDavid to nothing more than sheer coincidence. "My client had nothing to do with their death[s]," Diamond said.

Olga's lawyer could not be reached for comment that day.

From the time of their federal arrest, Helen and Olga had kept their lawyers busy seeking to be released on bail, which was consistently denied by the judge, who ruled that prosecutors had shown probable cause that the pair had committed murder and were flight risks.

Diamond questioned the federal government's motivation in filing the lawsuit against the women.

"The government is simply doing the dirty work of the insurance companies. Why should federal taxpayers finance a lawsuit designed only to benefit the insurance companies?"

While that argument went nowhere, it didn't stop Diamond from trying again and again.

Shortly before they were indicted on state charges, Diamond made one last attempt to have Helen released on bail.

U.S. Magistrate Judge Jeffrey Johnson denied the request, even though they had not been charged in the deaths of McDavid and Vados. In making his ruling, he relied on government evidence that FBI Special Agent Sam Mayrose had outlined for him, which included blood found in the Mercury Sable, lists of personal data such as Social Security numbers found in Helen's and Olga's homes, lists of life insurance premiums and payouts, what was found on their computer hard drives, photocopies of rent receipts and personal checks, and the monumental job of checking out their landline and cell phone records.

"These women . . . there is probable cause to believe, have committed murder," Johnson said.

Lawyers for Helen and Olga tried to convince the judge otherwise, saying that the women posed no flight risk or public danger. Diamond argued that Helen was a grandmother with little money available and no plans to flee.

"She wants to stay and fight the charges," he said.

When public defender Kim Savo brought up Olga's age and the fact that she didn't have a passport, she also had a hard time trying to get the judge to change his mind. Besides, the assistant U.S. attorney reminded the judge, when Olga was arrested, she'd told police that if she had a valid passport, she had plans to run to Canada.

"If she isn't a flight risk, what does that make her?" Johnson asked Olga's attorney.

"A frightened seventy-three-year-old woman," Savo replied.

As with earlier federal hearings, Helen's daughter Kecia

and Vados' daughter Stella were in the courtroom, sitting on opposite sides of the room. Stella spent most of her time staring angrily at Helen. Kecia waved at her mother and frequently wiped away tears during the hearing, but when she tried reaching out to touch Helen, a marshal warned her that she would be banned from sitting in the courtroom during the proceedings if she did so again.

Kecia began sobbing after the dressing-down.

Finally, on July 31, the Los Angeles County District Attorney charged Helen and Olga with four counts of murder, which also included the special circumstances of murder for financial gain and multiple murder.

In the indictment, prosecutors detailed eighteen overt acts on counts one and two and twenty-two overt acts on counts three and four. The overt acts listed specific particulars such as Helen and Olga filing a missing persons report saying that Paul Vados was missing and falsely claiming to be his only relatives, and having made fraudulent claims to dozens of life insurance companies between December 1999 and November 2000.

Among some of the other overt acts detailed were that Helen and Olga had created a rubber stamp in Kenneth McDavid's name; that they had applied for at least fifteen life insurance policies; that they'd purchased a 1999 Mercury Stable station wagon for $6,000, using the name of Hilary Adler; that the vehicle had been stored behind Helen Golay's home from January 20, 2004, to June 21, 2005, and was later found abandoned on July 19, 2005, five blocks from Olga Rutterschmidt's Hollywood apartment; and that Helen Golay had misrepresented herself to the Los Angeles County Department of Coroner, obtained the release of McDavid's body, and had it cremated.

The district attorney accused the two women of fraudulently cashing more than $2 million in life insurance claims on the two men they had befriended and were charged with murdering.

This made the two grannies eligible for the death penalty.

They were also charged with two counts of conspiracy to commit murder for financial gain.

In dismissing the fraud case, the United States Attorney's Office said they were agreeing to it with the understanding that they retained the option of refiling the charges at another time should the two women be acquitted of murder in state court.

Chapter 7

Court is Torture for Helen

After their federal arrest in May 2006, Helen Golay was known as inmate number 43630-112 and Olga Rutterschmidt as inmate number 43629-112, and their temporary home was the Roybal Federal Building in downtown Los Angeles.

But all that changed on Wednesday, August 16, 2006.

That's when Helen and Olga exchanged their confined living accommodations at the federal detention facility for typical 12-foot-by-8-foot cells at the Century Regional Detention Facility in Lynwood, California, shortly after they were re-arrested that same day.

Los Angeles police detectives had arrested the two women at 6:10 p.m. after a federal judge released Helen and Olga from federal custody—so they could be re-arrested on the state capital murder charges.

Thirty minutes after they were re-arrested, both women were booked on charges of murdering Paul Vados and Kenneth McDavid in order to claim insurance proceeds. Their arraignment was set for Thursday morning in Division 30 at the downtown Superior Courthouse, but in the meantime they were shipped off to spend the first of many nights at Lynwood.

"We owe a debt to the Los Angeles office of the FBI," said lead investigator Dennis Kilcoyne. "They put the federal case together so we could take both these women out of circulation before they could strike again. They gave us the breathing room to complete the homicide investigation."

Kilcoyne also gave thanks to the assistance of Rob Brockway from the California Department of Insurance to help locate the many policies the women had opened on their targeted victims.

The murder charges were based upon the totality of the circumstances behind the women's scheme, Kilcoyne said. The keystone in the case was connecting DNA found on a silver Mercury Sable station wagon to Kenneth McDavid's 2005 death. "We found tissue in three locations on the undercarriage of the car," Kilcoyne said. "We have records to show both women bought this car in 2004, which was the murder weapon, [and] that they stored it at Golay's house."

The detectives also released two photographs and three names of homeless men they were looking for, in hopes of finding them alive, and interviewing them: Nicolas Koos, born November 17, 1939; Jimmy Allen Covington, born August 9, 1960; and Scott Gones, no picture or birth date available. Brockway, who had located Covington months earlier, believed that he might have gone into hiding in the San Francisco area.

Helen and Olga were detained at the all-female Lynwood detention facility, located five miles south of downtown Los Angeles. Holding 2,200 inmates, the two-story concrete building is surrounded by a bustling industrial neighborhood that runs alongside train tracks near a busy freeway.

The prison, where Helen and Olga would spend the next two years, had been nicknamed the *Lynwood Hilton* when hotel heiress Paris Hilton began a 23-day stint there in May 2007. In fact, Helen's cell was one module over from Paris, Helen's lawyer, Roger Jon Diamond, said.

"They were in the same situation, in that Helen was in a cell by herself, a K-ten unit for 'keepaways.' Paris didn't want to mingle with the other prisoners, and Helen also preferred to be alone."

Hilton's short-lived stay at the facility was not unusual. She joined a list of actresses and personalities who have served sentences at Lynwood due to arrests for drunk driving or possession of small amounts of drugs. Other female celebrities who have briefly bedded down at Lynwood include Nicole Richie, the daughter of Lionel Richie, who was there for 82 minutes, and Lindsay Lohan, who spent 84 minutes there before being released.

It is common procedure for nonviolent offenders to be released from jail early when the facility is overcrowded.

Helen and Olga, who had been used to the finer things in life, soon learned that they had to make do with their frugal furnishings at Lynwood, getting by with a fixed small white stool and desk, two bunk beds each with a single green vinyl mattress, a steel toilet and sink, and a small window.

They were mandated by court order to be housed in separate units of the jail in the special-needs area. They had to take their meals in their cells. Like other inmates in their unit, once a day they were allowed out of their cramped space to shower, watch television in the day room, participate in outdoor recreation, or talk on the telephone.

Cell phones, BlackBerrys and Trēos were not permitted in the jail, not even for visitors.

Instead of the fashionable tight miniskirts that Helen often wore, she and Olga were now required to be satisfied with unspectacular orange prison jumpsuits. Helen in particular complained long and loud about her fashion attire, to no avail, constantly asking her jailers for her tweezers and insisting on wanting to wear makeup.

During her nearly 2-year stay at Lynwood, Olga became such a relentless whiner, bitching to her guards about the food, access to her favorite television programs, clothes, cellmates, showering, and recreation, that to shut her up, she was continuously thrown in the hole for days on end. The term frequently used by her jailers was that Olga was a *kvetch*.

Helen also kept her jailers on the go demanding anything and everything from new shoes—because her current ones were "worn out"—to makeup to thermal underwear and new clothes to keep her warm to wanting to be released to go vote.

Another demand Helen made, which the judge denied, was a cell for herself. Diamond said that Helen wanted to get rid of her cellmate, claiming that the woman had been harassing her and preventing her from concentrating on her case.

On entering the facility, both women were given a gift from the state: a kit that included a toothbrush, toothpaste, soap, a comb, deodorant, and shampoo, along with a pencil, stationery, envelopes, and stamps.

The Black Widows, as the media began calling Helen and Olga, made their long-awaited debut in court on August 17, 2006, on the ninth floor of the Clara Shortridge Foltz Criminal Justice Center in downtown Los Angeles. Foltz was the first female lawyer on the West Coast admitted to the California State Bar. She was also the sister of U.S. Senator Samuel Shortridge and a descendant of Daniel Boone. Her many trail-blazing accomplishments include becoming the first female clerk for the State Judiciary Committee, the first woman appointed to the State Board of Corrections, the first woman licensed as a Notary Public, and in 1930, the first woman to run for Governor of California, at the age of 81. This building has been the venue for, among many others, the O. J. Simpson and Phil Spector murder trials.

Everyone seated in the Department 102 courtroom awaited the arrival of Superior Court Judge David S. Wesley. Wesley is considered a down-to-earth judge, appointed to the Superior Court by Governor Peter Wilson in 1997. Prior to his appointment, Wesley served as a hearing judge of the state bar court for two years and subsequently was appointed a Superior Court commissioner, presiding over a juvenile court.

Last year, Wesley was named Judge of the Year by

Southwestern Law School, one of nearly two dozen awards he has received since 1990.

He has presided over dozens of felony trials, and also enjoys devoting a great deal of time and effort to the Los Angeles County teen courts, a program where juveniles accused of first-time offenses submit their cases to juries of their peers.

Prior to his appointment as a judge, Wesley joined the Los Angeles County Public Defender's office in 1972. He stayed there until 1981, when he entered private practice as a partner in Overland, Berke, Wesley, Gits, Randolph & Levanas, and there he remained until 1991.

Shellie Samuels, the deputy district attorney, had been assigned to take over the Golay–Rutterschmidt case as soon as Helen and Olga were arrested.

Samuels had grown up in the San Fernando Valley and, before attending law school, was a school teacher for two years. She has been with the district attorney's office nearly a quarter of a century. For almost nine years, her forte has been prosecuting gang-related cases.

"I didn't know much about prosecuting until my third year at law school. There was a program at Loyola, and I did a preliminary hearing and decided, 'This is what I want to do.'"

Once out of law school, she passed the Bar, was hired at the district attorney's office, and has been there ever since. "I knew that I would never be happy as a lawyer sitting in an office doing briefs," she says. Starting with misdemeanor cases, she moved on to preliminary hearings and spent time prosecuting juveniles before starting on felony and gang trials in 1984.

"It's a lot scarier now than it was back then, but I never had a witness killed," she says.

In 1993, she was the first woman to be presented with the Prosecutor of the Year Award by the Los Angeles County Association of Deputy District Attorneys, and has some fifty murder trials under her belt. "The only case I ever lost is Robert Blake, and I'm still not over it," she admits.

What does she think went wrong on the verdict? Samuels was asked. "Part of it was that Blake appeared sympathetic. He's a little man, and he sat in the defense chair with his little legs dangling, and then he would go out during a break for a cigarette and mingle with the jurors and sign autographs."

Samuels is married and had her first child when she was 41 years old, her second when she was 44.

"When I first got the Golay–Rutterschmidt case, the feds had the case as a mail fraud case. If they had gotten convicted in federal court of mail fraud, because of their ages, they never would have gotten out. But with the murder case, you really have to prosecute.

"There was another homeless man that they had approached that we considered putting on during the trial phase of the case. I don't recall his name, but he indicated to them that he wasn't interested in any of their 'help,'" Samuels said.

In reviewing the case, Samuels said it was her opinion that Fred Downie, the elderly man Kecia befriended, was "a very weird coincidence."

"The man had a house in Massachusetts, and Kecia started calling him 'Grandpa,' and she got him to move to California. He actually gave Kecia's half-sister Pamela money for her chiropractor business, and he gave money also to Kecia and Helen Golay.

"They didn't treat him so great," Samuels said. "What confused the investigative team after he ended up getting hit by a car that killed him, was when we learned that Helen and Olga didn't really have any insurance on him. It was the one that really got away. But they did get money anyway, because they fooled the woman who accidentally hit him and sued her, the insurance company, and the auto insurance company.

"Nobody would have issued them ten or twelve policies on these homeless men, claiming that they were employed and earning one hundred thousand dollars to one hundred sixty thousand dollars a year.

"Even if you make one hundred sixty thousand dollars a year, they are not going to issue ten policies on you, because at some point you are over-insured, and your life isn't worth it. The problem is that insurance companies don't share information.

"If companies didn't pay them off right away, they threatened to sue. Not only that, but Olga, who had already received maybe many millions of dollars, needed a copy of the autopsy report and death certificate on McDavid in order to collect on one of his many policies. But Olga sent a letter to the coroner's office asking them to waive the sixteen-dollar fee because she was a poor woman who couldn't afford the fee.

"Talk about chutzpah," Samuels says. "You kill a guy and then you don't want to pay for his autopsy report? It's just greed. That's the sad part. It's just pure greed."

On the opposite side of the room, at the defense table, inside the well of the courtroom, sat public defender Michael Sklar, representing Olga Rutterschmidt. Born in Detroit, Michigan, forty-seven years before, Sklar had gone West at an early age and graduated from California Western School of Law in San Diego. While in law school, he went to work for Robert M. Takasugi, the senior federal judge for the Central District of California, and the first Japanese-American appointed to the federal bench as an extern.

After graduation, he stayed with the judge, who recommended that he join the Los Angeles County Public Defender's office, which Sklar did on January 2, 1990. He has been there ever since.

Roger Jon Diamond, a criminal lawyer whose office in Santa Monica was just blocks from the real estate holdings his clients once owned, sat next to Helen Golay at the defense table.

Diamond admits he wanted to be a lawyer ever since he was 10 years old, when he started researching how he could get his neighbors' dogs to stop doing their business on his front lawn. Then, in high school, his civics teacher had him read a Missouri case about migrating birds that he said fascinated him because "there was a solution" to the story. "I love reading court decisions. Every night I read court decisions, and I keep track of the appellate decisions.

"I'm just addicted to the law, and I enjoy the whole process," he said. "To me it's like the Gary Cooper scene in *High Noon*—me against them—the FBI, the LAPD, the DA. It's me against them, and it's a great feeling.

"As a matter of fact, it has affected the Golay case, because it was on January twelfth, 2007, that I read a case that directly supported my argument that her right to a speedy preliminary hearing was violated, in that it must be held within sixty days of when she was arraigned, unless she waived that right.

"I immediately filed a motion to dismiss the Golay case. I was right on. If I hadn't read the advance sheets every day, I wouldn't have seen that case," he said.

As a result, Diamond filed a motion and forced the prosecution to refile charges not only against Helen, but against Olga as well.

"And so for about ninety minutes on January eighteenth, the date we were in court, Helen Golay had no federal case pending against her, because a judge dismissed the case and there was no state case pending against her, because that case was dismissed," Diamond said.

Of course, prosecutors promptly refiled murder charges against Golay, notwithstanding the fact that the two women were originally arraigned in September 2006 and should have had a preliminary hearing within sixty days.

"When I was with Helen in the lockup there, I said, 'You're a free woman right now,' because I said at the very beginning I would get the federal case dismissed, which is true, and I said I would get the state case dismissed, which is true, and so for a brief moment there, she had nothing pending against her, she was a free lady," he said.

Some states, such as California, rarely use grand juries in seeking an indictment. As an alternative, California prefers using the preliminary hearing route in criminal courts.

Defendants are automatically entitled to such a hearing. It is often referred to as a "prelim" and it is a formal proceeding before a judge in which evidence is presented so that the court may determine whether there is sufficient cause to hold the defendant for trial on a felony charge. In short, a prelim is a "mini-trial," where prosecutors present witnesses establishing that a crime has been committed and the defendant is responsible. Not every state holds a preliminary hearing.

At the end of the prelim, once the judge decides whether there is enough evidence to support the charges against the defendant, the accused can enter a plea. The prelim is used to flesh out the prosecution's case and to lock in their witness's testimony in preparation for trial.

The most notable difference between a prelim and trial is the burden of proof. At trial, the prosecutor must prove a defendant's guilt beyond a reasonable doubt. But at a preliminary hearing, the State needs only to present evidence to convince the court that there is probable cause to hold the defendant to answer to the charge.

In Diamond's motion to dismiss the case against Helen, he argued that Judge Wesley had granted Olga's requests for postponements over his client's continued objections.

When a date of February 20, 2007, was then set for a new prelim—thirty-three days later—Diamond objected, pointing out that he had to be in Orange County for a re-trial in another case.

"Orange County can wait," Judge Wesley replied.

Although Diamond was initially successful in dismissing the case, Deputy District Attorney Samuels did not view it as a setback to the prosecution case. "No, not at all. It's really not important except procedurally, as long as we don't go over the sixty days again, which we won't," she said. "Let's put it this way," she added. "We don't want another dismissal."

For months, the prelim had been marked by delay after delay. The delays were caused largely by Michael Sklar, who had joined the defense of Olga in July 2006, while

Diamond had been present from the beginning, with the federal arrest of the women.

Diamond continually sought a speedy trial, as guaranteed by the Sixth Amendment of the U.S. Constitution, but since both women were to be tried together, the judge felt obligated to be fair to requests from both defendants.

"There's tremendous work generated by law enforcement, and I'm working through their investigation and conducting one of our own," Sklar explained in arguing why he needed more time. Sklar informed the judge that he had received hundreds of pages of discovery and had hundreds of witnesses to interview.

So while Sklar kept getting postponements, Diamond kept filing motion after motion objecting to the postponements and also outlining dozens of Helen's complaints.

When the preliminary hearing was again delayed, Diamond was shocked that the procedure was taking so much time.

"The prelim is such a very unimportant procedure. It's an ancient relic from older days," Diamond said.

Finally, Monday, March 12, 2007, arrived, the day that everyone had been waiting for. According to the National Weather Service, the temperature in downtown Los Angeles was a balmy 80 degrees. The Black Widows' long-delayed preliminary hearing was about to take place, and the two women were about to get their day in court.

Helen again insisted that Diamond ask the judge to allow her to leave the courthouse and return to her cell in the Los Angeles County Prison after every hearing—otherwise, she'd be stuck in the courthouse until late at night before being returned to Lynwood, which meant that she would be getting back later than desired.

In denying her request, the judge ruled that Golay was not entitled to special treatment over the hundreds of other inmates who arrive at the courthouse daily and stay until the conclusion of the court day.

Outside in the ninth-floor corridor in Department 102,

there was an air of anticipation, as if the camera crew lining up outside the door were awaiting the arrival of Britney Spears, Paris Hilton or Lindsay Lohan, frequent guests to the courthouse.

Inside the wood-paneled courtroom, the fifty to sixty members of the audience sat quietly, speaking in soft tones, awaiting the appearance of Judge Wesley, who would swiftly open the door behind the bench and take his seat.

The spectator section was packed with young lawyers from the prosecutor's office, and detectives and investigators who had worked on the case for nearly two years. Dozens of reporters filled most of the other seats, poised to take down witnesses' every word with their blue and red pens and slim notebooks.

In the audience, sitting alone, was Kecia Golay, a blonde knockout, looking tanned, stunning, and elegant in her Ralph Lauren outfit, wearing sandals and sporting a $2,000 Cartier "Tank" watch on her wrist. As far as is known by detectives who worked the case, Kecia didn't have a job. But she did collect rent from all of her mother's properties, and had been living on the thousands of dollars Helen had accrued from the insurance scheme that got her into her latest legal jam.

Helen made her grand entrance into the courtroom wearing an orange prison jumpsuit. She looked haggard and worn-out compared to her mug shot, in which she was primped up in her 'sixties-style bouffant. Gone were her bleached-blonde tresses, replaced now with long, streaked, straggly ash-gray hair. As she was escorted to her seat by a court officer, Kecia began sobbing loudly and uncontrollably. Her non-stop weeping jag prompted a good Samaritan, seated behind her in the audience, to hand her a tissue.

Olga sat next to Sklar and, complementing her orange jumpsuit, courtesy of the state, she was using foam hair rollers as barrettes. She had a mousy look about her and turned around in her chair to see who was in the audience.

A few seats away from Kecia sat the relatives of Kenneth McDavid and Paul Vados. Sandra Salman, a stern look on her face, sat solemnly in her seat with her brother and other members of McDavid's family. Nearby, with her boyfriend, was Stella Carmen Vados, merely looking intently at the two women at the defense table, convinced they had taken her father's life.

At 9:47 a.m., after concluding another trial, Judge Wesley called the case against Helen and Olga to order. It had taken five attempts to get the preliminary hearing on the road.

No sooner did Judge Wesley deny media requests for cameras in the courtroom than Diamond was up on his feet wanting, again for the official record, he said, to make an issue of the conditions in the jail.

"Your Honor—Miss Golay advises me that today she was awakened at three o'clock in the morning. Of course, this is the first business day after daylight savings time, which makes getting up early even more severe on this particular day.

"But in general, by awakening Miss Golay at three o'clock in the morning, and putting her in a holding facility at the county jail, and then busing them here to the court, all of these things together operate to deprive her of her ability to concentrate and follow the proceedings, because she's so tired. And this is something that I guess will persist throughout the preliminary hearing. It will become more serious if there is a trial in this matter.

"And, also because she is exhausted, she cannot assist me in a way that a person should be able to assist an attorney during the proceedings. And therefore, her right to effective assistance of counsel under the Sixth Amendment is also jeopardized.

"So we respectfully ask the court to make an appropriate order directing the sheriff not to awaken Miss Golay until a reasonable hour, say seven, seven-thirty in the morning, so when she's brought here, she can function. Or, in the alternative, that she be permitted to be released on bail or on her own recognizance. Otherwise, it's just a terrible ordeal for her to have to endure. We did make this request once before, but I wanted to reiterate it now, Your Honor."

Judge Wesley wasted no time in denying Diamond's proposal. "I wish I could sleep in until seven-thirty in the morning and get to court on time and do all the things that I have to do. She is in custody. She has to be transported. I don't tell the sheriff how to do their business. If she needs to rest, she can take a nap at lunchtime in between the proceedings.

"But in the meantime, she's not suffering any more than any other inmate who has to be transported around the County of Los Angeles on any given day. And so the motion is denied.

"All right. Are we ready to proceed then?" the judge sharply asked Diamond.

"All rise," the court clerk said.

The first witness called was Robert Brockway. He testified that he'd begun working on the case in November 2005. Brockway was on the witness stand most of Monday as Shellie Samuels took him over the different insurance policies and claim forms that had been taken out on Kenneth McDavid and Paul Vados.

Using an Elmo, a high-tech overhead projector, Samuels displayed checks written and signed by Helen, and other documents that linked the victims to the two defendants.

Helen and Olga sat quietly as the prosecutors went over every insurance policy with Brockway.

The evidence that Brockway presented was, for the most part, quite cut-and-dried—and, because it was full of dates and figures, was very boring. Yet, every time he identified another policy it was very enlighting, and it looked as if he was striking another nail in Helen and Olga's coffin.

On one of the applications for insurance, Brockway pointed out to the judge that the women had represented that McDavid had $1.25 million in assets and $450,000 in bank loans.

On another policy, filed with another company, they'd

listed McDavid's assets as $700,000 and his annual salary as $72,000.

Samuels also displayed letters written by Helen, who'd threatened litigation against companies that were refusing her requests for life insurance payouts. Several of the replies indicated that the companies were refusing to honor Helen's claims "pending an investigation."

Showing Brockway various other documents, including an accidental life insurance policy, Samuels asked him about the different types of policies.

"This would not have been paid out if Mr. Vados had died of natural causes, correct?" Samuels asked.

"Correct," Brockway replied.

One other witness testified on the first day of the preliminary hearing. That was Maria Zamarripa, the former apartment manager at 861 South Fedora, where Vados had lived until his death in 1999. Speaking through a Spanish language interpreter, Zamarripa testified that she'd seen Olga stop by to visit Vados "on a regular basis . . . But on two occasions, I saw another person accompany her."

Asked by Samuels to look around the courtroom to see if the witness could identify the person she'd seen with Vados "on a regular basis," Zamarripa replied, "Yes, it's her."

"Are you pointing to the person at the end [of the defense table] or the person next to me?" Samuels asked.

"At the end of the table," she replied, indicating that she was referring to Olga.

"Did that person that you've identified at the end of the table ever come to you and tell you that Mr. Vados was missing?"

"Yes . . . She told me that he was missing and that she was looking for him," the apartment manager replied.

"Some time after that, did she come back and tell you what happened to him?" Samuels asked.

"Yes . . . She told me that he had died."

"Did she tell you what to do with his things?"

"Yes . . . to throw everything in the apartment away." There'd been nothing in the apartment worth saving.

On cross-examination by Michael Sklar, the witness testified that Vados "drank a lot" and "had a difficult time caring for himself."

On occasion, Zamarripa testified, "he was so drunk somewhere in the neighborhood" that she would go help him find his way home.

Zamarripa went on to testify that Olga would help him pay his rent and would bring him food.

By mid-afternoon, Brockway was back on the witness stand. One by one, he continued to detail the policies that had been taken out on behalf of the two victims. Throughout his testimony, Brockway described letters Helen had sent to a number of insurance companies in which she threatened litigation if the company didn't pay her. By day's end, Brockway had not concluded his testimony, and was instructed by the judge to return on Tuesday. Before adjourning at 3:30 p.m., Samuels advised the court that she anticipated calling another twenty to twenty-five witnesses before concluding the hearing later in the week.

Chapter 8

Helen's "Not a Spring Chicken"

Tuesday, March 13, 2007, day two of the preliminary hearing, began with Helen's lawyer, Roger Jon Diamond, leaping to his feet to seize upon the same theme he had brought up with Judge Wesley on Monday.

"Your Honor. Regarding the conditions of Ms. Golay in custody, she tells me that she was not able to take a nap yesterday. They provided her with some minimal food during the break, but there is no facility for taking a noon nap during the noon break.

"As far as her hours of sleep, yesterday I may have said we would like to have her get up at seven-thirty in the morning. Perhaps that was overstating my case.

"She was awakened yesterday at three a.m. and again today at three a.m. If they could get her up at six o'clock, that's three extra hours of sleep."

Diamond then spent another fifteen minutes eloquently presenting Helen's sleeping requirements. It was obvious that he was going on non-stop about her need to be alert because he was building issues to be brought up on appeal.

Next on the lawyer's agenda was another of Helen's complaints: food. "She tells me that she returned to the jail yesterday at around six-thirty. She missed dinner because they only provide dinner at five o'clock.

"And there's no way to sleep in the jail until after ten

o'clock at night because the TVs are on and the lights are on. So there is no way for her to get rest."

Diamond then spent thirty minutes and 1,500 words arguing that the preliminary hearing for Helen "is not fair" and violates her Sixth Amendment right to a fair preliminary hearing as well as her California statutory right to a fair hearing.

The lawyer then went on and on to blame the system for the problem before reverting to the same old argument of letting Helen sleep until six in the morning.

"She's exhausted. She's authorized me to tell Your Honor that she's seventy-six years old. She's not a spring chicken. It's very grueling upon her. She gets very little rest, minimal food. I think she got a burrito when she did get to the jail last night . . ."

Diamond again asked that the sheriff bring Helen to court "at a reasonable time" . . . or "in the alternative, release her on bail or on her own recognizance. There has to be some remedy to this continuing Constitution violation . . ."

The lawyer went on relentlessly, trying to get a positive response from the judge. But Judge Wesley ruled that while he was understanding of the problem, he again pointed out to Diamond that Helen was "awakened early and brought to the courthouse like every other inmate that has come to the court for the last twenty years that I know of . . . I'm sorry that she's uncomfortable with the conditions that she has while she's incarcerated in county jail . . ."

The judge recommended that Helen file an administrative complaint at the jail to alleviate the problem.

"After she has exhausted her administrative remedies, then I'll be glad to look at the issue, but until she exhausts her administrative issues at the county jail, I will not look at the issue," Wesley ruled.

But when Diamond suggested there was no time to do that unless Wesley suspended the preliminary hearing, the judge had done all he could to control his anger at the lawyer, and put his foot down at such talk.

"You have insisted all along that you have a speedy preliminary hearing. I would not think of putting this preliminary hearing off," the judge said. "If she is unhappy with her jail conditions, have her file a complaint in the jail. In the meantime, I'm not going to take any action, other than to make sure she gets a meal. I'm instructing the bailiff to make sure of that after court. If she is sent back late on a late bus, then she is to be given a full meal."

Before getting to the first witness of the day, Diamond had still another request on his wish list: He didn't want witnesses to be asked to identify Helen simply by scanning the courtroom to see whether or not a particular person was present.

His argument was that such identification is "inherently suggestive to ask a witness to look around the court, because most witnesses would believe that the person who looks like a defendant, namely somebody in jail wearing an orange jumpsuit, and sitting at defense table handcuffed, makes for a highly suggestive in-court identification.

"We respectfully request that if the district attorney plans to have an identification in court, that it be in a fair way by having Ms. Golay in a lineup with other persons, so that she's not singled out," Diamond said.

When asked by the judge if he had any case law to back up his request, Diamond had to admit he did not.

"As long as I can remember, and I believe that the case law does not support your position, the cases I have read do not support your position, so your request is denied," Wesley said.

"Are we ready to proceed?" he asked. "Call your first witness," the judge intoned.

With that, Deputy District Attorney Shellie Samuels promptly recalled Robert Brockway to the witness stand to complete his direct testimony on the insurance policies.

Brockway went through the mundane, unexciting routine of reeling off the items on the insurance applications. He detailed the $25,000 policy from an AARP benefit term life application and spelled out what the insurance company does once they receive an application.

"Once a claim is filed, the first letter to go out to the beneficiary from AARP is a letter giving their condolences for their recent loss," Brockway explained.

Brockway also apprised the judge that in the case of the AARP policy, Helen Golay received two settlement checks because she had increased the policy on Kenneth McDavid's life to $75,000.

For the next two hours, Brockway had the dreary task of going through all the policies taken out on Kenneth McDavid's and Paul Vados' lives by Helen and Olga. And then he had to show the court how the two women had filed claims to get back their two-year investment.

"Mr. Brockway, can you tell us, please, between the two defendants, how many policies for life insurance were sought on Mr. Vados' life?" Samuels asked.

"From Mr. Vados, eight policies," he replied.

"And as to Mr. McDavid, how many policies were sought?"

"Sixteen policies," came the response.

"And do you have the figures for how much, under the death—of the policies for the death of Mr. Vados, how much money was actually paid out to Ms. Olga Rutterschmidt?"

"Yes, I do."

"How much is that?"

"Two hundred forty-six thousand, three hundred forty-four dollars and twenty-six cents on the death of Paul Vados, based on the policies found on his life," came the reply.

"And how much did Ms. Golay receive?" Brockway was asked.

"Three hundred forty-seven thousand, eight hundred sixty-seven dollars and eight cents."

Brockway then repeated what he had found during his initial investigation—that Helen and Olga had taken out sixteen policies on Kenneth McDavid.

"And the total amount of all the policies, had they all been paid out, was how much?"

"If all the policies would have paid out, it would have been five million, seven hundred forty thousand dollars," Brockway replied.

"As it stood, how much did Ms. Golay collect on the death of Mr. McDavid?"

"One million, five hundred forty-two thousand, seven hundred sixty-seven dollars and five cents."

"And how much did Ms. Rutterschmidt get paid for the death of Mr. McDavid?"

"Six hundred seventy-six thousand, five hundred seventy-one dollars and eighty-nine cents."

With Brockway's direct testimony completed, Diamond started his cross-examination, going into a number of long-winded hypothetical questions. "Let's assume that a statement is submitted on an application for insurance that is not two-thousand percent accurate. There's a slight misstatement in there, for whatever reason. Let's say the person did not really have full-blown cancer, but had something similar to that.

"Would it be fraud for the insurance company to take the premium for a couple of years on that application, knowing that once a claim were made that the claim would be dishonored because the insurance company would then take the position that it was misled by the application?"

Samuels objected to Diamond's line of questioning, calling it "ambiguous and irrelevant."

The judge sustained the objection and did so again when Diamond persisted in elaborating his complicated question.

"It's compound and complex. It's multifaceted, and I'm not going to allow it," the judge told the lawyer without showing his displeasure.

"Correct me if I'm wrong, but one of the claims made by the insurance companies was that they did not know that there were multiple policies being sought for the same insured?" Diamond asked Brockway.

"That is true."

"But from your experience in the insurance industry, that an insured can have more than one policy on his or her life from more than one insurance company?"

"That is true."

"They can aggregate the policies, is that right?"

"Yes, but you can't overinsure," replied Brockway.

"But if somebody wants to insure somebody's life, who is to say whether one million dollars is too much or two million dollars is too much?"

"Well, that goes into their insurable interest."

"So there's nothing inherently wrong with getting more than one policy on one person, is it?"

"As long as you don't overinsure the person, that is correct."

Diamond then changed tactics and began another line of questions, asking this time about how insurance companies conduct business and whether they belong to a trade association where they can advance their common interests.

"There is not one organization that every insurance carrier belongs to so they can check on each other's claims or policies or insured. There is nothing like that," was Brockway's response.

When Diamond concluded, it was Michael Sklar's turn to grill Brockway.

In his concise cross-examination, Sklar got right to the point by showing Brockway a document on AAA Life Insurance letterhead. "Do you recognize this document, sir?" Sklar asked in trying to distance his client from Helen Golay.

"Yes, I do."

"That document was sent to you on your request?"

"Yes."

"Now, with regard to the second full paragraph that begins 'Also,' could you read that paragraph to the court?"

With that, Brockway grabbed a copy of the letter and began reading from the document. "'Also on May second,

2005, the agent, Jody Resnick, received a telephone call from Helen Golay. Ms. Golay wanted to increase the coverage from eight hundred thousand dollars to one million dollars on Kenneth McDavid. The application was sent out to her.' "

"This indicates that the request to increase the policy was within a couple of months of the date of Mr. McDavid's death, correct?"

"That's correct."

"In your investigation into this case, did you uncover any evidence that Ms. Rutterschmidt attempted to increase any of the policies that she was a beneficiary of within sixty days of the date of McDavid's death?"

"No."

Sklar next showed the witness a letterhead document from the MONY Life Insurance Company, dated June 6, 2005, that listed both Helen and Olga as beneficiaries.

After reviewing the documents handed to him by Sklar, Brockway told the judge that shortly before McDavid's death, Helen had attempted to delete Olga as a joint beneficiary, but that he wasn't sure whether Olga had ever attempted to remove Helen from a policy.

"Nothing further," Sklar said before sitting down.

Finally after a brief question to Brockway to name the five policies out of sixteen where both defendants—Helen and Olga—were beneficiaries, Samuels announced that she had no further questions of Brockway and said she was ready to call a new witness.

"Can you please state and spell your first and last name for the record?" the clerk asked the next witness.

"Luis Jaimes. L-U-I-S J-A-I-M-E-S."

Jaimes testified that back in June 2005, he'd worked for Brent Air Towing, which was under contract to AAA.

"Did you receive a call to go to an area near Santa Monica Boulevard and Westwood Boulevard in the late-night hours of June twenty-first, 2005?" Samuels asked.

"Yes."

Jaimes said he'd received the call at six minutes before midnight.

"Do you remember the car being a 1999 silver Mercury Sable?"

"Yes, one of those Ford model cars like a Sable or Taurus, something like that."

The driver said he couldn't recall the name of the person because he services "a good fifteen people a day . . ."

Samuels was about to show the witness photographs of a car for identification when Diamond abruptly interrupted the prosecutor's presentation to insist that "the district attorney show the witness pictures of five cars, not just one car. It's too suggestive," he said.

"You put on the case you want. She puts on the case she wants," the judge sternly told the outspoken Diamond, referring to Samuels. "Your objection is overruled," he advised the defense lawyer. "Go ahead."

After being shown the pictures, Samuels asked Jaimes whether he could recall if it was a male or female with the car.

"Female."

But when asked if he could see that female in the courtroom, Jaimes replied that he sees "so many people that I honestly don't remember any face."

"Do you recall if it was a young woman or an older woman?" he was asked.

"It was an elderly woman."

"Do you recall towing it to Fifth Street and Ocean Park Boulevard in Santa Monica?"

Jaimes said that he remembered towing the car in the city of Santa Monica, but could not recall the name on the AAA membership card and did not have any memory as to whether that person was Helen Golay.

On cross-examination, Diamond pressed the witness for his definition of "elderly."

"Would that be anybody over say forty-five, fifty years old?" Diamond wanted to know.

"I would say sixty, fifty."

"Fifty years old would be elderly?"

"Yes."

"What about forty-five?"

"I would say that's elderly too," the witness replied.

Jaimes' answer led to laughter in the courtroom.

With Diamond's cross-examination finished, Samuels picked up the pace by asking Jaimes if he considered someone forty years of age elderly.

"Yes."

"And how old are you?" Samuels wanted to know.

"I'm twenty-one."

"But *elderly* would also include somebody in their seventies?"

"Yes."

Sklar had but one important question to ask Jaimes about the elderly woman in his tow truck with him the night of June 21, 2005. And that was to get the witness to confirm that she was not towed to Olga's residence.

"You did not tow that vehicle to seventeen-seventy-six Sycamore in Hollywood, correct?"

"I remember towing it to the city of Santa Monica," he replied.

Samuels next called on FBI Special Agent Samuel Mayrose, who had the tedious task of going through all of the insurance policies that Brockway had detailed in his earlier testimony.

Mayrose also informed the judge that he'd assisted in the searches of Helen and Olga's residences and supervised the search. He further told Wesley that he'd also been responsible for subpoenaing the bank records for the defendants, including their checking and savings accounts.

Almost all of Mayrose's testimony was taken up with him identifying checks written by either Helen or Olga paying for either insurance premiums, or rent, or utilities bills on behalf of McDavid and Vados.

Mayrose's response to all of Samuels' questions was "Yes, ma'am," eventually leading to some chuckles in the courtroom when the prosecutor openly made reference to the agent's "brilliant 'Yes, ma'am' testimony."

By mid-afternoon on the second day of the prelim, Samuels called time-out on Mayrose's "titillating testimony" so that she could call on other witnesses in her presentation.

Sandra Salman had a determined look on her face as she approached the witness stand. She told the judge that she was Kenneth McDavid's sister and that the last time she'd seen her brother was in 1995.

She testified that the last time she'd heard from her brother was "a month before I was notified that he died. A month before he died, I received a call in May of '05.

"It was a message from him. I did not actually speak to him," she said.

In response to a question as to whether she was familiar with her family tree, Salman said she was.

"Is your family related in any way to this defendant, Helen Golay?" Samuels asked, pointing to Helen seated next to her lawyer.

"No."

"Is your family related in any way to this defendant, Olga Rutterschmidt?" Samuels asked, pointing to Olga seated next to Michael Sklar.

"No."

"Is Kenneth McDavid a cousin?"

"No."

Diamond, on his cross-examination of Salman, questioned her as to whether she knew that her brother had had an interest in screenwriting. When she replied negatively, Diamond asked what she recalled when her brother worked.

"I know that he worked in San Francisco prior to 1992. He was a disc jockey for a Marriott hotel," Salman said.

As to the message her brother had left on her answering machine, Salman said McDavid was calling "to get in touch with everybody and see how everyone is doing, and he apologized for not calling sooner."

Diamond asked several innocuous questions regarding her family tree, such as how many brothers and sisters she had—two brothers, one sister, Salman said. She also revealed that she was a nurse and mentioned that her mother had lived with her for the last two-and-a-half years since she'd had a stroke.

When Salman replied that she'd never gotten involved with her brother's insurance, it prompted Diamond to ask if she'd "basically lost all contact" with McDavid.

"Basically. I didn't even know he was homeless," she said, pointing out that "other than through my mom to see if she had heard from him, because normally he would make contact with her, not me."

Sklar pressed Salman in his cross-examination about whether her brother had ever given any indication that he wrote screenplays.

"Well, he wrote stories. He would write music. He would write songs."

"Did you not, in a conversation you had with Officers Sanchez and Kilcoyne, say that Ken called in May 2005 and you told them that he called about investing in a He-Man movie-type series?" asked Sklar.

"No, that's not what I said," she answered.

And with that response, Sklar abruptly ended his cross-examination of the witness.

Moments after Salman left the witness stand, Stella Carmen Vados, the daughter of Paul Vados, testified that she had not seen her father since 1996, three years before his death.

Stella Vados explained that she'd lost touch with her father when she moved from Southern to Northern California. She claimed her father had lived on Sycamore Street, but couldn't recall the exact address. She described how she'd tried sending her father correspondence at the Sycamore address, but had never gotten a response from him.

Stella Vados was asked a series of questions about her family tree, and whether Helen and Olga were cousins.

"No," she replied.

This time Sklar started the cross-examination of Stella Vados. In her testimony it was brought out that as a result "of this incident with your father, you've retained the services of the law firm of Allred, Maroko and Goldberg" to assist her and her siblings of recovering some money in a life insurance policy.

Stella brought out in her testimony that her lawyer at that firm was none other than Gloria Allred, who'd represented Amber Frey when Frey was a witness in the criminal case against Scott Peterson. She'd also represented Paula Jones in the sexual harassment case against former U.S. President Bill Clinton, as well as Nicole Brown Simpson's family during the O. J. Simpson murder case. Allred is also known for her criticism of pop singer Michael Jackson, and is the mother of truTV anchor Lisa Bloom.

"And have you been led to believe that the defendants in this case gained financially upon your father's death?" Sklar asked the witness.

"No, I didn't know before."

At first Stella Vados was vague and confused about the purpose of hiring Allred despite Sklar's persistent grilling of the witness. "It was advised. We'd do best to do so, since it's going to be claimed anyway," is how she explained hiring Allred.

"Since what's going to be claimed anyways?" Sklar asked.

"The money from the insurance . . . It's just going to be claimed. You might as well claim it."

Under cross-examination by Diamond, Stella Vados testified that her father, before he retired, had worked as a foreman at Apple Computer, and she said she was "very close" to him before he disappeared.

It was brought out under re-direct examination by Samuels that at some point in the last year, there had been an arbitration hearing in order to determine whether Stella Vados was entitled to a portion of the life insurance policy that had been taken out on her father by Helen and Olga.

"The arbitration was conducted in such a way that you

were kept in a separate room from the defendants, with your attorney talking to their attorneys, and then coming back to talk to you?" Samuels asked.

"Correct."

"And did you and your brother get any portion of the life insurance policy?"

"A very small amount," she replied, saying that she and her brother and sister each got $4,200.

"Were you aware of the total value of the policy?"

"It was something around twelve thousand dollars to fifteen thousand dollars to twenty-five thousand dollars or twenty-two thousand dollars, something like that."

Stella Vados said that while at the law office during the arbitration, she'd actually seen Helen Golay. "Yes, I crossed paths with her walking to the bathroom."

"And did she embrace you and tell you that she was your father's fiancée, and how good it was to meet his daughter? Did she say anything when she saw you?"

"Yes, she looked at me, and tried to cover her face and hide herself."

The witness said that at no time did Helen introduce herself to Stella Vados or tell her she was her father's fiancée. As for Olga, they did not speak to each other.

"Were you ever aware that the policy that you were seeking to get a portion of was in fact for two hundred thousand dollars?"

"Maybe, after I was sitting inside at that time."

"Are you aware that Gloria Allred and her firm are representing you in what is called 'pro bono'? That they are not taking any fee from you?"

"Yes."

Vados' daughter also testified that she had never attempted to receive any funds from any of the other policies on her father's life.

Throughout most of Stella Vados' testimony, she was unclear and appeared confused about what she was attempting to convey to the court. Her testimony was often punctuated with ambiguous non-sequiturs. Whether she was scared or overwhelmed at having to testify, the young woman gave prosecutors the answers needed in the case, namely that Helen and Olga were not related to Paul Vados.

Called as the next witness, Eli Burgos, the team manager for the automobile club of Southern California, was shown a document titled "Members Use History," which detailed the membership card used by Helen in 2005 and 2006.

Burgos testified that someone had used Helen Golay's membership number to have a car towed to a location near her Santa Monica home.

"Is there a call there for June twenty-first, 2005?" he was asked by Samuels.

"There is . . . The call originated at eleven-fifty-four p.m., and that's when it was received in our office," Burgos said, reading from the document.

Burgos said the caller had given the location of the distressed vehicle as a "Chevron station at the northwest corner of Santa Monica and Westwood."

"Does it say where it was towed?"

In responding to the question that the "tow destination is Fifth and Ocean Park in the city of Santa Monica," it was enough to link Helen Golay to the murder of McDavid, because not only was it the exact location of Helen's residence, but detectives always referred to the car as "the murder weapon."

Questioned as to whether the document he was reading indicated the type, make, and year of the car being towed, Burgos replied, "It is a '99 Mercury Sable, silver in color."

In his cross-examination of Burgos, Diamond delved into how long AAA kept its recordings of calls. Ninety days, unless they are subpoenaed, Burgos said, but in this case they were not subpoenaed. Diamond next raised another of his hypothetical questions, wanting to know what would happen if someone other than the card member used the card to call for service.

Burgos replied that the auto club could not determine who had placed the call.

"In theory, the tow truck operator should have obtained a signature on some form from the person using the service?" he was asked.

"Correct, in theory," Burgos said, but he admitted that quite often some of the tow operators forgot to get signatures.

In raising the question as to whether the tow truck operator had obtained a signature from the person using the AAA towing service, Diamond was attempting to distance Helen from the Chevron gas station the night of June 21, 2005, at 11:54 p.m., and was trying to suggest that someone other than Helen had used her membership card to get AAA membership service.

Meilisa Thompson, a neighbor of Helen Golay, followed Burgos to the stand. She testified that she'd known Helen for maybe two-and-a-half to three years, and that they would often see each other in the back alley because "our garage and trash cans are right next to her garage."

"Did you notice a vehicle that was parked behind your place and her place?"

"Yes."

At that point Thompson was shown People's Exhibit 78, a photograph of a car that had been previously identified as the 1999 silver Mercury Sable, and was asked if she had seen that vehicle before.

"Yes. That was the vehicle parked next to the garbage cans."

Thompson testified that what had alerted her to the vehicle was that parking was a problem in the neighborhood and she'd become aware of how long she parked in the alley and how long other cars were parked there.

"So I did notice this particular car there more than any other car. That was the one reason I noticed that car."

"How long would you say that car was parked there?" she was asked.

"Over a month, over a month . . . It could have been as much as six months," was Thompson's reply.

Thompson said she'd actually called the city of Santa Monica about the garbage cans in the alley that belonged to Helen Golay. "There were three large garbage cans that were right across the alley from our house, and they drew a lot of unsavory people . . . people rummaging through those cans. So I actually was in contact with the city, requesting them to move the garbage cans to the back of the alley," Thompson testified.

Samuels then showed Thompson another photo, which the witness identified as the vehicle parked next to the garbage cans—only this time there was red paint on the car.

Thompson explained in her testimony that about a year later, she'd noticed that the garbage cans had been vandalized, and that there had been red paint spotted on apartment buildings and on the car that was parked there.

"So I took photos of these garbage cans, specifically to try to send to the city in hopes of just having evidence to have them please move the garbage cans, because nothing had happened in about a year.

"Inadvertently I took pictures of this car, which also had the red paint, and I thought to myself later, if I ever found out who the owner was, I would give them a copy of the photo to help them out, perhaps for insurance purposes."

Thompson said that one day she was outside of her house and noticed Helen Golay interacting with the car. "Not necessarily with a key, but intimately, like checking it out, so that in my head, I made a note to myself that she's the owner.

"We were not super-friendly, so I didn't feel the need to give her the pictures," Thompson testified.

The witness said that her "feelings had changed on supplying the owner with these pictures because . . ." she didn't like Ms. Golay. "Actually, when I saw the paint and realized the car belonged to Ms. Golay, I felt it was karma. And I wasn't going to help her out by giving her the photos.

"She was looking into the car and didn't realize I was seeing her do this. At some point, the car was gone."

On cross-examination by Diamond, Thompson said that just before the arrest, she and Helen had run into each other in the alley and chatted about her grandchild.

With tears in her eyes, Thompson recalled the conversation. "I actually felt like that was the warmest conversation I had with Helen," she said, her voice cracking.

Chapter 9

Murder Most Gruesome

Those in the audience who were still hanging around in Judge David Wesley's courtroom on the second day of the prelim dreaded the next witness Shellie Samuels was about to call.

He was Dr. Solomon Riley Jr., the deputy coroner with the Los Angeles County Coroner's office, who'd conducted the autopsy of Kenneth McDavid under Coroner's Case Number 2005-04721.

The coroner started by noting rather off-handedly that McDavid was 71 inches tall, or five-foot-eleven, and weighed 194 pounds.

Riley said he'd seen the body after it had been washed and photographed, and noticed that McDavid showed multiple lacerations to his scalp on the right side.

So much for the niceties of the autopsy. What Riley was about to describe was not for those with weak stomachs.

An external examination of McDavid, Riley said, had shown that there were scrape marks at the left shoulder region and the back of the left arm, and a pattern scrape mark across the front of the right side of his torso.

"There was also a laceration to the upper lip. There were abrasions on the face in addition to the other locations that I had mentioned up to this point. There were scrape marks on the back of both sides of his hip region."

Riley wasn't through detailing the horrific injuries sustained by McDavid. "There was bleeding beneath the scalp. There was also bleeding on the surfaces of the brain itself. There was a fracture of the thoracic spine, the upper thoracic spine. There were also lacerations of the cord adjacent to the spine fracture, lacerations of the upper thoracic cord. There were fractures of the sternum, the mid-portion of the sternum. There were fractures of the upper three ribs on the right side and of the eighth and ninth ribs on the left side at the back. There were also fractures to the right side of the pelvis."

"Would these be what you would refer to as *compression injuries*?" Samuels asked.

"These are injuries that could only be sustained by having the body crushed," Riley said softly, in describing the violent and brutal way McDavid was murdered. "It would appear that the most significant crush injuries occurred to the upper torso where the spine was broken and the spinal cord was broken. I think the injuries to the scalp might have been due to the effect of possibly having the body dragged to some extent."

"What is it exactly of these injuries that caused Mr. McDavid to die?" Riley was asked.

"The most severe problem that the decedent would have encountered as a result of these injuries would be the ability to breathe properly, both because of fractured ribs on both sides and paralysis of the respiratory muscles, as a result of spinal laceration," he replied.

"Did you find any significant injuries below Mr. McDavid's pelvis?"

"I found no evidence of lacerations or long bone fractures . . . I found no injuries to the thigh bones or to the leg bones," the coroner said.

But when Samuels tried to query further, as to whether the decedent had been standing when he was struck, there was a series of objections from Olga's lawyer, Michael Sklar, that prevented the prosecutor from trying to lay the foundation that would allow the coroner to answer whether McDavid had been standing or lying on the ground at the time he was hurt by the car.

Whether the coroner was going to answer that question became so heated between the lawyers and the prosecutor that the judge called for a fifteen-minute recess and informed the lawyers that court would remain in session until five o'clock.

While Dr. Riley was unable to answer specifically as to whether McDavid had been standing or lying down when he was struck, he did say that death in any case would have been "fairly rapid" because the spinal cord laceration in the upper thoracic "might cause paralysis of many of the muscles of respiration, so the death would be fairly rapid."

Turning to another area that needed clarification— McDavid's toxicology report—Riley described the substance that had been found in McDavid's system when he died.

"The heart blood showed zero-point-zero-eight grams percent alcohol, drinking alcohol, and it showed small amounts of a tranquilizing drug, zolpidem. And a therapeutic range amount of hydrocodone and a drug used to treat epileptic seizures, topiramate."

Riley went on to explain that a combination of these drugs would produce drowsiness. He amplified his answer by saying that zolpidem was a type of sedative, probably an anti-anxiety drug, and that topiramate was used to treat seizures.

In taking over the cross-examination, Diamond asked the witness whether or not McDavid had first been struck by a vehicle and then knocked down and run over, or whether he had simply been run over.

"The significant injuries would have been sustained when he was down, the crushing injury to the upper torso," the witness said.

Although both defense lawyers appeared satisfied with their questioning of Riley, Samuels was obviously disappointed that the coroner could not initially answer the crucial question as to whether McDavid had been standing or lying down. The answer to that question, an essential part of the prosecution's case, meant that the prosecution still had more work to do if they were to successfully convict Helen and Olga, since the state contention was that McDavid had deliberately been lying down when he was killed, and was not involved in a normal pedestrian hit.

Day three of the preliminary hearing began with the same broken-record dilemma. As Diamond got to his feet to start the *kvetching* going about Helen's need for sleep and food, a chorus of moans and groans could be heard in the courtroom from the spectator section.

"It's now nine-twenty-five, Your Honor. Ms. Golay advises me that after the court session yesterday, she was kept here at the criminal court building until ten p.m. Then she was taken by bus to the Twin Towers, where she was taken off that bus and put in a holding facility for a while, and then taken back to the women's jail in Lynwood, and did not arrive at the women's jail in Lynwood until five minutes to midnight, last night, and she was not able to get to sleep until one o'clock in the morning.

"She's exhausted, and then they awakened her this morning at three a.m. She had an hour or two of sleep. She's exhausted and she protests the situation. The conditions under which she is undergoing in this preliminary hearing were such that she cannot function properly.

"I understand that she believes one of the problems is that Olga Rutterschmidt apparently was taken on an earlier bus, because there is, I understand . . . an order that keeps the two of them separate, so apparently the sheriff feels they cannot use the same bus."

When the judge learned from Diamond that both Helen and Olga were classified as K-10s, he explained to the lawyer that it meant that the two women were to be kept away from everybody, not just each other.

Diamond corrected the judge, saying, "But Helen did

have a cellmate . . . She is a K-ten, not a keepaway," Diamond said.

"K-ten is keepaway," the judge told him.

"That's inconsistent with being a K-ten, since they gave her a cellmate. Anyway, Your Honor, we would like the prelim dismissed and start over when she's refreshed and has some ability to function. She's exhausted. And if necessary, she's willing to take the stand and testify to support what I'm representing to the court, which is they're just brutal in terms of the rest that she's getting—or *not* getting— at the county jail."

Judge Wesley, who has been described by other defense lawyers who have appeared before him as "very neutral," listened patiently to Diamond's complaints about his client's problems. "Well, fortunately for her, we should be done today or tomorrow, and she can catch up on her sleep. I feel for her plight, except I have no control over what the sheriffs do in county jail. She is in custody. She is a prisoner in custody. She's being treated like a prisoner. She doesn't like that," he admitted wearily.

"I'm sorry that she doesn't like that. But the fact of the matter is that the sheriff's department controls the transportation and housing of prisoners. The court does not, and so she'll have to catch her rest whenever she can catch it."

While the purpose of Diamond's persistently bringing up Helen's lack of beauty sleep may have seemed annoying to those listening to his remarks, actually it was an essential part of the lawyer's hidden agenda to build a solid appeals record. And if sounding like he was making a nuisance of himself by constantly raising Helen's need for sleep, so be it. It was all part of Diamond's overall strategy. He was keenly aware that once the prelim was concluded, should the judge rule that there was enough evidence to take the case to trial, Diamond could later use Helen's sleepless nights in jail in his appeal to overturn any adverse verdict.

Never one to raise the white flag and surrender, Diamond took another tack and told the judge that, even though both women were classified as K-10 prisoners, he couldn't see any reason why they couldn't be transported on the same bus.

Exasperated, Judge Wesley had had enough of Diamond's maneuvering and delaying tactics. "Again, don't tell the sheriff how to do his business. If he feels they have to be on separate buses, they have to be on separate buses," the judge scolded the lawyer. "So your motion to dismiss the preliminary hearing is denied."

"And that's based on federal constitutional grounds, Your Honor?" Diamond asked, getting in the last word in the argument.

"Understood. Call your first witness," Wesley directed Samuels without even looking at the lawyer or taking a pause.

"The People call Officer William Fernandez."

The testimony of Fernandez was merely to establish that on November 17, 1999, at 10 p.m., a missing persons report on Paul Vados had been taken at the Wilshire police station.

"And did you take that report from a woman by the name of Olga Rutterschmidt?" Samuels asked.

"Yes."

And did she give you also the name of Helen Golay as another individual that was looking for Mr. Vados?"

"Yes."

"And did she tell you when they last saw him?" Samuels wanted to know.

"Yes. I believe it's November fifth, according to the report . . . in 1999," he added.

The report that the officer was reading reflected what Olga had told the officer, in which she said that she had gone to Vados' apartment around six that evening and couldn't find him.

It had been eight years since he had briefly had contact with the two women. In the cross-examination, Fernandez was unable to identify either Olga or Helen in the courtroom. "I couldn't tell you at this point who they were if they're in this room either," the officer said. "It's so far back."

The reason the prosecutor asked the witness whether Helen was the name of the other person seeking to find Vados was to show that there was the furtherance of conspiracy between the two women as outlined in one of the counts in the indictment against them.

Vados' body had been found on November 8, 1999, at 4:50 a.m., in an alley west of La Brea Avenue and south of Oakwood Avenue in Hollywood. Perhaps because it was their first murder, Helen and Olga were novices and had overlooked the obvious. As it turned out, they'd blown it. In their attempt to cover their tracks, making sure that there wasn't any evidence that could lead to their front door before murdering Vados, the women took what they thought was the precaution of stripping him of all vestiges of identification.

Only after bumping off their prize cash cow—who had been grazing in their pasture for the last two years—did they realize that they couldn't collect a dime on the insurance policies that they had been paying unless they produced proof that Vados was officially dead.

And the only proof the insurance company would accept was an official death certificate from the city. But Vados was lying on a cold gurney in a freezer at the medical examiner's office with a beige tag on his toe indicating that his name was John Doe.

So, having killed Vados, they now had the unceremonious undertaking of raising him from the dead by filing a missing persons report. And having filed a missing persons report, they had to wait it out until authorities matched the report to the unclaimed John Doe and then go through the charade of identifying him as Paul Vados.

Harry Klan, a criminalist for the Los Angeles Police Department assigned to the serology DNA unit for the past seventeen years, was the next witness to take the stand. He testified about examining the 1999 Mercury Sable, license plate 5RKZ444, and the undercarriage to see if he could find anything relating to a homicide.

Klan admitted that he'd collected the evidence, but did not analyze it, testifying that he had been able to extract about a dozen items from the car.

In his testimony he described collecting a red stain, presumably blood, from the lower control arm of the undercarriage, which he'd placed into a vial with a sterile cotton swab.

"Basically, in a nutshell, you say you collected three bloodstains from one particular portion of the vehicle, is that right?" Diamond asked on cross-examination.

"In a nutshell, yes," came the reply.

"And you're saying they were all three near each other by the right rear wheel?"

"Right. In fact, I can tell you item fifty-seven was one foot, five inches to the right of the center bolt. Item fifty-nine was one foot, nine inches right of the center bolt. Item sixty was one foot, eleven inches right of the center bolt. So they were all within about six inches of each other."

Diamond tried to suggest that the stains could also have been made by a mechanic working on the vehicle and cutting himself. But Klan put that notion to rest, saying that "it took six people probably a better part of an hour to even find the stains."

Klan explained that they were difficult to find because the stains "were old and weathered, and they were no longer red. That I would normally associate with dried blood. These were kind of brown, if not even a little bit gray."

On re-cross, Klan brought out that hair had also been collected from the undercarriage side of the driver's door, underneath the car.

Los Angeles police DNA expert Stephanie McLean was the next witness. After detailing her extensive DNA training under the National Forensic Science Technology Center, she testified that she had been involved in analyzing material removed from the undercarriage of a 1999 silver Mercury Sable station wagon.

Her testimony included describing her examination of the bloodstains that Klan had itemized.

"And what was your finding?"

"That the DNA profile obtained from items fifty-seven, fifty-eight, and sixty matched the DNA profile obtained from Kenneth McDavid," McLean said.

"And did you determine that the combination of genetic markers would occur in approximately one in ten quadrillion unrelated individuals?"

"Yes, that's correct."

Another witness, Mario Medina, a car salesman who works for Mexicar Auto Sales in Los Angeles, testified that he'd sold the 1999 Mercury Sable with the last four digits of the VIN number being 4946, license number 4FYR482, on January 20, 2004, to an elderly woman.

"Can you look around the courtroom and tell me whether either one of the ladies who came to purchase the car is present in the courtroom?" Samuels asked.

"Yes, I believe it was the lady at the end of the table," he said, indicating where Olga Rutterschmidt was sitting.

"And is that the lady who gave you this driver's license and said that she was buying the car for her friend?" Samuels continued, referring to Hilary Adler.

"Yes."

Samuels next showed Medina a motor vehicle purchase order pre-computed finance charge, bearing the name *Hilary Adler* of 823 South Croft Avenue, Apartment B, in Los Angeles, and asked, "And where did you get that address?"

"It was given to us by the lady that purchased the car," Medina said, adding that she was the person he had just identified in court.

It was Medina's testimony that Olga had brought a license with her to complete the sale, and had supplied Hilary Adler's driver's license to him. "We figured it was something legal. We never thought it could be something that was going to be used for the wrong purpose," Medina said.

Medina's testimony was crucial to the prosecution's case, and was key to connecting the dots that would go to prove at trial that Helen and Olga had used the Mercury to kill McDavid in the back alley hit-and-run.

The real Hilary Adler followed Medina to the witness stand. She testified that she did not know Olga and had never asked her to purchase the Mercury for her. Samuels wasted no time in asking the witness a series of questions that caused Olga to look pathetic and turn pale.

"Ms. Adler, back in 2004, did you purchase a Mercury Sable, a 1999 Mercury Sable?" she was asked.

"No."

"At some time prior to January 2004, did you either lose or have your purse stolen?"

"Yes."

"And was your wallet in there?"

"Yes."

"And your driver's license?"

"Yes."

"Do you have any memory as to where it was that this purse went missing from?"

"Yes, I do."

"Where was that?"

"At the Spectrum sports club in Santa Monica."

"And did you ever give the woman at the end of the table, by the name of Olga Rutterschmidt, permission to buy a car in your name?"

"No."

"Did you ever give your driver's license to either one of these women?" Samuels asked, pointing to both Helen and Olga at the defense table.

"No."

On cross-examination, Adler told defense lawyers that she was "absolutely" certain her purse had been stolen in April or May of 2003 at the Spectrum Athletic Club.

"How do you know that?" Diamond asked.

"Because I was in the actual change rooms in the locker room and I had my locker open. And I turned around for a few minutes to talk to someone, and when I came back, my whole purse was stolen."

Adler said she'd looked for the purse and it was nowhere to be found.

On redirect, Adler said that she had never lived on South Croft Avenue, the address supplied to Medina by Olga at the time the Mercury was purchased.

Prosecutors suspect that either Helen Golay or her daughter Kecia, both members of the sports club, was behind the theft of Adler's purse.

Samuels brought on Danielli Cosgrove, the resident manager at the Palm Court Apartments, to testify that Kenneth McDavid had been a resident in apartment 410 of the building and that his rent had been paid monthly by Helen Golay.

She said that Helen had rented the apartment for McDavid on September 1, 2002, and was initially paying $875 a month, but that the rental was increased later on to $900 a month.

Cosgrove readily identified both Helen and Olga seated at the defense table, but testified that she hadn't met the two women until December 2004 when "there was a problem when McDavid, he brought other people into the apartment."

The resident manager said both Helen and Olga had told her to "get rid" of McDavid's visitors. When Cosgrove informed them that she couldn't do that, since Helen was the actual tenant of that apartment, the women went "ballistic." The next thing that happened that Cosgrove was aware of was that Helen and Olga kicked the homeless people out, including McDavid's friend Patrick Lamay, and changed the locks.

It was during the testimony of Detective Rosemary Sanchez that Patrick Lamay, the elusive roommate of Kenneth McDavid, surfaced.

Tracking down Lamay hadn't been easy. He was nowhere

to be found in Los Angeles. Sanchez checked hospitals, the jail and Motor Vehicles, and came up empty. The detective had gone back to McDavid's old apartment to re-interview Danielli Cosgrove, who recalled that Lamay might have lived in Michigan before moving in with McDavid.

Sanchez then learned that while living at Palm Court, Lamay had had contact with his mother in Michigan. While trying to trace the location of Lamay's mother, Sanchez also ran a "Triple I" check with Lamay's name through a state computer that tied in with thirty-four other states. Within an hour after feeding Lamay's name into the computer, Sanchez learned that he had been convicted of a minor sex crime and was doing jail time at the Washtenaw County Jail in Ann Arbor.

On October 17, 2006, Sanchez said, she and FBI Agent Sam Mayrose had flown out to Ann Arbor and interviewed Lamay at the jail, where he told Sanchez that he'd met McDavid at a church in Hollywood, and a few days later, Lamay and his girlfriend, Aimee, had moved in to the small apartment with him.

Lamay related to Sanchez that during the time he and Aimee were in the apartment, Olga had come over a couple of times. "One time she came by and just walked in. She had the keys to the apartment and walked in. She told McDavid that he couldn't have anybody living there, because that wasn't part of their arrangement."

On another visit, Lamay said, Olga had come to the apartment with somebody "armed with a gun, and removed his belongings and put it out in the hallway."

Lamay said that he'd seen Helen at the apartment "one time." On that occasion, Lamay said, McDavid had also invited Daniel McKelvie and Stephanie Stevens to move in with him.

"She too had a key to the apartment," Lamay said, referring to Helen. "She opened the door real quick, peeked in, shut it, and then about ten minutes later, she came back with two police officers and wanted the police to evict everyone in the apartment." But because Lamay had paid for

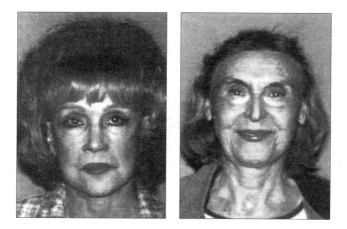

"The Girls," Helen Golay and Olga Rutterschmidt, convicted in a plot to murder men and collect on their insurance.

LAPD

A home owned by Helen Golay in Santa Monica.

Yvonne Adler

Hollywood Presbyterian Church, where homeless are fed and where Helen and Olga found their victims.

Chris King

"The Murder Weapon": The Mercury Sable station wagon used to kill Kenneth McDavid.

Police investigators search the undercarriage of the Mercury Sable station wagon, where they found McDavid's DNA.

Paul Vados's body at the crime scene, where he had been run over.

The alley in Westwood where the body of Kenneth McDavid was discovered.

"You can't have that many insurances…you were greedy."
Olga, from the surveillance video at the Parker Center in
Los Angeles.   *LAPD*

The investigative team: (l-r) Dt. Rosemary Sanchez, Lead
Dt. Dennis Kilcoyne, Special FBI Agent Samuel Mayrose,
and Investigator for the State Department of Insurance Robert Brockway.   *Jeanne King*

Supervising prosecutor Pat Dixon, lead prosecutor Truc Do, and Deputy District Attorney Bobby Grace.

Yvonne Adler

Michael Sklar, who represented Olga Rutterschmidt in court.

Tracy Collins

Kecia Golay, daughter of Helen Golay. The defense claimed that it was she who killed McDavid.

LAPD

Roger Diamond, the lawyer who defended Helen Golay.

Judy Burgdorf

Detectives Lee Willmon and Nelson Hernandez.

Jeanne King

The one who got away: Jimmy Covington, almost a victim of Helen and Olga's deadly plot.

Jeanne King

the utilities in his own name, the police informed Helen that they couldn't evict him.

Lamay said that after Olga had left his belongings out in the hallway, he'd come back to the apartment two weeks later to make sure he didn't have any other personal things left there. What he found was Olga in the apartment again, this time with an armed guard. He and Olga started arguing, ostensibly over the fact that he didn't belong there.

Lamay told Sanchez that he'd called the police and the FBI, and notified them of the situation, but was told that since no crime had been committed, there wasn't anything they could do.

The last time Lamay had seen his friend, he said, was in April or May 2005, shortly before McDavid was murdered.

Diamond's first cross-examination question of Sanchez was to ask the reason Lamay was in jail. Told that it had to do with "some sexual charge," Sanchez replied that Lamay had eventually been convicted. In response to another question by the lawyer, the detective observed that Lamay would be willing to come to Los Angeles and testify in the event that the case went to trial.

Samuels was rushing to get through with her list of witnesses because of Diamond's constant complaints about Helen being either too tired or too cold or too hungry. Besides, the judge had indicated that he had another trial to start on Thursday.

Rigo Bonilla followed Sanchez to the stand. He had been assigned in November 1999 to the West Traffic Division as a collision investigator. At 6:40 in the morning on November 8, 1999, he testified, he'd gotten a call to go out to the rear alley just west of La Brea Avenue and south of Oakwood.

"What was the situation when you arrived? What did you see?" he was asked.

"There was a dead body, a male."

"Could you tell by looking what kind of injuries were sustained?"

"It didn't look real to me. I thought he was a fake at the

time when we first arrived, because his body was all twisted, and I really thought it was a fake," he said.

After a closer look at the body, Bonilla determined that the body was in fact a real human being.

Samuels showed the witness a diagram so that he could identify where the impact had happened in relation to where "the baseball cap was left behind.

". . . And the dotted line that you have going to the little stick figure that's presumably the body, it's curled around, is that a little bit of artistic line on your part?" the prosecutor asked.

"That to us indicates that the body was thrown, you know, airborne, and landed to approximately where it's located at."

Bonilla then went through a long list of technical measurements as to where Paul Vados' body had landed when he was hit by the car, but the witness could not determine whether the victim had been standing or lying down at the time he was hit.

On cross-examination, Sklar wanted to know if Bonilla was determining the point of impact according to where the baseball cap had been found.

"No, when a vehicle hits a pedestrian, it's going to get thrown forward, assuming that the vehicle was traveling northbound."

"Okay. So . . . your conclusion that it was a vehicle that hit the pedestrian was your speculation?" Sklar asked. "Was it a guess or— What was it based on?"

"It was his body and his injuries at the time. I mean, he looked bad."

"So you assumed it was a vehicle that hit him?"

"Correct. I mean, he wasn't shot or stabbed or beat up."

Detective Dennis Kilcoyne took the witness stand next and testified on direct that he had interviewed Kecia Golay, Helen's daughter, and that she'd told him she had never heard of either Paul Vados or Kenneth McDavid.

She stated to the detective that her mother had never been engaged to either Vados or McDavid that she was aware of, and that her mother had had a boyfriend for more than twenty years—Gary Hilaiel. She also confirmed to Kilcoyne that Olga and Helen had met at a Santa Monica health spa and had been friends for twenty years.

Sklar's cross-examination of the detective brought out first-hand details about Kecia.

"On or about June twenty-seven, 2005, was Kecia Golay convicted of stalking?" Sklar asked the detective.

"I believe so."

"And on or about January of 2003, was Kecia Golay convicted of petty larceny with a prior felony?"

"I believe so."

"And on or about October seventeen, 1993, Kecia Golay was convicted of petty theft with a prior different crime?"

"I believe so," replied Kilcoyne.

"And on or about July 1989, Kecia Golay was convicted of theft of an access card?"

"I believe so."

"I have nothing further," Sklar said, sitting down at the defense table.

Kilcoyne also testified that the Mercury had been registered under two different license plate numbers. The Department of Motor Vehicles, he said, had reported that on January 20, 2004, the vehicle that he'd identified by the last four digits of the VIN as being 4946, with a California license number of 4FYR482, had been sold by Mexicar Auto Sales to a Hilary Adler residing at 823 South Croft Avenue in Los Angeles.

"That address is non-existent," Kilcoyne said.

The next documentation of the vehicle, Kilcoyne said, showed that the Mercury had been impounded by a tow lot on July 19, 2005, from 1739 North Vista Street in Hollywood, which he said was "four to five blocks from Olga's residence."

The Mercury had been "marked" by the traffic cops on July 12, 2005, but wasn't officially removed to the police garage by Hollywood Tow until July 19, Kilcoyne explained.

"The Mercury apparently stayed at Hollywood Tow for some time until it was 'lien sold' on November seventeenth, 2005, and then sold to Martha and Jose Canteros of Los Angeles."

Kilcoyne said he'd interviewed Jose Canteros, who informed him that when he'd purchased the Mercury from Hollywood Tow, it had no license plates, and had been replated. An inquiry with Hollywood Tow could not explain what had happened to the license plates while it was in their possession.

That same car had been caught on a surveillance camera in the alley in Westwood on the night McDavid was killed—the same night that Helen's AAA membership card had been used for a tow service to respond to a location near where the murder had occurred.

Though there is no surveillance video, Kilcoyne said, there are still time-lapse photos taken from the alley that show the Mercury Sable.

"What I've seen, you cannot make out who was in the car."

The purpose of calling Rick Constantinescu, the owner of the Hollywood Rubber Stamp Company in Hollywood, as a witness was for him to identify Olga as a long-standing customer of his, and to confirm that she'd used the name of Olga Smith in ordering dozens of rubber stamps.

Because Olga had had rubber stamps made up bearing the signatures of Vados and McDavid, the two men were never aware that dozens of insurance policies had been applied for and were issued in their names. Had the two victims been made aware of the existence of these rubber stamp signatures, it might have alerted them to what these two women were up to.

Dr. Louis Pena, a forensic pathologist and deputy medical examiner for the Los Angeles County Department of Coroner, testified that on November 10, 1999, he'd conducted the autopsy on the body of a John Doe who was later identified to be Paul Vados.

One by one, Pena methodically went through all of the

fractures, bruises and abrasions on Vados' body, from his face to his ribs to his toes.

As with the autopsy on McDavid, Vados' breathing, he said, had already been impaired by the breaking of his ribs and the puncturing of his lungs.

"What actually caused Mr. Vados to die?" Pena was asked.

"That would be the extensive loss of the blood . . . which means a decrease in oxygen getting to the brain, and basically the person would go unconscious. And respiratory and heart functions would subsequently cease."

"Is it your understanding in most of the cases you've done that people were standing or walking when they were hit?"

"Yes."

"In automobile versus a pedestrian, and the pedestrian is killed due to the accident, have there been injuries to the legs?"

"If it's an adult being struck with an auto front, an adult is going to get struck somewhere on the legs," was the best answer the medical examiner could give.

Samuels was frustrated. It seemed that no matter how often the prosecutor asked the question, and she must have posed it at least a half a dozen times, she could not get the witness to answer whether Vados had been lying in the alley before he was run over. It was obviously an area that the prosecution was going to have to work on if they were to prove that the victims in the case had deliberately been run over while they were lying on the ground.

Chapter 10

The Beginning of the End

As the prelim hearing progressed to its wind-up, Multidis-ciplinary Accident Investigation Team (MAIT) Supervisor Donald Karol was called to the stand to go into detail on the possible connection between the 1999 Mercury Sable and the murders.

Karol, who worked for the California Highway Patrol, familiar to millions of television viewers as CHiPs, was a specialist in accident reconstruction and what is technically called "auto versus pedestrian" accidents. His testimony before Judge Wesley was crucial to the court in making a ruling as to whether the case would ever go to trial.

Before testifying, Karol explained that MAIT is a team of investigators composed of experts in accident reconstruction, automotive mechanics, and traffic engineering; California Department of Transportation engineers; and officers with advanced education in math and physics, and in human factors.

In qualifying as an expert witness, Karol said he had investigated and testified in about 100 fatal automobile versus pedestrian traffic collisions, and said that he believed it was possible that a hit-and-run was a likely explanation for McDavid's death.

As part of the investigation, Karol said he'd inspected the Mercury Sable three times at the Los Angeles Police

Department's Scientific Investigation Division over at Piper Tech.

Karol said he had been present when red stains were removed from a rod near the back rear tire.

"Did you look at the front of the car, the front bumper, the grill area, the hood area, and the windshield area to see if you observed any signs of possible contact or impact with a pedestrian?" Samuels asked.

"Yes . . . I didn't observe any obvious signs of contact of the bumper or the grill or the hood area that would, in my opinion, be consistent with the impacting of a pedestrian with the front of the vehicle."

"Did you observe any damage to the undercarriage, which would have caused the car to stop; in other words, cause the car to be unable to continue driving after coming in contact with, say, a human body by rolling over it?" he was asked.

"Yes . . . the back near the right rear of the vehicle is where the fuel filter is located, and there was a hose clamp attached to the fuel line right forward of the fuel filter."

Karol further explained that the fuel line had looked as though it had been repaired, and the clamp had the appearance of having been used to repair the fuel line.

"And if the fuel line was to be damaged in some way, or separated from the fuel filter to which it is attached, would that cause the car to stop working?"

"Yes . . . It basically would cause the car to be the same as if one ran out of gas," Karol said.

Karol said he'd visited the scene where McDavid was killed, and driven the distance from the alley where his body had been found to the Chevron station where Helen had made the call to AAA.

Samuels pressed Karol to explain how far the car could go before it would no longer be able to continue.

"There is a considerable grade at that location, going down towards where the Chevron station . . . that would cause [the car] to roll."

Karol later testified that the distance from the Chevron station to where McDavid's body had been found was less than half a mile.

"So even if the car would no longer go because of lack of fuel, at the end of the distance from the site of the accident to the location where the car was towed by Triple A, is it a fairly steep grade going down?"

"Yes, ma'am."

And how could Karol tell that the damage in the vicinity of the fuel filter would cause him to believe that the fuel line was damaged?

Karol said that when he'd inspected the right rear of the car, where McDavid's blood had been found, he discovered "a wiping of the surface of the undercarriage. There's a number of smudge marks along the damage area."

"From the documents and photographs you reviewed, in your inspection of the 1999 Sable, do you have an opinion whether Mr. McDavid was standing upright when he was hit?"

"Yes . . . It is my opinion that Mr. McDavid was not standing upright when he was struck."

"And what is that opinion based upon?" Samuels asked.

Karol took a deep breath before explaining how he arrived at his opinion that McDavid had been murdered.

Choosing his words carefully, Karol said that he had reviewed the preliminary hearing witnesses who had already testified in the preceding three days. He was also keenly aware that while his response might seem lengthy, he knew that what he was about to say was perhaps most crucial to the case since it could convince the judge that McDavid was deliberately murdered and not accidently killed by a car.

On a couple of things, Karol said. "The first being the lack of any obvious lower extremity injuries such as deep bruises, or contusions, or fractures to his lower extremities, his legs.

"It's also based upon what I saw regarding the fact that

his glasses were damaged on the ground, and in the photographs I observed. There was grease all around the glasses, in particular around the right opening of his glasses, which was consistent with all of the grease that I observed in the photographs of Mr. McDavid with grease and grime over his right eye, which to me indicates that his glasses were still on when the car ran over the top of his body.

"In most cases, the glasses, from all of my testing and collisions that I've gone to, the glasses come off quite easily when a vehicle will strike them. So that seemed to indicate to me that he was near the ground when he was struck by the vehicle."

And what convinced Karol to believe that McDavid was run over rather than being hit?

"Well, all of the crushing injuries that I saw to his ribs area, plus all the grease and grime that were on his clothing. That tied in with a lot of the wiping that I saw under the undercarriage of the car, which indicated he was run over."

"What about the scrapes on his body? Were they consistent with being gouged by the vehicle undercarriage components?"

"When I observed the body of Mr. McDavid, I saw some gouges on the front and in the rear, which were unusual from being in contact with a roadway. To me it appeared to have been made [when his body was] in contact with sharp objects from the undercarriage of the vehicle."

"What direction do you believe the vehicle which struck Mr. McDavid was traveling prior to impacting him?"

"I believe it was heading south in the alley," Karol replied, based on his observation of the physical evidence that was on the alley surface. "It indicated a dragging of the body in a southerly direction."

Diamond couldn't wait to cross-examine Karol, initially asking superfluous questions as to whether a man or woman had been driving the Mercury, how many people had been in the car, and if the car could still have functioned after hitting a pedestrian.

Karol patiently explained to the lawyer what he had testified about in his direct examination.

"Would it not have stalled immediately?" Diamond asked.

"It may have if the [fuel] line was completely torn. With a small crack in the line, it could actually have proceeded a little bit further past the body," Karol replied.

Asking a series of hypothetical questions, Diamond was unsuccessful in trying to get the witness to say that perhaps the person who'd bought the Mercury after it had been abandoned had repaired the fuel line, and that it was that person's blood underneath the car.

The last three witnesses that Wednesday included Kelli Blanchard, a coroner's investigator who described the condition of McDavid's body when she'd arrived on the scene. She'd noted in her report the grease mark on the body, the tire marks to the left upper thigh of the jeans, and that the eyeglasses were broken.

Once back at the coroner's office, Blanchard had taken fingernail samples from the body before heading to the complex where McDavid had last lived, and learned from the resident manager that Helen Golay was the tenant of the apartment.

Blanchard testified that she'd called Helen, who'd returned the call the same day, and claimed to have been McDavid's cousin.

On cross-examination by Diamond, it was learned that Helen had informed the coroner that she would contact a funeral home, since, she said, McDavid was not married and had no other living relatives.

The next witness, Selena Barros, was another coroner's investigator who'd responded to the scene where Paul Vados had been killed. It was Barros who'd noted that there wasn't any identification on Vados, resulting in his being sent to the coroner's office as a John Doe until his identity could be determined.

William Leaver, an examiner of questioned documents

for the Los Angeles Police Department, was the last of the twenty-five witnesses Samuels called on during the preliminary hearing in the state's effort to get the judge to say there was sufficient evidence for a full-scale trial.

Leaver had been asked to examine a number of insurance policies taken out on the lives of Vados and McDavid by Helen and Olga, and to compare handwriting against documents that had been generated with a stamp impression.

As a series of different insurance policies taken out on behalf of Vados or McDavid were reviewed, Leaver was asked the same question: whether the signature at the bottom of a questioned document was an original signature or a stamp impression. Leaver's answer was that known signatures would be listed under *exemplars* in his report and those not listed as copies would be original.

Because cross-examination by the defense lawyers had not concluded by five o'clock, Leaver returned to the witness stand on the fourth and final day of the preliminary hearing to complete his testimony.

Day four, on Thursday, March 15, 2007, began with Diamond as usual making another motion that Helen had been kept at the criminal court building on Wednesday evening until 8:30, did not get back to her cell at Lynwood until one a.m., and was awakened at three a.m. Diamond argued that these late nights were affecting Helen's ability to concentrate, and she was unable to communicate properly with him.

Helen had also asked for bedroom slippers and again wanted a cell of her own. She got the slippers, but was denied private accommodations.

As for the rest of Diamond's motion, the judge assured him that if the case went to trial, special arrangements would have to be made regarding ample rest for her each day. "I accept your representations if you're telling me that's how much sleep she's getting. I accept that. The motion is denied, though. Now have a seat."

The defense lawyers breezed through Leaver's cross-examination. Then Samuels again called up Samuel Mayrose, the FBI agent, to ask whether Kecia Golay had been shown certain documents and asked if she recognized her mother's handwriting when he'd interviewed her.

Mayrose was shown a series of checks and insurance policies, and testified as to which signatures Kecia had recognized as her mother's.

In his cross-examination of Mayrose, public defender Sklar asked him if the search of Olga's apartment had turned up any bottles of hydrocodone. The agent said none had been found.

Sklar obviously raised that particular question because McDavid's toxicology report had indicated that hydrocodone, marketed as Vicodin, was found in his body, and five bottles of the same drug had been found in Helen's medicine cabinet. By showing that the drug had not been found in Olga's home, Sklar was attempting to distance his client from Helen.

Detective Dennis Kilcoyne was briefly recalled to the stand by the prosecutor and testified that both Olga and Helen had refused twice to provide handwriting samples.

Finally, after hearing from 25 witnesses, the preliminary hearing was over and it was time for closing arguments. Diamond went first and wasted no time in the proceedings. He simply didn't offer any closing statement.

Instead he got up, approached the bench and told Judge Wesley:

"Your Honor, because of the conditions at the jail and Ms. Golay's not being able to get sufficient sleep, we ask that the charges be dismissed. And if the DA wants to refile, then there would be a separate issue. We'll submit it on that basis."

"Thank you," Wesley said. "That motion is denied."

It was now time for the summing up, so that the judge could determine whether there was sufficient evidence to bring Helen and Olga to trial.

In his closing argument, Sklar began by also asking the

judge that the murder charges against Olga be dropped. Although admitting that her participation in the insurance fraud was inappropriate, that didn't connect her to the murders.

He touched on what he said were significant areas of testimony that had been covered in the last three-and-a-half days of the hearing to back up his contention that Olga had been Vados' friend and was trying to help the former homeless man back on his feet.

He reminded the judge that it was Helen, not Olga, who'd called the insurance company seeking an increase in the policy about a month before McDavid was killed.

Sklar summarized some of the evidence presented at the prelim with regards to Vados by reminding the judge that Ms. Zamarripa, the apartment manager at his unit, believed that Olga had been a friend of Vados, regularly visiting and bringing him food.

The defense lawyer tried to shift suspicion from Olga to Helen by pointing out that Olga had filed a missing persons report for Vados and had paid a life insurance premium on him after he had died, suggesting that she'd been unaware of his death.

"The fact that she had filed a missing persons report for Mr. Vados further indicates that she had a friendship with him and that she cared for Mr. Vados, and that she was clearly concerned about his disappearance," the lawyer said.

In recapping the testimony, he brought out that Helen had upped McDavid's life insurance about a month before he was killed, and had tried to eliminate Olga's name from the policy. "This suggests that [Helen] might be anticipating the death of McDavid," Sklar said.

He also mentioned the earlier testimony from FBI Agent Mayrose that bottles of hydrocodone, the painkiller found in McDavid's body, had also been found at Helen's home, but not in Olga's apartment.

Sklar asked the judge to consider the fact that the Mercury had been stored behind Helen's Santa Monica address for at least six months prior to McDavid's death, and that

Helen's neighbor testified that she had never seen Olga in possession of the vehicle.

The lawyer also tried to cast doubt about Olga's involvement in the murder of McDavid by bringing up the testimony of the tow truck driver who said that after picking up the elderly woman at the Chevron station, he had dropped her off in Santa Monica near Helen's address, and not in Hollywood where Olga lived.

Another factor that the lawyer said strongly pointed to Olga's innocence was a letter *she'd* written to one of the insurance companies seeking the return of a premium she had paid after McDavid's death. "This indicates that she wasn't aware of the death of Mr. McDavid at the time she sent the premium," Sklar said.

When Shellie Samuels had been assigned the case by the district attorney, she knew that the case was unique because of the defendants' age and the fact that they had no prior arrests. "It kind of boggles the mind to accept the fact of what these women were willing to do. People tend to think that women of that age aren't going to do something this awful," she said shortly before she began her closing remarks to the judge.

Samuels' closing was concise and to the point: "The only reason for committing insurance fraud is if you know that this person is going to die. One of the victims was fifty years old, and the insurance policies were taken out by a woman who was in her seventies. So she certainly wasn't going to sit around and wait for him to die of natural causes, not to mention that some of the policies were for accidental death only.

"Therefore, the only purpose for taking out these policies was in fact that the women knew that these men were going to die in a timely manner, so that they could collect."

In further explaining the prosecutor's theory of the case, Samuels said that the women had supported the men during the two-year contestability periods, housing and feeding them and paying for their monthly insurance premiums. "This was a huge investment by these women," she told the judge.

Samuels stressed that prosecutors had the proof that Olga had actually bought the car. "I believe it's quite clear that this is the car that was used to kill Mr. McDavid.

"And I would also like to remind the court that the premium payment made by Olga Rutterschmidt after the death of Mr. McDavid was by automatic debit. So what she did was forget to call the bank and tell them to stop taking money out of her account," Samuels said in explaining why Olga had inadvertently paid the premium.

Samuels summed up her case by saying that it was "quite clear that these women had a conspiracy going here to take out policies on homeless men whom they believed didn't have any family members who would care about them enough to inquire, and lie about their relationships to these men, lie about the value of these men's [lives] monetarily . . . in order to get multiple insurance companies to insure them."

The prosecutor also took the opportunity to accuse Helen and Olga of taking advantage of the fact that antitrust laws would keep the insurance companies from having a single clearing house where they could go and find out what other policies had been taken out on a person, making it a simple matter to defraud them of millions of dollars.

"I believe there was no reason for doing all this insurance fraud but for the fact that you intend to kill this person at the end of the two-year period of contestability.

"The only way for the fraud to pay off is to kill these victims," she said.

And now it was up to Judge Wesley to rule, and while everyone in the courtroom waited in anticipation for his decision, Helen appeared relaxed. Her feet lay loose as she continued to doodle and scribble on a legal pad. But all the while, Olga trembled anxiously, and appeared quite animated as she spoke nervously with her lawyer.

"All right," Wesley began. "It appears from the evidence

presented that the following offenses have been committed and that there is sufficient cause to believe the following defendants guilty. I order that the defendants be held to answer to stand trial on murder and conspiracy charges," he ruled.

Helen sat expressionless at the news that she was going to stand trial for murder and conspiracy. Olga, on the other hand, was taken aback, stunned at the judge's ruling. She opened her mouth in disbelief, bit her lip, shook her head "no, no" several times, and then buried her face in her right hand and began crying.

Wesley further ordered that the women be held without bail, which meant that they would remain in jail pending their arraignment on March 29, 2007.

Chapter 11

Life or Death, That is the Question

At 9 a.m. on Thursday, March 29, three weeks after the preliminary hearing had concluded, Judge David Wesley ordered that Olga and Helen be arraigned on charges that they'd murdered two homeless men.

Television news cameras and photographers waited patiently outside in the hallway of Department 102 on the ninth floor at the Clara Shortridge Foltz Criminal Justice Center on arraignment day for a chance to grab a seat when the deputies opened the doors.

Once inside the small courtroom, everyone spoke in hushed tones, waiting for the main event to begin. The small talk among reporters was to see what the two Black Widows would wear when they made their long-awaited appearance. It was like a scene in a Hollywood movie plot.

Finally, a young sheriff opened a side door inside the well of the courtroom and out scurried two septuagenarians, their handcuffs removed, wearing the latest trend in stylish daywear—orange Los Angeles County prison jumpsuits. They quickly took their seats at the defense table, next to their respective lawyers.

A few minutes later, the wood-paneled door suddenly opened behind the bench, and as Judge Wesley walked over to his chair, the clerk uttered those two well-known words to the audience: "All rise."

The two women looked contrite as Judge Wesley wasted

no time and began reading aloud the charges the two faced.

When asked how she was pleading to the charges of murder and conspiracy, Helen Golay said, "Not guilty." Olga Rutterschmidt answered the same.

In April, Roger Jon Diamond had formally challenged the court on the issue of whether the preliminary hearing that had just concluded was valid, since Helen had been denied "sufficient rest." The judge ruled that it was, and turned down Diamond's motion, instead setting up a series of scheduled dates for pre-trial hearings.

By May 2, 2007, the first of many pre-trial hearings was to begin. The only problem was that every time a hearing was scheduled, one of the defense lawyers or the prosecutor would cancel the session at the last minute. Judge Wesley also tried setting a tentative trial date of May 23, 2007. But like the pre-trial hearing dates, the trial date came and went, new trial dates were set up and canceled, and hardly anyone in the media paid any attention or raised questions as to the cause of the long delays.

In fact, every time the defense lawyers met with the prosecutor, all that was accomplished was that a number of minor housekeeping chores were handled, including such mundane issues as granting Helen a waiver of personal presence—court permission to remain in her cell at Lynwood unless her appearance in court was absolutely essential to the case.

At one of the pre-trial hearings, Samuels advised the court that she intended to further examine the Mercury Sable, and asked the lawyers if they wanted to be present during the testing. Of course they wanted to be present. That decision took less than one minute to resolve.

Another issue of great concern to the defense was that the prosecutor had yet to determine whether the trial would be a capital case, and as a result there had not been a decision as to whether they would be seeking the death penalty or life without parole when the trial began.

It normally takes about four months for a special committee at the Los Angeles County District Attorney's Office to decide whether prosecutors should seek the death
penalty against a defendant, said Samuels. Prosecutors
were trying to accelerate the process of whether to go or
not go for the death penalty because the judge had ruled in
January that Helen's right to a speedy hearing had been
violated.

Nevertheless, Diamond constantly used the delay by the
death penalty committee to remind reporters that Helen
was not guilty. "She is innocent, and she hopes to win in
court," he would say.

Diamond's tactic was to call the prosecution's case
against Helen "very weak," arguing that there were no eyewitnesses to the men's deaths. Surveillance tapes did not
show who had been driving the Mercury Sable allegedly
used to kill McDavid, or whether there was more than one
person in the car. Most important, the tow truck driver
could not identify Helen as the person who'd wanted the
Sable towed to the rear of her Santa Monica home the night
McDavid was killed.

By September the earlier trial dates were but a memory
as the case continued to move at a snail's pace.

About the only positive news for the defense came in
October when prosecutors announced that they would not
seek the death penalty against either of the defendants, but
would ask for life without parole if the women were convicted of both first-degree murder and the special circumstance allegations.

While the committee that handled death penalty cases
did not explain their decision, the reason was fairly obvious: if convicted at trial, both women would be in their
mid-seventies. Appeals on death penalty cases are costly,
and can take five to ten years or longer before the United
States Supreme Court hands down a final decision. Olga
and Helen would be around 85 to 90 years of age before
they could possibly be executed by lethal injection. And by

then, there would no doubt be such an outcry from the public about executing such elderly women that the committee reasoned that it wasn't worthwhile to suggest the death penalty.

A number of other delays were caused by the defense requesting more time for investigation that still needed to be conducted. As a circumstantial case, there were matters that had to be resolved because of the massive amount of material that the lawyers had to review.

In any event, the decision to not execute the Black Widows was a major victory for the serial killers.

Chapter 12

Can They Convince a Jury?

New Year's Eve 2008 came and went at the Lynwood jail, and was rather uneventful for Helen and Olga, who were waiting for a new trial date. The biggest excitement for the girls was being let out of their tiny cubicles for one hour a day to exercise, shower, and make telephone calls. It was certainly a far cry from the lush Pacific beaches of Santa Monica and mountain walks in Runyon Canyon, where Helen and Olga used to go almost every day.

The wheels of justice were beginning to grind to a halt as February approached and word trickled out that the district attorney's office had reassigned Deputy District Attorney Shellie Samuels to another high-profile case, and Truc Do, a nine-year career prosecutor, would be taking over the job of prosecuting the Black Widows.

Truc Do had less than two months to become well-versed in the case. To her credit, she had already overseen trials for fifty-seven felonies, including murder, attempted murder, sexual assault, robberies, carjackings, and shootings.

Do, 37, had come to the United States at age 3 with her family, escaping Vietnam before the April 1975 fall of Saigon. A magna cum laude graduate from the University of California, Los Angeles, Do got her law degree in June 1997 from the Stanford Law School, where she was the associate editor of the *Stanford Law Review*.

After a two-year stint with a private law firm following graduation, Do joined the district attorney's office in April 1999, and was soon handling some of the top murder cases in Los Angeles County.

In April 2007, she prosecuted Chester Dewayne Turner, one of the most prolific serial killers in Los Angeles. From 1987 to 1988, he lured ten women to secluded areas with the promise of drugs, then sexually assaulted and brutally murdered them.

The case had remained unsolved until a "cold hit" on California's DNA database linked Turner to all eleven murders. A jury convicted him of ten first-degree murders and one count of second-degree fetal murder—one of the victims was pregnant—with the special circumstances of rape-murder and multiple murder. After learning of the eleventh victim in the penalty phase of the trial, the jury recommended, and a judge sentenced Turner to death.

Another of Do's big cases was that of two 21-year-old men—Carlos Argueta and Enrique Gonzalez. In October 2006, over a period of five days, they went on a shooting spree with a World War I submachine gun. In the first shooting, the two attacked a car with three people in it, and killed a 21-year-old man. Twenty-four hours later, Argueta fired twenty-one rounds at the backs of four children, ages 12 to 15, killing a 12-year old boy, and injuring a 13-year-old girl and a 26-year-old man who'd walked into the line of fire. Two days later, Argueta and Gonzalez chased down two witnesses who had testified against Argueta's younger brother, and shot at them. In separate trials, juries convicted both men of two counts of murder and six counts of attempted murder. A jury recommended, and a judge sentenced Argueta to death while Gonzalez was given life in prison without the possibility of parole.

Do spent an inordinate amount of time going over every detail in the case, reading through thousands of pages of reports so that she would be up to speed when the trial testimony began.

Seated next to Do in the second chair at the prosecution

table was Robert (Bobby) Grace, who has been an outstanding prosecutor in Los Angeles for twenty years. During his tenure, he had been assigned to the Hardcore Gang, Family Violence, and Major Crimes Divisions of the office. Like Do, Bobby was also known for trying complex, high-profile cases. He has worked on over fifty murder cases and over twenty special circumstances murder cases that involve the death penalty.

Bobby has teamed up with Do on other cases, including the prosecution of Chester Turner.

Bobby received a special commendation in 2004 for his prosecution of Henry Hayes, a Los Angeles minister accused of murdering his wife and 7-year-old daughter. He was having multiple extramarital affairs, and sought to start a new life by killing his family, and trying to make the crime scene look like a residential robbery gone bad. Hayes was convicted of two counts of special circumstance murder for the shotgun killings of his wife, Vangela, and daughter, Teanna, and sentenced to life without the possibility of parole.

After months of delays and rescheduling, the often-postponed murder trial of the *People of the State of California* vs. *Olga Rutterschmidt and Helen Golay* was set to get underway on Tuesday, March 11, 2008.

Helen and Olga must have sensed that things were about to get hot, because both began complaining to their jailers about anything that came to mind. As one deputy at Lynwood remarked, "They are a general pain in the ass."

At 8:15 a.m. the corridor outside the courtroom was like a three-ring circus as nearly one hundred potential jurors waited patiently for the doors to open. There weren't enough benches to seat everyone that had been called as potential jurors, so they either sat on the cold marble floor or just stood around waiting for the doors to the courtroom to open.

A pool of eighty-five potential candidates had initially been summoned. It was one of the smallest jury pools called by the county; surprising, considering the extensive pre-trial publicity that the case had generated over the past three years.

Some who were lucky enough to find seats on the plastic benches that lined the corridor spent the time waiting to get into the courtroom dozing. But most tried to keep themselves busy by reading newspapers or paperbacks, solving crossword puzzles, or, in the case of one brave woman, knitting. Others made do by squatting on the floor or simply standing and milling around aimlessly.

The courtroom was nearly empty, with the exception of the two prosecutors, two defense lawyers with their clients, the sheriff's deputy, Gloria Armenta, the court clerk, and court reporter Phyllis Young. Once the door opened, the sixty seats inside were quickly filled and the screening process got underway. Judge Wesley let it be known at the start of the session that television and still cameras were barred from the courtroom, although he would allow one pool photographer.

Unlike with most big-name trials, the Golay–Rutterschmidt jury pool was not given a lengthy questionnaire to fill out; nonetheless, the screening process was grueling.

The judge began by advising the potential panel that prosecutors planned calling on some ninety witnesses. He also told them that the trial would take about a month, and that if a juror could not be away from their business that long, they were to notify the clerk when their name was called.

Over the next day and a half, the prosecutor and defense lawyers got down to the nitty-gritty of selecting the panel. Jurors were asked routine questions such as whether they had difficulty speaking or understanding English, whether they knew the defendants or the lawyers, whether pre-trial publicity in the case would influence their decision process, and whether they could be fair.

Several jurors were excused after saying they were very familiar with the case, and had formed an opinion as to the guilt of the two women and didn't feel they could be fair.

Others were eliminated for appearing too eager to serve as jurors on the case. A few jurors admitted to never having heard of the two Black Widows. Once the pre-trial publicity questions were out of the way, the members of the pool were put through an extensive *voir dire* process. (A voir dire examination occurs when a judge or attorney questions prospective jurors to determine their qualifications for jury service.)

On Thursday, March 13, Court Clerk Gloria Armenta swore in the nine-man, three-woman jury panel, and four alternates, who would determine the case, and Helen and Olga's fate.

The judge ordered the panel to return to the courtroom on Tuesday, March 18, to hear opening statements.

By 8:30 a.m., spectators were already lined up outside Department 102 waiting for court officers to open the door. In many ways, the scene was reminiscent of shoppers just before Christmas, waiting for Wal-Mart or Macy's to open.

It was media madness as reporters from local TV and radio stations, wire services, and the area's numerous weekly and daily newspapers, including the *Los Angeles Times*, rushed to grab seats as soon as the door was flung open. With Judge Wesley's permission, the pool newspaper photographer positioned himself in the back left-hand corner of the courtroom. A couple of courtroom artists took up seats nearby.

Everyone in the room seemed antsy, fidgeting, waiting for the two women to make an entrance into the courtroom.

All eyes were fixed on the door through which, in moments, Helen and Olga would be taken from their holding cell to be seated at the defense table.

It wasn't until 9:34 a.m. that Helen arrived. Her handcuffs were removed and she took a seat next to her lawyer, Roger Diamond. Gone was her former signature dyed-blonde teased bouffant. What showed loud and clear now were her jailhouse roots. And although she did not wear her orange jumpsuit, the best she had been able to scrounge up was a pair of brown slacks, a nondescript blouse, and a dingy sea-green sweater.

Olga then made her grand entrance into the arena of court opinion. She seemed bewildered, almost unsure of her surroundings. She looked at the audience tentatively before acknowledging her lawyer, Michael Sklar, whom she sat next to. She wore her long dark hair, now peppered with flecks of white, slicked back and held together with a couple of barrettes.

Both women looked haggard and every bit their age.

With members of the prosecutor's staff, and investigators and detectives who'd worked the case for two or more years taking up the first two rows in the spectator section, and the media taking up the rest of the available seats, all that was missing to get the show on the road was for Judge Wesley to make an appearance.

The two defendants did not have any family members or friends in the courtroom. Stella Vados, the daughter of Paul Vados, and her boyfriend sat on the left side in the second row. Sandra Salman and her brother sat behind the Vados family. Gloria Allred, the attorney who represented both the Vados and Salman families, sat next to Sandra Salman.

All eyes were fixed on the front of the courtroom, waiting for the judge to take his seat at the bench. When he did, the room came alive. Earlier, jurors had been taken to a special area behind the courtroom and, when everything was ready to begin, Judge Wesley buzzed twice, signaling to them that it was all right to enter and be seated.

At 9:45 a.m. Truc Do, looking stunning in a two-piece black suit and white blouse, and wearing a gold heart-shaped art deco pin on the lapel of her jacket, faced the jurors and began her opening remarks by taking them through a history of the case.

"These women looked at their victims, Paul Vados, Kenneth McDavid, and Jimmy Covington, homeless and destitute, and saw a profit in their plight, a profit of two-point-eight million dollars. These women looked at these victims . . . and took advantage of their plight. They made two-point-eight million dollars by murder, murder to collect life insurance benefits of men who had nothing.

"This is what this case is about. You will hear evidence that the defendants hatched a murder plot, a plot to murder for money that began with finding the perfect victim. They specifically targeted homeless and destitute men because they understood that this class of victim are desperate and needy enough to take what they had offered."

Do went on to tell jurors that Golay and Rutterschmidt had offered the homeless men help, giving them shelter, paying their rent, and providing them with food, not out of kindness or compassion, but as a hook into their plot. And once their victims were hooked, the defendants took out life insurance policies on them.

The prosecutor explained that the biggest lie the defendants had told was that they were related to the victims. "Golay was always the fiancée, Rutterschmidt was always the cousin . . . and they would name themselves beneficiaries," Do told jurors.

"Their murder plot was simple. The victim died, they get paid. Using this murder plot, the defendants applied for twenty-six life insurance policies on three men, men that were not their lovers, not their friends, not their family."

The prosecutor explained to jurors the two-year incontestability clause that governed California insurance law. By waiting the two years before killing them, the defendants were able to collect their money, because the insurance companies could not challenge the validity of the policies.

"And each time the victim died, after the two years had passed, it would always be in the same manner, in what looked like a staged hit-and-run accident. This was part of their murder plot. The victim would always be run over, crushed to death, in an alley, with no witnesses, and it always looked like an accident.

"You will hear evidence that in 2002, the defendants entered Mr. McDavid's life. They offered him something he desperately needed: shelter, a place to live. He thought he was getting a helping hand from the defendants. But that some time after he moved in, the defendants told him he had to sign a life insurance policy as an act of good faith. You will hear that Mr. McDavid believed them. He believed that he had to sign in order to continue living there, in order to stay off the streets.

"What he didn't know was that for the next two years, from November 2002 to March 2005, these women fraudulently applied for eighteen life insurance policies on his life, asking for a total of five million, seven hundred thousand, nine hundred dollars.

"You will hear evidence that they used a signature stamp of Mr. McDavid's signature to complete these applications. You will hear from the owner of the store who will testify that the defendant, Olga Rutterschmidt, bought this stamp of Mr. McDavid's signature, and that she was, in fact, a regular customer at the store."

Do went on to tell jurors that a questioned-document examiner, an expert on the matter of handwriting, would be testifying to tell them that this stamp had been used on seventeen of the eighteen applications for life insurance on McDavid.

"You're going to hear evidence in this case that the defendants made up a screenplay, claiming that McDavid wrote a two-million-dollar screenplay called *Checking Out*, and that was their investment.

"So after they put Mr. McDavid in this apartment, they waited for two years, with murder on their mind. And during those two years, they waited for their fraud to be incontestable.

"Ms. Golay, you will hear, paid forty-two thousand dollars and change for all of the premiums on these policies, that she paid over twenty-one thousand dollars in rent. This is significant. You're going to hear that the total cost that these ladies paid out of pocket for their murder plot was over sixty-four thousand dollars, for a potential return of three million, seven hundred thousand and forty dollars. That's how much money they had invested in McDavid. And all they had to do is monitor him and make sure that he was still on their hook for those two years, or else they don't get paid.

"After putting all that money into Mr. McDavid, his life was theirs," Do said.

"You're going to hear from four witnesses in this case, Patrick Lamay, Jose Luna, Douglas Crapeau and Danielli Cosgrove. These four witnesses will tell you the lengths that these two women went to protect their interest in Mr. McDavid. You're going to hear that in late 2004, these women began to feel that their money, their interest in Mr. McDavid, was being threatened."

The prosecutor said that Patrick Lamay had met McDavid at the same church where homeless people got hot meals on Sunday morning. The two had become friendly, and McDavid had invited Lamay into his small studio apartment to get off the street.

"You're going to hear Mr. Lamay tell you that he then invited several more people into the apartment, and it was there that he met Olga Rutterschmidt, who became very angry when she saw Lamay and all these other people living with Mr. McDavid.

"'You can't have these people here, based on our arrangement,' Olga told McDavid. So Mr. Lamay asked him, 'What kind of arrangement do you have with these women?' and McDavid told him, 'They got me this apartment. They paid for the rent, and after I moved in, they told me I had to sign a life insurance policy as an act of good faith. And I believed that I had to sign in order to stay in this apartment.'

"You will hear Lamay testify that to isolate McDavid, Olga Rutterschmidt hired and brought in armed private guards to get these people out. And that he also then met Helen Golay, who came into the apartment with police to evict these people.

"You're going to hear from Jose Luna, who owned a

security company. He will testify that in October 2004, Olga Rutterschmidt hired him as an armed security guard with only one purpose, and that was to watch Mr. McDavid.

"You will hear from Douglas Crapeau, an acquaintance and neighbor of Olga Rutterschmidt, who will testify that he agreed to help her, and came to the apartment building where McDavid lived, with a loaded thirty-eight revolver that he had concealed, and that Ms. Rutterschmidt had him use the weapon to threaten those in the apartment."

Do pointed out to jurors that after McDavid had been removed from the apartment, Helen and Olga continued to monitor him by paying for him to stay at local motels.

She told the jury that on the backs of the registration cards at these motels, Helen Golay's name could be found, with her driver's license number, and that jurors would also see evidence of a credit card bill showing that she'd paid the rental for these motels.

"You're going to know from the evidence that at eleven-forty-five p.m. on June twenty-first, 2005, Ms. Golay and possibly other persons or by herself, ran over McDavid with a silver station wagon.

"You're going to hear about two businesses in this alley where McDavid's lifeless body was found had surveillance cameras—the Bristol Farms . . . and a Copy Express office.

"You're going to see the surveillance film and the surveillance photographs from these two businesses. And what you're going to see is that at eleven-forty-five p.m., a silver station wagon turns off Westwood Boulevard, west of Ohio and south through this alley."

Do said that as the station wagon had slowed down at that location where McDavid's body was found, it stopped, turned off its lights for four minutes and twenty-nine seconds, and, when the lights were turned back on, the car goes in reverse and then forward.

"What you're going to hear now is that at eleven-fifty-four p.m. that night, Helen Golay called Triple A for tow service on a silver Mercury Sable station wagon at a Chevron gas station at the end of the alley, about a thousand feet from where Mr. McDavid's body was found.

"You're going to hear evidence [from] the tow truck driver, who will tell you that he towed a Mercury Sable station wagon with an elderly woman, whom he could not identify, to Fifth and Ocean Park in Santa Monica, where the defendant Golay lives."

Do told how on June 21, 2005, at midnight, a witness who had been playing backgammon at a nearby store went to the alley where his car was. That witness, Yoram Hassid, called his friend to lock up his business because there was a drunk guy sleeping in the alley.

About an hour later, two more men (Behrooz Haverim and Masoud Khalifian) who had also been playing backgammon tried to get to their car, but couldn't because McDavid's body was lying in the middle of the alley. When they looked closer at the body of McDavid, they noticed he was lying in a pool of blood, and they called 911.

Do described the horrific injuries sustained by McDavid to the jury, including detailing the gruesome autopsy that was conducted on him. "You will hear evidence that he had a laceration in his head, deep enough to cause bleeding in the brain. He had multiple broken ribs, his spine had been broken—all injuries that the coroner will tell you are called *crush injuries*. He was crushed to death."

After McDavid had been murdered, Do said, Helen went to the coroner's office and claimed McDavid's body, saying she was a relative, and had him cremated. To this day, both Helen and Olga refuse to divulge where McDavid's ashes were interred, if indeed they were.

"You will hear evidence that a few weeks after Mr. McDavid's murder, a Mercury Sable is dumped point-fifty-four miles from where Olga Rutterschmidt's apartment building is. It was found abandoned at North Vista Street in Hollywood, and according to the impound document, was first noticed at that location on July twelfth, 2005. And it sat there until it was impounded on July nineteenth, 2005.

"You will hear proof that when the car was towed, it

went to an impound yard and ultimately sold to Jose Quintero in what is called a *lien sale*. The police tracked down Mr. Quintero and found this vehicle."

The police purchased the Sable from Quintero, paying him $4,000, and the vehicle was then examined by authorities, who found McDavid's DNA and his blood on the undercarriage. They also found that the fuel line had been damaged and repaired.

"You are going to hear evidence that Ms. Golay and Ms. Rutterschmidt bought this vehicle, this murder vehicle, on January twentieth, 2004. Mario Medina will testify that on that date, Olga Rutterschmidt wanted to buy that Mercury Sable station wagon, and told him that she wasn't buying it for herself, but for a friend, and gave him the driver's license of Hilary Adler.

"Not only did the defendants purchase this vehicle on January twentieth, 2004, you're going to hear evidence that Ms. Golay actually stored the vehicle at her home . . . before the murder."

Do pointed out that the car had been cited by the city of Santa Monica for unlawful parking at an alley near Golay's home on January 5, 2005. And that a neighbor had seen the murder vehicle near her home on April 8, 2005, when she noticed that someone had splashed red paint on it.

"When the murder weapon was recovered, not only did they find McDavid's DNA and blood, but it still had the red paint on the front driver's-side wheel. With all of that evidence, you're going to know that these defendants are guilty of Mr. McDavid's murder, because they had the murder weapon and they had the motive."

During Do's seventy-five-minute opening statement, jurors were shown pictures of the victims' bodies, receipts for rent, insurance premiums, the check to buy the station wagon, and a rubber stamp with McDavid's signature that was used to sign one of the insurance policies.

Jurors were also shown a photo of the Hollywood apartment building on Cherokee Avenue where Olga and Helen had rented the studio apartment for McDavid for $875 a month.

"You're going to hear that these women were so greedy that they actually attempted to hook another victim in through their murder plot, a man named Jimmy Covington, who was also homeless and destitute at the age of forty-five."

Do said that Covington would be testifying how he had been sitting outside a building and was approached by Olga, who asked him if he was homeless. When Covington had told her yes, Olga said she helped homeless people get off the street, and gave him some money and a place to stay in a building that was rented by Olga and Helen.

Then Olga began demanding documents and answers about his family. Covington got suspicious and walked away from Olga—just in time.

"But that didn't stop the two defendants from fraudulently applying for an eight-hundred-thousand-dollar life insurance policy on Covington," said Do.

"The defendants believed that they could get away with this bold murder plot because they had gotten away with it in 1999 with Paul Vados. We do know that, like the other two victims, Vados also took services from this church in Hollywood. Pastor Suhayda will testify that Mr. Vados was also among the many who needed the church's help."

The prosecutor let jurors know that from February 1997 to August 1999, Olga and Helen had applied for eight life insurance policies on Vados, worth $879,500—a plot identical to the one that was used with McDavid. For two years, they paid Vados' rent, paid for his insurance premiums, and monitored him.

"Mr. Vados, just like Mr. McDavid, was found dead in an alley on November eighth, 1999, from massive blunt-force injuries. It was the same scene, middle of the alley, no witnesses, literally crushed to death, all these grease marks to his clothing and on his body.

"For six years, Mr. Vados' death remained classified as an accident. But the evidence is going to show that these women thought they had gotten away with murder and six hundred thousand dollars.

"The evidence is going to show you that the defendants are guilty of both murders, beyond a reasonable doubt. Their guilt is evident in these numbers, a clear motive to kill. Their guilt is evident in the fact that they were found with the murder weapon that killed Mr. McDavid. They were arrested on May eighteenth, 2006, by the joint task force of federal agents and LAPD detectives. And when they were arrested, they were told that they were being charged federally with mail fraud charges, but that they were being investigated for the murders of Paul Vados and Kenneth McDavid.

"At this time, the police did not have the evidence of the Triple A call or the evidence of the Sable station wagon with Mr. McDavid's DNA on the undercarriage, and the women knew that.

"So on May eighteenth, 2006, the detectives put these women into a room together and secretly recorded a conversation . . . and when you watch this videotape of the defendants speaking . . . you are going to hear, in this tape, Ms. Rutterschmidt very angry with Ms. Golay because Ms. Golay has, on the side, taken out additional policies that she [Rutterschmidt] wasn't going to be able to profit from. And so, immediately after Detective Kilcoyne tells them that they are being investigated for murder, Olga Rutterschmidt turns to Golay and tells her, 'You are greedy, that's the problem.' "

Do gave the jury a taste of what was on the tape, mentioning that Helen tells Olga over and over to "*Be quiet. Don't say anything. They could be listening, be careful what you say*," and that Helen assures Olga that all the authorities have against them is the mail fraud charges and nothing else. "Helen Golay thinks that she's getting away with murder again," the prosecutor told the jury.

"You'll also hear on the tape that Golay tries to clue Rutterschmidt in to lies, saying that *Kenneth wanted all of this. Kenneth loved both of us. We were like his family.*"

But then Olga speaks up, saying, "Yeah, I was the cousin, and you were the fiancée. Baloney."

"What is most chilling in this recorded conversation is that all they could talk about was money. All they could talk about was how they were going to collect the rest of the money that they wanted from the insurance company.

"There was one-point-five million dollars that remained on Mr. McDavid's life that had not yet been paid, and these women were intent on collecting every single penny of that amount, so they started this murder plot with greed. And you're going to see that even when the jig was up, these defendants remained greedy until the very end."

Do asked jurors to deliver justice and return verdicts of guilty against both of these defendants because "the evidence is overwhelming that they are guilty beyond a reasonable doubt."

Helen and Olga seemed unmoved by the hard-hitting opening by the prosecutor.

When Do showed the broken bodies of Vados and McDavid, and also described the injuries to the bloody victims, jurors cringed and momentarily looked down at the floor. But Helen and Olga merely stared ahead, never once blinking or even taking a quick peek.

Most of the time during Do's opening remarks, she took jurors through a paper trail of the evidence, showing them photos and checks written by the defendants in a PowerPoint-style presentation. For their part, Helen and Olga spent the morning doodling or jotting down notes on yellow legal pads, pretending not to hear the prosecutor speaking when she asked jurors to find them guilty.

Both defense attorneys informed the judge that they were postponing their opening statements until the conclusion of the prosecution's case.

Golay's lawyer, Roger Diamond, appeared confident as he spoke with reporters outside the courtroom in the corridor. "We have evidence to show she's not guilty. They have over one hundred witnesses, but they have no eyewitnesses, no confession, and no fingerprints. It's all circumstantial," he said, predicting an acquittal. "Somebody's dead. That doesn't necessarily mean they were murdered."

Diamond claimed he had a "dynamite defense" that would prove no murder ever took place. Of course, he didn't share his thoughts with the media on what he planned to tell the jury that would convince them to acquit Helen.

Sklar made no comment as to why he was forgoing opening statements until later in the proceedings.

With the defense refusing to give a hint as to how they planned to exonerate the women, it was anyone's guess as to how they would proceed. Veteran defense lawyers claim that the usual reason for taking a pass on the introductory remarks is so the lawyer can switch defenses after the prosecution has put on their case. "It's very old-school," says criminal defense lawyer Stephen Somerstein.

If the lawyers for Helen or Olga were going to push for a psychiatric defense, the girls could refuse any such proposal offered by their lawyers. Besides, if they were going to go for a psychiatric defense, prosecutors should have been notified of that tactic months earlier.

There are only a few decisions a client must make when going to trial: whether to plead guilty or not guilty, whether to go to trial with a jury or have a bench trial where the judge decides the outcome, and whether to testify. Decisions such as tactics and strategy are almost always left to the lawyer—who, of course, is obligated to consult with his client.

Chapter 13

It's Show and Tell Time

With opening statements out of the way, the prosecution team was off and running. Day after day during the first week of the trial, witnesses took the stand offering evidence intended to prove that Helen and Olga were guilty of murdering two homeless and destitute men.

The prosecution had informed Judge David Wesley and the two defense lawyers that they intended to call ninety witnesses in presenting their case, many of whom had testified a year earlier at the preliminary hearing.

Kicking off the list of witnesses was the group of three men who had found McDavid in the alley behind Bristol Farms shortly before midnight on the night of June 21, and called the police.

The tow truck driver, who was next on the stand, testified that he had been called to the gas station at the end of the alley by someone using the AAA membership card of Helen Golay. While the driver couldn't identify the "elderly woman with wrinkles who was over forty years of age," he did say that he'd towed a 1999 silver Mercury Sable station wagon to Santa Monica behind Helen's home at Fifth Street and Ocean Park Boulevard.

The jury listened intently on Thursday, that first week, when the prosecution had the car salesman on the stand. He identified Olga as the woman who'd bought the Mercury from his dealership in January 2004. A neighbor of

Helen's followed him to the stand and spoke about having seen the Sable parked in the rear of her home in the alley for more than a year. She recalled taking photos of the vehicle at some point, after observing that it had been vandalized when someone splattered red paint on one wheel. She testified that she had planned to show the photos to the city fathers in hopes of getting protection for the area.

Brenda Heavens was one of several traffic officers to testify that they'd found the Sable abandoned on a street in Hollywood near Olga's apartment in July 2005. Heavens testified that she'd ticketed the car, and showed a copy of the $47 citation to jurors that also indicated that a radio call had been received at her office complaining about the station wagon parked in the alley.

Eventually the vehicle was impounded and then resold at auction. Police tracked it down. The new owner, Jose Adrian Quintero, upon learning that the vehicle had been used in a murder, no longer wanted it, and it was sold to the Los Angeles Police Department for $4,000, where it underwent an exhaustive inspection.

At 11 a.m. on Friday, March 21, John Kolter, the state's star witness, was called to the stand. It was going to be his job to lead jurors through a high-tech reenactment of the examination of what prosecutors referred to as *the murder weapon*.

Kolter, a CHP officer assigned to the Southern Division Multidisciplinary Accident Investigation Team, otherwise known as MAIT, specializes in responding to major catastrophic traffic accidents.

Back in 2004 when Olga and Helen had bought the station wagon, it probably cost them around $10 to $15,000. Unlike most murder weapons—revolvers, for example, which can be hidden in a purse or carried tucked around your waist—the weapon they'd purchased was bulky. It weighed 3,493 pounds, was 70.8 inches wide, had a height of 55.1 inches, and was 191.9 inches in length. But it was just as deadly as any pistol or 9mm Glock.

As a professional automobile technician for about eleven

years, Kolter said he was certified by the National Institute for Automotive Service Excellence, and is licensed as a state smog inspector, having investigated several hundred vehicles.

It was on Tuesday, June 6, 2006, Kolter said, that he and other officers from the MAIT team had responded to the LAPD holding facility at the Scientific Investigation Division, where he inspected the vehicle and undercarriage for any damage.

One of the first things he noticed was that there was red paint on the front wheel tire. "It appeared to be dried red paint. It was splashed onto the wheel at some point in time. I don't know when or where exactly," Kolter said.

He testified that when he began, he measured the clearance from the ground to the undercarriage. "I pretty much crawled under the car and measured various pieces of equipment under the car from the ground to that item."

"Could you tell the jury what the lowest clearance is from the ground to the undercarriage on this Mercury Sable?" Deputy District Attorney Truc Do asked him.

"The lowest clearance is zero-point-fifty-five feet."

"How many inches is that?"

"About six-and-a-half," he replied, showing jurors what that measurement looked like on a normal twelve-inch wooden ruler.

"When you say the lowest clearance is six-and-a-half inches, at what part of the undercarriage is that clearance?"

"According to my notes, it is the clearance at the front cross member," Kolter said, explaining that the "front cross member is going to be where the front suspension attaches to, and where the engine sits on, this piece of metal at the front of the car, basically between the front wheels," indicating the front bumper.

"What is the largest clearance from the ground to the undercarriage on this Mercury Sable?" the prosecutor wanted to know.

"According to my notes, it's the rear clearance at the

fascia, which is a covering on the bumper. It's in the back."

Truc Do pressed the witness, asking if he could be more specific as to the clearance.

"One-point-fifteen feet," Kolter replied.

"Which is how many inches?"

"It's about fourteen inches," Kolter said, pointing to a photograph that he said "is in the back by the rear bumper."

Kolter said that with the assistance of other officers, the vehicle had been hoisted up to examine the undercarriage, and that was when a criminalist collected possible samples for DNA testing.

The witness also said he'd examined the undercarriage for what is called *contact damage*, saying that "contact damage is where two components or two bodies come together.

"When I say *bodies*, I mean, like, two cars come together where the two components of the cars, like the front of one car and the back of another car, where the front bumper and the rear bumper come in contact with each other and cause damage to each other. That is contact damage."

"And did you find any damage on the contact area?"

"Yes. We found one major area of contact damage," he said, holding up a diagram for jurors to look at as he zoomed in on the PowerPoint presentation board to explain further what part of the undercarriage they were looking at.

"This is the floor pan on the passenger side or right side of the vehicle, and the specific area is going to be the floor pan in this area to the side of the exhaust. This is the exhaust pipe running down the middle of the car. Fuel tank is here. This is a floor pan that runs under the car, and it's basically where the seats are bolted to and the seat belt and things like that."

"And what kind of contact damage did you see there?"

"The floor pan was pushed up in that area and, when compared to the other side, they're basically going to be symmetrical as far as clearance. This side was the side that had contact damage and was wiped clean in comparison to the other side and areas around it. There's a line, that's dirt, where it's been wiped clean."

Kolter explained that the passenger side of the Mercury's floor pan was pushed up an inch, and that the dirt and grease had been wiped clean, suggesting that the car had run over something. But Truc Do pressed on with more questions, wanting to know whether, other than the significant displacement of the right floor pan, there was any other damage to the undercarriage that had been repaired.

"The fuel line had been repaired," Kolter answered firmly.

Using a pointer on the diagram to indicate where the fuel line would be on the Sable, Kolter explained to the panel that the fuel line travels inside the frame rail, up the passenger's side of the vehicle. "The fuel line is going to be there," he said indicating on the diagram that it was all on the passenger's side.

"When you said that the fuel line had been repaired, could you tell the jury what a fuel line is?" the prosecutor asked.

"A fuel line is a section of tubing that carries gasoline or— The engine burns from the tank to the engine, so it can be burned," he replied.

"And what happens to the vehicle if the fuel line is broken?"

"The engine is gong to stop . . . because no more gas is going to it."

"And what was it that made you think that the fuel line on this particular vehicle had been broken and then repaired?"

"The addition of a hose clamp that's normally not there," Kolter said.

Kolter explained to the jury that in his experience in making many fuel filter repairs and fuel tank repairs that the tubing is attached onto that fitting without a clamp.

"It's fused together like two pieces of plastic. They're,

like, welded together, and they're in one piece. Even though they're in two pieces here, this line and that tube are supposed to be together as one without a clamp there. It's basically called an *interference fit*, where the tubing is smaller than the fitting. And when they build this tubing, or assemble it, they press this tubing onto that fitting and the barbs create a seal that's very difficult to break off."

"It's what would be called an *after-market repair*?" he was asked.

"That's correct."

"Did you notice anything about the tubing itself to indicate further damage and repair?"

Kolter said that what he'd wanted to inspect was if the tubing had been cut or broken, and said that when he'd had the tubing magnified, he noticed two levels of tubing, which meant that this tube had not been cut by a mechanic. It was simply how it had come from the factory: The tubing had come off the fitting and was put back on the fitting with a hose clamp.

"That's one of the main reasons Ford doesn't recommend clamping devices is because it's plastic. You put a metal device on plastic, that tubing could distort, possibly leak. This type of repair is also a violation of the Clean Air Act. Again, tightening the clamp distorts this tube," Kolter said.

"Based on your expertise, how would you describe the quality of this repair?"

"It's a quick and dirty repair to get the car back on the road. It's not correct. It's a violation of Ford recommendations. It's a violation of the Clean Air Act. It's not appropriate, and could be dangerous, actually."

Kolter also revealed that he, along with MAIT officers and Detective Dennis Kilcoyne, had participated in an additional test out at the site where McDavid's body was found, to determine whether or not there was a slope to the alley.

The witness disclosed in his testimony that it had been "a controlled test" of the Sable to see if, with the fuel line cut, it could roll far enough along that death alley with the downward grade to reach the Chevron gas station where Helen Golay had called AAA for a tow back to her home.

The lights in the courtroom were dimmed and the jury was shown a DVD, which Kolter narrated for the panel. Kolter is shown in the driver's seat without gas in the tank, with the engine off, no brake application, and just using gravity.

The witness told the panel that as the car moves down the alley, the vehicle picks up quite a bit of speed and the Mercury slowly accelerates until it rolls southbound from the alley to the Chevron station.

With that dramatic demonstration out of the way, the prosecution informed the court that they had nothing further to ask of Kolter.

The questioning of Kolter was so thorough and informative that both defense attorneys declined to cross-examine him.

After Kolter's testimony, the jury recessed for lunch and at 1:40 p.m., the twelve jurors and four alternates were taken down to the bus bay area in the basement of the criminal court building to view the murder weapon up close.

Once in the basement, the judge instructed the jurors that they would be permitted to walk around the vehicle, that they could look underneath the Mercury Sable and that they could also look inside the station wagon without touching it.

"Ladies and gentlemen of the jury, you are going to be permitted to walk around this vehicle. I don't want you touching the vehicle," Wesley cautioned. "You can walk around it; look at it as much as you want. We're not going to open it up, and you're not going to touch it. You can take as long as you want.

"When you feel you've had enough time to look at this vehicle, let me know, and we'll be out of here. No questions will be asked or answered while you're in here. This is strictly a viewing," the judge said.

The jurors were an odd group as they cautiously crouched

down on the ground and strained for a view of the under-carriage. One bold juror got down on his knees and then lay flat on his stomach in a rather peculiar position just to look at the low clearance, which Kolter had testified was about six inches at its lowest point.

In inspecting the undercarriage, the jury was already aware that traces of hair and blood had been found that matched McDavid's DNA. The jury also looked at the Mercury's floor pan with dirt and grease wiped clean, suggesting that that was the spot where the car had struck McDavid, as Kolter had testified.

As jurors went through the chore of their brief assignment, Helen and Olga, straight-faced, with vacant stares, stood casually against the basement wall with their hands cuffed behind them.

In less than ten minutes, the viewing was over and the jurors were back in the courtroom, where the judge dismissed them for the weekend with the admonition that they were not to speak to anybody or form or express any opinion about the case until it was finally submitted to the entire panel at its conclusion.

"You are also to avoid any newspaper stories or television stories about this case," the judge warned them.

"The viewing was kind of a show and tell," Kilcoyne observed after the panel's inspection. "The jurors were hearing a lot of dry testimony all day, seeing pictures and documents. This was an opportunity for them to physically look at the real vehicle."

During the second and third weeks of testimony, jurors heard again from a number of prelim witnesses, among them: Helen's neighbor, Meilisa Thompson, who'd taken photographs of the red paint on the Sable; Sandra Salman, who spoke eloquently about her brother; and Stella Vados.

Robert Brockway, currently with the Department of Justice, who'd been working as an investigator for the California Department of Insurance back in 2005 when he began looking at the policies Helen and Olga had taken out on McDavid, explained the different types of life insurance that were out there for people to buy.

"There's *whole life*, there's *term insurance*, as well as *accidental death and disability*," Brockway began.

"*Whole life* is where the premium is set throughout the whole insurance policy and a portion of that premium goes towards an investment for the insured, and, depending on the policy, depends on when the insured can withdraw on that account or take dividends.

"In basic terms, it is permanent life insurance, so that if a husband wanted to insure his wife for the benefits of their kids, that insurance would cover her entire life."

Brockway was asked whether accidental death and dismemberment and term life were as expensive, or whether it was a cheaper type of life insurance.

"Whole life is going to be the most expensive, because the premium, like I say, stays the same, and a portion of the premium is invested for the insured. That means if a person [who] has taken out a whole life insurance policy continues to pay the premiums, there are no expiration or time issues. Then it doesn't matter when the person who is insured expires, or dies."

He next explained *accidental death and dismemberment*, which he said was usually a type of policy that's offered through your employer that will cover you in case you're injured at work. It should not be confused with workers compensation, Brockway said.

Brockway further made it clear that should you lose a limb or die while at work, benefits are paid based on a schedule, and the schedule is based on your injury, and depends on how much money is paid out to you.

"*Term insurance* is pure insurance. Your premium that you're paying on a monthly basis goes directly toward the insurance. None of it is taken out and put aside as an investment. It's just pure and simple, just insurance, and it is the cheapest," he said.

"Under any of these types of insurance, is suicide ever covered?" the prosecutor wanted to know.

"No, suicide is not going to be covered."

Brockway then was asked to give jurors some definitions that are used in the insurance business.

"Could you tell the jury what an *insured* is?"

"The *insured* is the person that the insurance policy is on. The easiest way, if I was to take out an insurance policy, I would be the insured, and my wife or children would be the beneficiary."

"Another term used in the insurance industry is called *beneficiary*?"

"The *beneficiary* is going to be the person who receives the funds upon the insured's death."

"Okay, there's another phrase that commonly comes out with respect to life insurance policy, is called an *insurable interest*?"

"The easiest way to remember *insurable interest* is the relationship that you have between the insured and the beneficiary. The common denominator with all of those is that there is a strong relationship where the insured is more valuable alive than dead.

"The insurable interest prevents anyone from taking out a policy on any individual and then causing their death. And the relationships are commonly either blood, marriage, or monetary interests."

The prosecutor asked Brockway why the insurance industry or the law requires that there be a bona-fide insurable interest between the insured and the beneficiary.

"Because it prevents an individual from taking out a life insurance policy on anyone and then causing the person's death," he said, adding that the person insured has to be worth more alive to the beneficiary than dead. "And when we're talking about worth, monetary interests can also be emotional or financial," he said.

Another definition the prosecutor wanted Brockway to explain was for *underwriting*.

"After a life insurance application is completed, the

agent or broker will send it to *underwriting*, where underwriting will check the information that is provided to make sure that it is accurate and correct."

Brockway explained that every carrier has a different underwriting process, depending on the amount of the insurance for the applicant.

The prosecutor then had Brockway read to jurors California Insurance Code Section 10113.5(a), which relates to the contestability issue.

"'An individual life insurance policy . . . in this state shall contain a provision that it is incontestable after it has been in force, during the lifetime of the insured, for a period of not more than two years after its date of issue, except for nonpayment of premiums . . .'

"It's pretty much a balancing act between the insurance carrier and the insured. During that first two-year period, an insurance company can cancel an insurance policy for any reason, and refund the premium to the applicant or the insured.

"After that two-year period, the policy is in force, even if there is some type of misrepresentation discovered."

In other words, he told the jury, if you're inside the two-year period and the person who took out the policy got it through fraud and deception, the company can cancel the policy.

"If the person dies within the two-year period, does it usually trigger an investigation by the insurance company?" the prosecution asked.

"Yes, any claim is going to trigger an investigation. But if it happens within the two-year period, it will be a more thorough investigation, where more will need to be done prior to the claim being paid. That is because an insurance carrier knows they have the authority under the California law to rescind the policy if there is fraud."

"So if the person dies after the two years has elapsed, does it become increasingly hard, if not impossible, for the insurance carriers to deny a claim to pay money if there is fraud or deception?" the prosecution asked.

"Yes, they're kind of stuck."

The defense questions on cross-examination were rather routine and didn't elicit any new information. But on re-direct examination, Brockway told jurors that the total amount of coverage sought on McDavid's life had been $5,700,095. And on just thirteen of the seventeen policies that were issued, Helen and Olga had been paid $2,215,338.94—$1,540,767.05 to Helen and $674,571.89 to Olga.

Chapter 14

Witnesses for the Prosecution

The prosecution called many unforgettable witnesses to the stand during the four-week trial. All contributed significant testimony that may have seemed of no consequence, but in the end provided jurors with tiny pieces of the puzzle that together proved beyond a reasonable doubt that Helen and Olga were guilty as charged in the indictment.

But a turning point was reached toward the end of the second week, on Thursday, March 27, 2008, when prosecutor Truc Do called Jody Resnick, the AAA life insurance agent, to the stand during the afternoon session.

The questioning of Resnick started out fairly routinely. No sooner had Resnick completed her brief testimony, though, when reporters made a mad dash to corner her in the corridor. Resnick revealed that she had received a mysterious telephone call from a woman with a heavy accent who'd identified herself only as Olga.

"I want to report a fraud. I'm the fiancée, she's not the fiancée," an out-of-control Olga had shrieked into the phone, livid that her partner had secretly screwed her by changing the beneficiary on an insurance policy by just listing herself as the recipient.

During her brief moment on the stand, Resnick had divulged that on May 2, 2005, seven weeks before McDavid's death, she'd received a phone call from Helen Golay ask-

ing that a term life policy on his life be increased from
$800,000 to $1,00,000. By May 2, McDavid had been
locked out of the apartment that Helen had been paying
$875 or $900 a month in rent for, for two years. To keep
tabs on her investment, Helen had begun housing McDavid
in a number of inexpensive motels in the Hollywood area.
The question everyone wondered was whether Helen had
raised the ante, calculating that McDavid's days were num-
bered because he was becoming a problem to handle.

Resnick's supervisor at AAA for the last twelve years,
Ganae Smith, was the next witness to testify. She acknowledged that the $800,000 policy had been issued, and that it
had initially named Kecia Golay and Sophie Golay as contingent beneficiaries, to share the proceeds 50–50.

Smith was shown another document indicating that on
September 5, 2003, Helen had requested that the contingent beneficiaries—Kecia and Sophie Golay—be removed,
making Helen the sole beneficiary of the $800,000 policy
at that point.

"Do you know how much in premium was paid on the
life of this policy?" Smith was asked.

"Yes . . . Nine thousand, nine hundred eighteen dollars
and forty cents."

"Was there ever a claim for payment of benefits by the
sole beneficiary, Miss Golay?"

"Yes . . . by Helen Golay on September sixteenth, 2005."

The prosecutor's next question went for Helen's jugular
when the witness was asked to look at the claim that
Helen had sent to AAA, and read to the court the date
given for Kenneth McDavid's death.

"June twenty-second, 2005," replied Smith.

"At some point when you were at your job, you looked
up this file? Did you think anything unusual between the
time that the date of death is listed and the time that the
date the person filed a claim for benefit payments?"

After an objection by defense lawyer Diamond was
overruled, Smith replied that the date between McDavid's

death and the date the claim form was filed was "unusual," and caused her to further look into the claim.

"It was kind of spaced out. Usually when we see someone pass away, they usually file the claim right away. And this one just kind of struck me as strange that several months had passed from the time McDavid died to the time there was a claim for benefits," Smith said.

What she did next, Smith said, was to research Helen Golay's AAA membership and look at her roadside service.

"I actually saw a tow around that same date of the death, like a day before," Smith said. "The date was the day before the claimant actually passed," she added, referring to McDavid.

Smith testified that she also noticed that the address the tow service had responded to was similar to the one where McDavid had met his fate.

Smith said that Rob Brockway from Insurance Services had been in touch with her and was making inquiries about policies taken out in the name of Kenneth McDavid, and notified him of her research regarding McDavid and Helen Golay.

"Okay. So was it you at Triple A that found that roadside service, the tow service, and then forwarded it to the law enforcement agency?"

"I did," she said.

Smith said she'd delved further into other applications for life insurance policies that were connected to Helen Golay. She testified that she'd found three other policies being processed, one in Kenneth McDavid's name, and the other going to a Jimmy Covington.

"Was death benefits paid out on McDavid?"

"Yes, it was payable to Helen Golay in the amount of eight hundred ten thousand, five hundred fifty-six dollars and thirty-nine cents, which included what was due on the policy, plus interest."

Smith said that she'd forwarded the information on Jimmy Covington to Rob Brockway, but had not questioned

Helen as to Covington's relationship to her or Olga Rutterschmidt.

That wasn't the end of her dealings with Helen. Smith
had had occasion to call her at her home number after AAA
underwriters had a question regarding Helen's relationship
with McDavid.

"She stated that she was Mr. McDavid's fiancée, and
that they were scheduled to be married in December, or
something like that," Smith said.

Truc Do then handed Smith another document. It was
an application for life insurance in the name of Jimmy
Covington for $800,000. It listed Helen Golay's home
phone number and her Santa Monica address on his membership application.

Smith said that because a medical exam scheduled for
May 4, 2002, had never been completed, the policy was
never issued.

Other witnesses to take the stand also offered evidence
that pointed to the guilt of Helen and Olga. Five experts
from the coroner's office described the horrific injuries sustained by McDavid and Vados, and showed jurors the
gruesome autopsy photos of both victims. The witnesses
explained to the panel how the injuries had all been alike,
and that the men had been lying down on the ground and
not standing when they were deliberately run over.

Seven hard-nosed homicide detectives and officers from
the Los Angeles Police Department, who'd formed the inner core of the investigation into the girls' nefarious activities, detailed the information they'd uncovered over a
period of nearly eighteen months, which resulted in the arrest and indictment of Helen and Olga.

Not to be outdone as witnesses were members of the
California Highway Patrol and the LAPD Scientific Investigation Division, who testified about the DNA and blood
found on the undercarriage of the Mercury Sable station
wagon.

Twenty-eight representatives from some of this country's best-known insurance firms, including JP Morgan

Chase & Co., Mutual of New York, First Federal, AARP
Life Insurance, and John Hancock, all of which Helen and
Olga had used to take out policies on McDavid and Vados,
were called to testify. Most of what these men and women
had to tell the jury was rather cut-and-dried. But it was
mandatory that they testify so that the jurors knew insurance policies had been taken out on these homeless men,
what the amounts of the policies were, what premiums had
been paid, and how much these defendants had collected
in benefits as a result of the deaths of the victims they'd
insured.

The jurors also paid close attention when Pastor Charles
Suhayda, the minister of the Hollywood Presbyterian
Church, got on the witness stand and identified Helen Go-
lay and Olga Rutterschmidt.

Pastor Suhayda told jurors he was responsible for community ministries at the church, which focuses on low-
income and homeless persons. As such, he runs programs
specifically designed to aid people in those areas.

"There are a number of programs. The first one is called
The Lord's Lighthouse Ministry. It was established in 1990
to work with some of the homeless and very low-income
people in Hollywood. We try to deal comprehensively, in
other words, physically, emotionally, and spiritually, with
people's needs. That particular program has as one of its
components a hot meal that we serve every Sunday at two
o'clock.

"The other program that we run is the deacons' grocery
program, and that has been at the church since the seventies."

After being shown a photograph of him, the minister
told jurors that during his time at the church, he'd come to
know Paul Vados, who, Suhayda said, had participated in
two programs offered at the church.

"I first met him through The Lord's Lighthouse Ministry on Sunday afternoons," Suhayda said. "And he was one
of our guests. As part of what I do, I go out and I meet
people, greet people on the street as they're waiting for the

meal. And so I would interact with the guests on the side-walk."

Suhayda was also shown photographs of Kenneth Mc-David and Jimmy Covington, and disclosed that both men also took part in The Lord's Lighthouse Ministry.

The minister said that "not everybody comes regularly to the programs," but recalled Vados and McDavid as be-ing "regular guests," while Covington participated in the services "occasionally."

He described McDavid as "a quiet person, sort of shy, a little bit withdrawn, an introvert."

Truc Do got right down to the nuts and bolts of why he was testifying. "Do you see anyone here in court that you've seen at your church?" Suhayda was asked.

"Yes."

"Would you please point them out by telling us where they're sitting and what they're wearing?"

"The lady in the gray suit with the pink blouse," he said, indicating Helen Golay, who at that very moment looked bored to death, staring blankly at the ceiling.

"Anyone else that you've seen at your church?"

"The lady with the black jacket and the white blouse," he said, pointing to Olga Rutterschmidt, who appeared to be trembling in her seat.

The pastor said that both women had come to the church "together. It was on a Sunday afternoon, and then we had The Lord's Lighthouse Ministry on that day. The meal times are served at two o'clock, and by two-forty-five to three o'clock, most folks have finished eating, and they'll be on their way. And it was at that point that one of our volunteers came over and introduced me to the two ladies." He recalled speaking with the women for "just a few minutes."

No one needed to be Sherlock Holmes to figure out why Sunday was the day that Helen and Olga would show up at the church to go fishing for new targets.

The pastor hadn't asked Helen and Olga any questions, but merely told them about the church and the services that they provided to the homeless.

The purpose of calling Olga's neighbor Douglas Crapeau to the stand was to inform the jury that she had asked him to accompany her to Kenneth McDavid's apartment in 2004 "and to bring a gun," so that the homeless people staying with McDavid could be "evicted . . . thrown out."

"And did you agree to bring the gun?" Deputy District Attorney Bobby Grace asked.

"Yes."

Crapeau said that when they'd reached the apartment, Olga had opened the door with a key. He said that when he'd stepped into the apartment, he saw "a slightly built person about a hundred and thirty, a hundred and forty-five pounds, that appeared more scared of Olga than she should have been of him.

"Suddenly I felt a tugging on my right arm. Olga was pulling my arm with the gun in my hand out of my pocket and saying, 'Show him the gun. Show him the gun,'" she kept telling him.

"What happened basically is that she pulled the gun clear enough out of my pocket to be seen."

"And did the defendant, Olga Rutterschmidt, say anything to you at that point when she pulled on your arm?"

"Yes, she said, 'Show him the gun. Show him the gun.' "

"Besides the person that you just described, was there anybody else in the apartment?" Grace asked.

"I didn't notice anybody, because at that point I just said, 'This is bullshit,' and wanted to leave immediately."

Crapeau was asked what the next thing was that had happened after the gun was exposed.

"I could see that there was no threat there, and I was angry at what she had been pulling on me, and I turned around and left with the comment that I previously made here," Crapeau said.

"What did the defendant, Olga Rutterschmidt, tell you was your purpose for being at the apartment?"

"It was to protect her from a violent street person."

Grace then changed the topic and wanted to know whether Olga had ever discussed her religious beliefs with him.

"Yes, she described herself as an atheist."

Jose Luna, owner of a private company, Luna Security, also testified that he had been hired by Helen and Olga to secure the apartment that McDavid was living in with a few other homeless friends.

Luna recalls Olga yelling at them and saying, "They should get out of the apartment." He said Olga told him she wanted a young man and woman kicked out. Luna said they'd gathered their clothes and left, but that "the older guy, who was in his sixties"—referring to McDavid—was to stay.

"Olga told me to make sure that nobody comes in and out of the apartment," Luna said.

Luna's orders were that he was to stay inside the apartment daily from one p.m. to one a.m. for at least a week, and he would be paid partially in cash and partially by check issued by Helen Golay.

Patrick Lamay was called to testify on March 26, 2008. He had testified a year earlier, during the prelim. As he approached the stand to be sworn in, Detective Rosemary Sanchez removed his handcuffs and stood near the witness stand throughout his testimony.

But before he was going to be permitted to speak, the judge announced that a 402 motion was going to be held regarding Lamay's testimony. A 402 motion is a request that the court consider the admissibility of evidence prior to it being presented to the jury.

Lamay started off by explaining to the court that he was currently in the custody of the state of Michigan for a felony criminal sexual conduct. He went on to testify that in 2004 he had lived with Kenneth McDavid at 1843 North Cherokee for two or three months.

Then the prosecutor got down to specifics as to why Lamay's testimony was essential to the case. He was asked if during the lunch hour he had been taken to the district attorney's office on the seventeenth floor of the criminal court building by Detectives Kilcoyne and Sanchez, where an audiotape was played for him.

The tape had two voices on it: the first, a woman's,

identified by the prosecutors as an insurance agent for United Investors; the second voice was purported to be that of Kenneth McDavid.

Because Lamay had lived with McDavid, he was asked if he'd recognized his voice.

"No, I did not," Lamay said.

"Are you saying that it was not his voice on the tape?" Lamay was asked a second time.

"Absolutely, I'm saying it's not his voice."

The tape had been made by the agent at United Investors, who was attempting to speak to Kenneth McDavid regarding a policy that he'd had taken out on his life. The telephone number that the agent had used to call McDavid was Helen Golay's private number, and when the agent called, Helen disguised her voice by pretending to be McDavid.

The tape was played for Lamay several times. Although jurors were not present, it was obvious to those who heard it that the voice was definitely not a man's, but that of a woman speaking in a deeper tone.

During a hard-hitting cross-examination, Diamond questioned Lamay about how often he'd spoken with McDavid when they'd resided together, and the number of times they'd spoken by phone.

"We were working at an agency as telemarketers. And so I probably called over to his house about seven to probably twelve times at least," Lamay replied.

Diamond then questioned him about his felony conviction. The defense lawyer suggested that Lamay had received an inducement to testify for the prosecution in exchange for leniency in his sentence.

"Absolutely not. None," Lamay replied firmly.

"Now you are expected to go before the parole board of Michigan in May 2008?"

"No. I've already gone before the parole board."

"And you expect to be released in May of 2008?"

"There are no guarantees," he said.

Diamond became more antagonistic and aggressive

with Lamay, trying to imply that he was only testifying that the voice on the tape was not McDavid's because he had already made a deal with Michigan authorities.

"And what is your interest in testifying here today?" Diamond asked, sarcasm dripping from his voice.

"To get justice for a friend of mine," was Lamay's reply.

"And that would be Mr. McDavid?"

"Yes, sir."

"When you say 'get justice' for him, how does this case relate to Mr. McDavid as far as you know?"

"I was contacted by the detective, Rosemary Sanchez, who told me that Mr. McDavid was no longer living."

It appeared that Lamay had wanted to say how upset he'd been to learn that his friend had been murdered, but Diamond cut him off, saying, "No further questions."

After Lamay's brief testimony, both defense lawyers suggested that they wanted a further hearing to determine what promises had been made to him.

"Is there any document with respect to communications with Michigan with respect to getting this witness here?" the judge asked.

"Yes. It's called an executive agreement between the governors' offices. It's the equivalent of a removal order. And I will represent that there have been no promises. No deals of that nature with this witness. This witness is here on his own accord," Truc Do informed the judge.

"Fine. Then we're going to proceed," Wesley said.

Two days later, on Friday, March 28, Lamay was re-called to the stand, and with the jury present, was briefly asked about his felony conviction. He said he was serving a 2- to 15-year prison sentence, and that while he was in California, he was in the custody of the Los Angeles Police Department.

Truc Do then had Lamay describe for jurors the story of how he and McDavid had met at the Presbyterian church, and how he and his friends had moved in with McDavid, until Olga showed up one day and ranted and raved about their being in the apartment, and got pistol-packing guards to oust them.

In court, Lamay was asked if he could identify anyone he had met at the apartment.

"Yes, the lady in the teal-colored coat," he said, indicating Olga Rutterschmidt.

"Did you meet anyone else that you see in court?"

"Yes, the lady in the gray coat," he said, indicating Helen Golay.

Lamay described the scene inside the apartment as chaotic. "Olga was quite erratic and excited. It was a lot of yelling and screaming. She definitely did not want me in the apartment at all."

Lamay had started removing his clothes from the apartment to his car, which was parked out in front of the building, and said that as he was leaving, he'd seen Olga outside the apartment building.

"While I was finishing up putting my things away, she came outside the apartment, and I noticed her walking with the security guy. And I was just finishing up putting my things away, so I closed the lid to the trunk and told my girlfriend to sit in the car, and I followed her on foot.

"She went down to the very next street and then went west on that street. And so I followed her far enough behind where she didn't see me. And then I saw her starting to open up a car, and I made a notation of the car and license plate."

He said that he'd jotted Olga's name on a slip of paper with a notation that her car was a light blue Honda Civic with a California plate number 4VWB627. He'd kept the memo, and, when he later learned that McDavid had been killed, turned it over to authorities.

Lamay wasn't quite sure of the importance of his having recorded the car information, but prosecutors felt it provided evidence that tied Olga and Helen to McDavid's apartment.

Had Lamay ever asked McDavid what his arrangement

was with Olga and Helen, and what he had to do in order
for them to pay his rent?

"He said that after he had been living there for a little
bit of time, they approached him and asked him to sign a
life insurance policy as an act of good faith."

"Did you ask Mr. McDavid if he had any kind of relationship with the women who he signed the life insurance
policy for?"

"Yes, I did. I said, 'Ken, are these women your lovers or
your significant others, or are they family to you?' "

"And how did he respond?"

"He said no, they were not."

After he had been kicked out of the apartment, he returned about two weeks later to see how McDavid was
doing, but was unable to go inside because "a Hispanic
middle-aged gentleman with a pistol" had prevented him.

"The security guard stopped me at the door and said I
was not allowed to be in the apartment."

Lamay had tried asking McDavid how he was doing,
but instead the security guard had responded for him.

"Mr. McDavid cannot talk to you," the guard said.

It was the last time Lamay saw his friend alive.

Just before Lamay completed his testimony, which also
included a lengthy cross-examination by Diamond asking,
among other questions, whether McDavid had written
movie scripts, prosecutors played the audiotape in front of
the jury and asked Lamay if the voice on the tape was his
friend.

"No, it is not."

Chapter 15

The One that Got Away

Perhaps the most dramatic moment at the trial of the two Black Widows came shortly before the prosecution was about to rest its case by putting Jimmy Covington on the witness stand. His testimony brought chills to the jurors as they listened to his story of how he'd been an intended target of Helen Golay and Olga Rutterschmidt.

During the initial phase of the investigation, after Helen and Olga's arrest, California detectives became aware that the girls had applied for an $800,000 life insurance policy from AAA. But where was Jimmy Covington? The Los Angeles Police Department made a public appeal to the media about Covington and two other homeless men who authorities believed might also have been targeted by the women.

Stories about the homeless men began to circulate throughout California newspapers seeking information in an effort to find them. Brockway and Mayrose had located the elusive Covington early on in the investigation, but lost track of him as the case was getting closer to trial.

By then, Covington was living as a transient in San Rafael, California. He learned that Helen and Olga had been arrested after a friend of his read about it in the *Los Angeles Times* and recognized Covington's name in the article.

At first, Covington was reluctant to come forward, fearful for his life. As he told reporters after he testified, "I could have been run over by a car and killed."

Both the police and Sam Mayrose of the FBI convinced Covington he would be safe, and brought him to Los Angeles, where they put him up in a local motel until it was time to testify.

The 48-year-old Covington took the stand and said that back in 2002 he'd been living on the street in Hollywood, homeless. And like others in a similar situation, he went to the First Presbyterian Church of Hollywood to get help, which included dinner on Sunday afternoon. From "time to time" he would get pieces of clothing and some groceries at the resource center.

"In 2005, I was sitting on the steps of an office building across from the Bally's health club that I used to go to work out in Hollywood, when a woman approached me.

"She asked me if I was homeless," he said. "I said, 'Yes, I am.' And then she identified herself and said her name was Olga. She spoke with an accent," Covington recalled.

"I'm going to ask you to look around this courtroom and tell me if you recognize the person named Olga who approached you outside the building here," Truc Do asked.

"The woman in the blue jacket. That's her," Covington said from the witness stand, pointing to Olga, who was sitting next to her lawyer, Michael Sklar.

"Did she say anything back to you after you said you were homeless?"

"Yes. She said, 'I work with homeless people, and I can get you some benefits. I can help you get a place to stay, and give you a temporary place to stay, and help you get some money in approximately thirty days.'

"I asked her how she could do that. She said that I had to fill out some forms. She said that she works with a place for the homeless and if I would fill out some paperwork, telling a little bit about my homelessness and other questions about my background, any disabilities or anything like that, that she could put me up in a room right there temporarily for a while and process the paperwork and give me a little money every day, and then—until the paperwork was finished—

and in approximately thirty days, she would come up with around two thousand dollars."

"Did you believe her?"

"Sort of. I somewhat needed her help. Yes, I considered it, and after talking for about fifteen minutes, she put me up in a room in the building. She took me inside the building. We went into the lobby and then we went to the right, up the staircase and up to the second floor to an office room."

The prosecutor later showed that Helen and Olga had rented an office in the building where Covington was staying, and were using it to house the homeless on a temporary basis.

"The room was furnished. It had a desk on the left-hand side. It had a computer on the back of the desk, and it had a futon in the back room."

Olga told Covington he could stay in the room "temporarily," and that she would return the next day for him to fill out some paperwork.

"She told me I had to follow these rules in order to stay there. She said I had to keep it very clean. I had to keep it very quiet. I had to fold the futon back when I left, and I had to stay gone from the room all day long, until around three or five in the afternoon, before I could come back."

"Did she give you keys?"

"There was an alarm, a button and a key too. I had a key to the front door and a key to the room, and there was an alarm on the side of the wall when I would come in the door. She showed me how to punch the alarm code, too.

"At first she seemed real concerned and kind of anxious and sincere," Covington said.

The first day that Covington was in his new home, Olga stayed twenty minutes. "I just sat at the desk and she brought me paperwork. The forms had questions about my full name, my background, a little bit where I worked, my medical history, my identification number, my Social Security number, and my homeless information . . . You know, the amount of time I lived on the street, and where I lived."

Over the next few days, Olga brought him about ten pages of printed forms to fill out.

"Did you give her your driver's license?"

"Yes."

"And did she also ask you questions about your family and your family history?"

"Yes. It was basically where I was from, where I was born, how long I lived there. She asked questions about whether I had any severe illness. And I told her about my chronic nerve damage and asthma problems."

When Covington hesitated in answering Olga's questions, she buttered him up, reiterating how she could help him, working her charm on him. She told him how she had helped other homeless people before, and that she was eager to get him a place to stay.

"Did she lead you to believe she cared?"

"Yes."

Day after day, Olga cajoled Covington to give up more information about himself, but when she began asking questions about his mother, and wanting to know his mother's maiden name and other personal background information, Covington balked. No amount of flattery could get him to change his mind.

"I refused, and I said I had to think about it."

Olga wasn't about to give up, and kept stopping by again and again, mostly at night, Covington said. He told about one nighttime visit made by Olga that was scary.

"I was in bed on the futon when she came in at three o'clock in the morning, and I was asleep. She didn't even knock. She just put her key in and turned it, and just came right in."

When asked by the prosecutor whether Olga ever delivered on her promises to help him, Covington said that "other than sleeping in the room for seven nights and the fifteen dollars she gave me to go to Burger King, where I bought a hamburger, that was it."

"What about the two thousand dollars she promised you, to get you in thirty days?"

"Never seen any of that," he said.

"What caused you to leave?"

"She was asking for too much personal information, and she wasn't paying me every day like she said she would, and she was coming up and yelling at me and coming in at all hours of the night and getting me real upset and telling me I got to fill this paperwork out and I got to do this now, and she just started screaming and being real belligerent and real abusive to me.

"At first she seemed like she cared, but over the course of the seven nights that I stayed there, her behavior changed. She was verbally abusive and real upset.

"She would say, 'What's wrong with you? Why don't you fill this out? We need to get this paperwork done. We need to do this now.' And then she would open the doors and slam the doors on her way out . . . things like that. I was getting uncomfortable, and so I left."

"Did you ever give her permission to apply for a life insurance policy in your name as the insured?"

"No, I didn't. I was never aware of that."

"Did you ever become aware that there was an application for a life insurance policy with Triple A, naming you as the insured for eight hundred thousand dollars?"

"No, I never noticed that."

On cross-examination by public defender Michael Sklar, Covington said that Olga had insisted she worked with people who helped those who were homeless, and that she had a partner who was the boss, referring to Helen Golay, whom he could not identify in court.

Outside court, Covington told reporters he now believed he could have been the third victim in the case if he had not walked away.

"I feel blessed by Jesus and God, who looked out for me," he said.

"And I pray for them, too, that they'll have their souls saved," he said, referring to Helen and Olga.

Chapter 16

"Kecia Did the Murder"

Monday, April 7, turned out to be a lucky day for defense lawyer Roger Jon Diamond. Judge David Wesley agreed to hold an early morning hearing without the jury present to determine whether the lawyer could pursue what is called a *third party culpability* defense that Kecia Golay, the daughter of Helen, had murdered Kenneth McDavid and framed her mother for his hit-and-run killing. The street expression used in New York City or Washington, DC, for that particular defense is SODDI—Some Other Dude Did It.

What Diamond hoped to create, should he get a favorable decision, was doubt among the jurors regarding Helen's responsibility for the murder.

Usually judges are reluctant to go along with third party culpability defense questioning of witnesses, as it severely limits the questioning.

Diamond began by outlining his theory for the judge, naming Kecia Golay as the person who'd murdered Kenneth McDavid by running him over in the Mercury Sable.

"We have her driver's license and we also have the testimony of Detective Kilcoyne, who verifies that the date of birth of Kecia Golay is January twenty-ninth, 1964. Why is that important? Because the tow truck operator said that the person whom he picked up on the evening of June twenty-first and June twenty-second, was a woman above forty. If the court will do the math, if Ms. Golay was born in January twenty-nine, 1964, she would have been above forty when the tow truck operator picked her up."

Diamond reminded the judge that when the tow truck operator testified, he did not identify Helen Golay as the person who'd sat right next to him in the truck driving back to Santa Monica.

In addition, Diamond told the judge, he planned to call Andrew Zanger, an attorney who'd handled Kecia's last criminal case, in which Kecia had pleaded guilty to stalking and destroying her boyfriend's apartment. It resulted in her being incarcerated at the Los Angeles County jail, co-incidentally in the same jail where her mother had briefly stayed last year.

The judge kept insisting that Diamond further detail his theory on how he planned to let the information into the trial.

"The theory is this," Diamond said eagerly. "One of the possible motives that Kecia Golay would have in this case is an intense hatred towards her mother. It is very erratic. She acts bizarre, and she is not able to function properly.

"We have the probation report in the case that Mr. Zanger handled, reflecting a report by Kecia Golay's psychiatrist or psychologist, where he says in his report that Kecia has an intense hatred towards her mother. They fight back and forth. They sue each other.

"In addition to that, she has a number of theft convictions, stealing things from department stores. We will prove that it was Kecia Golay who stole Hilary Adler's purse. One way we can do that is that she had the opportunity to do that, and the fact that she has been convicted numerous times, including for theft felonies."

"What other evidence do you have?" Wesley wanted to know.

"We have Phillip Samovar, another attorney who represented Kecia Golay, and also has represented Helen Golay in civil litigation. Phillip Samovar more than anybody else can testify as to the relationship between Kecia Golay and her mother in terms of the bizarre activity that has occurred. In fact, they sued each other once or twice. Helen Golay sued Kecia Golay. Kecia Golay sued Helen Golay. This is most bizarre for a mother and daughter to be suing each other.

"We can show that Kecia Golay on a number of occasions physically assaulted, trespassed in the home of Helen Golay, and that Helen Golay was fearful of Kecia Golay."

Diamond then raised a third angle to all this litigation. "There was a hatred by Kecia towards her mother because her mother would not approve of Steve Taracevicz as being the boyfriend of Kecia Golay."

The lawyer insisted he had documents and interviews that law enforcement had conducted with Taracevicz to back up these allegations. "Also, Kecia provided statements against her mother the day she was arrested on May eighteenth, 2006. Kecia went down voluntarily and spoke with the FBI and the police, and gave statements against her own mother, which shows the hostility of Kecia towards her mother."

Deputy District Attorney Bobby Grace told the judge that prosecutors didn't know who the driver of the Mercury Sable was, but that it was their position that it was one of the two defendants or an unnamed co-conspirator.

After the hearing concluded, the judge ruled that Diamond had "enough basis to put on a third party culpability defense" and gave the lawyer the go-ahead to argue that Kecia Golay had murdered Kenneth McDavid and framed her mother for his hit-and-run killing.

After an abbreviated morning session in which the prosecution put on two witnesses, the state wrapped up its case after nearly one month, and 4,627 pages of testimony by parading ninety witnesses and presenting at least 277 exhibits for the jury to consider when they began their deliberations. At that point, Truc Do stood up and quietly informed the judge that "The People rest."

It was now going to be up to the defense to put their best foot forward to the jury. But before they could begin, pub-

lic defender Michael Sklar made a motion to dismiss the
conspiracy to murder and the murder charges against his
client Olga Rutterschmidt.

His argument was that there had been no evidence that
Olga aided and abetted a perpetrator in the commission of
that act.

"There has been no evidence submitted that Ms. Rutterschmidt committed an act . . . that caused the deaths of
either Mr. McDavid or Mr. Vados. The only evidence presented by the district attorney with regard to Ms. Rutterschmidt is her conspiracy to commit insurance fraud."

Diamond's motion to dismiss was on similar grounds.
However, he also emphasized that "there has been zero evidence that Ms. Golay was involved in the murder of Mr. Vados. We move to dismiss the Vados count as to Ms. Golay."

Judge Wesley swiftly rejected the defense team's motion, and in the same breath ordered Diamond to deliver
his opening statement.

After a rather long-winded explanation of why opening
statements are different from closing arguments, Diamond
began by telling jurors that "essentially what we have here
is Ms. Golay involved, arguably with Ms. Rutterschmidt,
in some kind of insurance shenanigans that may or may
not rise to the level of outright fraud."

From there, instead of getting to the heart of his opening, he explained that insurance was a difficult and complicated area of the law and whether or not the beneficiary
of a policy has an insurable interest isn't the issue, but that
the matter was "sort of lurking in the background here.

"So, the question now is, Who killed Mr. Vados and
who killed Mr. McDavid? There is apparently a lot of evidence that, at least with respect to Mr. McDavid, that he
was struck, not by a hit-and-run driver, but by somebody
who deliberately ran into him or ran over him with an improper purpose, which obviously would be murder. And so
we have a lot of evidence that a murder took place.

"That is the *what* of 'what, when, how, where and who.'
We have a lot of evidence with respect to McDavid as to

what happened. We basically have no evidence as to what happened with Mr. Vados.

"The testimony is, the evidence already established that . . ."

Diamond never got the chance to finish the sentence, because Judge Wesley interrupted to remind him that he was delivering a closing argument, not an opening statement. Diamond protested that the evidence on Vados would show that the crime scene was "basically washed away by a heavy downpour the night he met his untimely death." But the judge didn't seem amused by the lawyer's delaying comments and insisted that Diamond stay the course on his opening remarks.

"So we'll focus now on Mr. McDavid, because he's the key to this case. Who murdered Mr. McDavid? There is one answer to that question, because that is the question presented: Who did this dastardly act? Not how it was done. The evidence is pretty clear as to how it was done," Diamond said, pausing to emphasize his last words.

"Who did it?" he said, looking intently at the jurors.

"Kecia Golay . . . Helen Golay's daughter," Diamond answered.

Diamond then delved into the evidence, which he claimed would establish that Kecia, not Helen, had committed the murder of McDavid. By then, the lawyer had the jury spellbound. Even the badly behaved mouse that kept playing hide-and-seek behind the vents in the courtroom was utterly silent.

"Number one, Kecia Golay obtained a driver's license from a Hilary Adler because Kecia Golay, the evidence will show, was a member of the Spectrum club in Santa Monica at the same time that Hilary Adler was a member of the Spectrum club in Santa Monica.

"We will show you the corresponding membership list that shows every time you go to a club, a health club, such as Spectrum club, and your card is swiped, a record is made of the visit and your particular guest of that club at that time.

"The evidence will show that the times that Hilary Adler was there . . . in April and May 2003, her purse was stolen. Who stole the purse? The only evidence shows that it was Kecia Golay who was there at the same time that Hilary Adler was there."

Helen appeared crestfallen as Diamond spoke. When he walked over to her and placed his hands on her shoulders in an attempt to console her, she became tearful, and began dabbing her eyes with a tissue.

"I know she's not going to like this, but Helen Golay is a little old lady who could not have done what is claimed she allegedly did in this particular case, which is to lift a man weighing almost two hundred pounds, five-eleven or so—he's just short of six feet—and put him in an alley and then run him over. That is not what happened in this particular case.

"She is now seventy-seven years old. In 2005, in June, she was seventy-five years old. I don't mean to be critical of women. I know in this age, we have to be politically correct, but she lacked the ability, given her age, not her gender, her age, to do this.

"Kecia Golay, the evidence will show, was a regular member of the Spectrum club, obviously in good shape, working out all the time. She, rather than Helen Golay, would be in a position to carry out this dastardly deed. So the evidence will be, and is, this joint attendance at the Spectrum club when Hilary Adler's purse is stolen.

"What else do we have? We have Mr. Medina, the used car salesman who sold this car on January twentieth, 2004. If you remember, he did not identify Helen Golay as being one of the purchasers of the vehicle. We don't have any evidence that Helen Golay purchased the vehicle.

"More importantly, we have phone records from Kecia Golay's cell phone. We have evidence to show you . . . that the cell phone that was used to call the Mexicar used car business was Kecia Golay's cell phone.

"In fact, cell records show on January twentieth, 2004,

a call was placed from Kecia Golay's cell phone to the car dealership.

"The evidence will also show that on the night of the unfortunate death to Mr. McDavid, it was Kecia Golay who drove the vehicle. Kecia Golay whose address was frequently given as four-twenty-four Ocean Park, the same address of her mother, Helen Golay . . . that was the address used by Kecia Golay in addition to a residence about half a mile away, at six-oh-nine Marine, where Kecia also maintained a residence."

Diamond slowly pulled apart the prosecution case bit by bit to show Kecia's involvement in the murder of McDavid. He pointed out that Kecia had had her own prescription drugs in her mother's medicine cabinet at the Ocean Park Boulevard address, and that she had a key to the home.

"The evidence will show that on the night of June twenty-first, 2005, Kecia Golay placed calls on the cell phone because the cell phone was her cell phone. We have undisputed physical evidence showing that the cell phone was registered to Kecia Golay."

Diamond brought out that when Kecia had made a call on her cell phone at 11:51 to AAA for tow service, she was not a member, that her mother was the AAA member.

"Kecia Golay did not anticipate that when she ran over Mr. McDavid, the fuel hose would disconnect, causing the car to malfunction. This was an unanticipated situation that occurred, catching Kecia Golay off-guard."

The lawyer reminded jurors again that Kecia was in fantastic physical condition, and was capable of putting the body of McDavid into the alley and running him over.

"Indeed, it was Kecia Golay who was present, because we know from the testimony of the tow truck operator, when asked to describe the person who was with him, riding back to the area where both Kecia and Helen resided, the Ocean Park, Marine Street area . . . he testified that he could not identify Helen Golay. He could not identify her in the courtroom . . ."

At that moment, Truc Do cut Diamond off sharply to

object to what he was saying to jurors. At a sidebar, out of the presence of the jurors, the prosecutor argued that Diamond was essentially arguing to the panel and not telling them what evidence they were going to hear in the case from the defense.

"I agree with you," Wesley told the prosecutor. Annoyed at the way Diamond was presenting the defense, the judge let him have it. "I've warned you once. I will cut off your argument entirely. This is an opening statement. This is not argument," Wesley told the lawyer.

"I can't refer back to the evidence at all?" snapped Diamond.

"Not really. This is supposed to be what you're going to be presenting to them," the judge reminded him.

"So I can't, in opening statements, refer back to testimony that's already in the record?" an irritable Diamond wanted to know.

"No," the judge said firmly.

"Okay."

After being turned down by the judge, Diamond resumed his opening statement to the jury, promising that he would no longer refer to evidence that had already been submitted to the jurors, and he would only give the panel "additional evidence."

Starting again to resume his opening statements, Diamond apparently went off on another approach. "The evidence will show that my client is not in a position to testify and explain this case . . ."

Truc Do objected again, and the judge sustained, but that didn't stop Diamond from speaking.

"The evidence will show that lurking in the background . . ."

"Your Honor, it's again argument and relevance," Deputy District Attorney Bobby Grace said, jumping up from his seat.

The judge then called the lawyers to the bench for another sidebar out of the presence of jurors.

Wesley wasted no time letting Diamond know he was

annoyed. "What makes you think you can argue to the jury, or make an opening statement that your client can't testify in this case because she has a federal case pending, with impunity?" he asked.

"That she could testify, but this is evidence as to why she won't," was Diamond's insignificant reply to the judge.

"Well, you cannot do that," the judge said. "That's totally improper. They're going to get a jury instruction from me that tells you there's a lot of different reasons why a witness does not testify. And if you want to go ahead and put a specific one on, you're going to open up the door to all kinds of testimony."

Diamond persisted in trying to explain the defense position to the judge, but Wesley kept insisting it was not an opening statement and that Diamond couldn't do that.

Finally, Diamond agreed and said he would only inform the jury that Sam Mayrose, the FBI agent, would again be testifying, but would only say that the federal case could be refiled. (When the federal case against Helen and Olga was dropped in August 2006, it was with the understanding that if the State failed to get murder convictions, the federal government could pursue the mail fraud charges.)

With the wind taken out of Diamond's sails, he resumed speaking to the panel. He informed them that he expected Mayrose to testify regarding documents seized from the homes, and that he expected others such as attorney Eric Meller to testify about five lawsuits he had filed for Helen against insurance companies that had refused to pay claim benefits.

"We expect Mr. Meller to testify that he filed the cases, but that they cannot be pursued because Ms. Golay is now in custody.

"We also expect Mr. Phillip Samovar to testify concerning some litigation between Helen and Kecia to show that Helen had filed a restraining order against her daughter.

"The evidence will also show that Ms. Golay has not been identified by Mr. Medina as being the person who purchased the vehicle.

"The evidence will show that the cell phone that was used was a cell phone of Kecia Golay. The evidence will show, through the witnesses, that it was Kecia Golay, for reasons to be explained later on, that she is the one who drove over Mr. McDavid and killed him."

At the conclusion of Diamond's opening statement, the judge took the unusual step of dismissing at least half a dozen witnesses whom Diamond wanted to call on behalf of Helen Golay. The judge turned down Diamond's request that he be allowed to bring out that Kecia had charmed Fred Downie, the 97-year-old man from Massachusetts, to California, where he was killed by a car while crossing the street near Helen Golay's home.

After his death, Kecia had made a windfall by collecting on a wrongful death lawsuit. Then, not satisfied with the money and property that she got from Downie while he was still alive, Kecia had further profited from his death by filing a lawsuit against the city of Santa Monica and Cheryl Clark, the driver who'd struck and killed Downie.

"This gave Kecia the idea that she could get money through the death of old people and through her own deranged thinking, and that got her involved with the McDavid situation," Diamond told the judge.

"This has nothing to do with this case," Wesley stated to Diamond, adding that there wasn't "any illegality involved by Kecia on this point."

Diamond said he had no plans to call Kecia during the defense case, because he assumed she would invoke the Fifth Amendment protection against self-incrimination.

Wesley also pointed out that Phillip Samovar's testimony was "irrelevant," as was that of other witnesses Diamond planned to call to testify.

The judge's decision left the disappointed lawyer with the option of relying on the testimony of Eric Meller, and a few prosecution witnesses who had already testified, to convince jurors of his theory.

Meller's testimony on the witness stand was brief. An attorney for thirty-six years, he testified that he'd first represented Helen in some civil litigation involving real estate, and that more recently, she had retained him to file five lawsuits against five insurance companies that had refused to pay claims.

He explained that as a result of Helen's arrest in May 2006, it was impossible to pursue the cases on her behalf, because she was in the county jail, and that he then opted out of representing her.

On Tuesday, Diamond called just four witnesses to the stand, including Michael Jones, a forensic audio and video specialist who conducted a series of different video sequences showing cars going in and out of the alley the night of June 21 and ending at midnight on June 22 with the ambulance that had been called for McDavid.

During his presentation, Jones kept commenting on what he thought was "significant" or what "intrigued" him as he showed the video sequences, saying that "they were curious" to him.

Prosecutors objected to his testimony and the judge concurred with them by refusing to allow him to testify before the jury regarding his conclusions as to what interested him. The judge ruled it was "irrelevant to this case."

Diamond had wanted Jones to tell jurors that the car that had made the four-minute, twenty-nine-second stop in the alley was not the murder weapon. But Judge Wesley made it clear to the witness and to Diamond that it was up to the jury to decide.

With Diamond's obtuse arguments virtually thrown out the window, there was not much left for the defense.

Kecia Golay could not be found to comment on the fact that her mother was accusing her of murder. Lead Detective Dennis Kilcoyne had reached out to Kecia by telephone to inform her of Diamond's argument.

"She appeared a little surprised, but was standoffish," Kilcoyne said. "She said this was an ongoing nightmare."

After the verdict, Truc Do revealed that police had Kecia's phone under surveillance and it was her belief that "mother and daughter were in on the entire scam about naming her as the murderer" for purposes of the defense.

Chapter 17

The Prosecution Speaks—Closing Arguments

With the public defender presenting no witnesses on behalf of Olga, Michael Sklar simply informed the judge that he was resting his case based "on the state of the evidence."

Judge Wesley scheduled final arguments to begin Thursday, April 10, at 1:30 in the afternoon, almost one month after the trial had started.

The eighty-seat courtroom was packed to the rafters waiting for the jury to enter to hear closing arguments in the case. The front-row seats were taken up by prosecution staff members and detectives who had worked on the case. In the audience, in the back row, was Pat Dixon, one of Los Angeles District Attorney Steve Cooley's most trusted aides, a frequent observer at the trial of Helen and Olga.

Dixon's appearance during the closing arguments was considered significant by veteran courthouse observers. Head of the Major Crimes Division, Dixon has been a prosecutor for three decades. In 2007, he had worked with veteran prosecutor Alan Jackson in prosecuting "Wall of Sound" producer Phil Spector for allegedly murdering actress Lana Clarkson in his home, a case that ended in a mistrial. It was retried in the fall of 2008. A jury verdict was expected in April 2009. Dixon also recently teamed up with Jackson to successfully prosecute Michael Goodwin for the murders of car-racing legend Mickey Thompson and his wife.

Also seated in the crowded courtroom was lawyer Gloria Allred, who represented Stella Vados, and Sandra Salman, the sister of Kenneth McDavid, who was accompanied by her brother, Robert.

In closing arguments, it would be up to lead prosecutor Truc Do to sum up the prosecution's case to jurors first since they have the burden to prove beyond a reasonable doubt their case. After Truc Do wraps up her case, it will then be up to the two defense lawyers to tear into her theory of why Helen and Olga are not murderers and rip the state witnesses to shreds. Bobby Grace, the deputy district attorney, would then have the last word in rebutting the two defense attorneys' remarks.

"Good afternoon, ladies and gentlemen. On behalf of Mr. Grace and I, let me first thank you in advance for your jury service in this case," Truc Do began her two-hour summation.

"The defendants made six hundred thousand dollars on the life of Paul Vados. They collected their profit and they buried Paul Vados in an unmarked grave. They took a man who, through human circumstances, lost his family, and made that loss permanent to his daughter, Stella Vados. They did not care for Paul Vados in life or in death. They sought only profit.

"They made two-point-two million dollars on the life of Kenneth McDavid. They took their profit. They cremated his remains. And to this day, his remains are unknown to his family. They took a man who, through human circumstances . . ."

At that moment, defense lawyer Roger Diamond stood up and disrupted the prosecutor's closing remarks, and asked that a sidebar be held outside the presence of the jury.

Diamond, Sklar, Do, and Grace huddled around the bench of Judge Wesley as Sherry Quenga, the court stenographer, squeezed in between the lawyers to record Diamond's objections to the prosecutor's comments.

"It's so inflammatory," Diamond protested. "It's not based on any evidence of the record. There's no evidence as to where his cremated remains are or whether the family has them or does not have them. There's nothing in the record on that. It's so inflammatory. I move for a mistrial."

The no-nonsense judge was obviously irate at Diamond, for he didn't even ask the prosecutor or Sklar to respond.

"Motion for mistrial is denied," Wesley told Diamond, who promptly took his seat and did not raise any further objections during Truc Do's closing argument.

"The defendants collected their profit on the life of Mr. McDavid," continued Do. "They had his body cremated. And his remains are unknown to his family even to this day. They took this man who, through circumstances, became disconnected with his family, and made that irreversible to his sister, Sandra Salman, and his brother, Robert McDavid. They did not love Kenneth McDavid or care for him in life or in death. They sought only profit."

Truc Do told the jury that Vados and McDavid had believed that Helen and Olga were their friends, and were rescuing them from sleeping on the streets. "Jimmy Covington, the only victim who got away, told you that he believed Olga Rutterschmidt was sincere when she offered him help for the homeless.

"This case is about murder, conspiracy to commit murder, to collect life insurance benefits. Murder for profit. It is not, as the defense will argue to you, a case about insurance shenanigans, questionable insurance practices, gambling, investments, or insurance fraud. It is murder for profit."

The prosecutor went on by talking to the jury about the charges against the defendants and to explain the instructions that the court had read to them in an effort to help them understand how the law applies to the evidence in this case, and to give them a framework to look at the evidence when they are back in the deliberation room.

She spoke to the jury about conspiracy; she asked that when deliberating, they question why the defendants had applied for so many insurance policies if they didn't intend to kill their victims.

"What we have in this case is that the victims are worth more dead to the defendants . . . Victims like Paul Vados, who was destitute, had nothing to offer these women while he was alive. Mr. Kenneth McDavid, who was literally homeless before they plucked him off of that church premises and put him in their apartment, was worth nothing to them alive. And Jimmy Covington. When you look at this question of whether there's intent to kill behind their applications to insure another human being's life, this is what to look at.

"What else do you have in this case?" she asked, pointing out that every single document that had been mailed out for these policies had gone to the home of Olga Rutterschmidt or the home of Helen Golay. "It's one thing to commit insurance fraud. It's one thing to lie to the insurance companies. But you have to ask yourself, why lie to the victims?

"Remember Patrick Lamay? He told you that after hearing the discussion between Olga Rutterschmidt and Mr. McDavid about the arrangement that they had, Mr. McDavid told him that after they got him off the streets and moved into the apartment that they paid for, these women approached him and said that he had to sign a life insurance policy as an act of good faith.

"You heard from the testimony of Stacy Pederson from United Investors that Helen Golay applied to insure Kenneth McDavid for a policy worth one hundred thousand dollars, in which she was the sole beneficiary. The signature on this application is a stamp that matched one of the rubber stamps that you have in evidence, testified to by Mr. Constantinescu, that Olga Rutterschmidt bought.

"What else do you know about this? Miss Pederson testified that there was a phone call after several attempts were made to talk to Mr. McDavid to verify that in fact he was applying for this policy. And the contact information is, again, Miss Golay. The phone is Miss Golay."

The prosecutor urged jurors to listen to the tape recording again, because "perhaps you may have not realized that at the time you were listening to that phone call, you were listening to Miss Golay's voice. That Miss Golay called in and pretended to be Mr. McDavid's secretary, which you know is a lie, because the man did not have a job. And when you listen to the voice that comes on to the call and says, 'This is Kenneth McDavid,' did you realize that that was a woman?"

Truc Do then played the audio recording for the jurors.

The prosecutor then went into other areas of evidence that she'd presented. She dealt with the fact that there were questionable medical interviews, she spoke about the rubber stamps that Olga had bought for victims, she re-capped the testimony of Jimmy Covington, who'd successfully gotten away from the defendants' scheme, and then explained in court how their scheme had worked.

"I want you to think about this question with common sense. What is the average life span of a white male in this country? Is it seventy? Seventy-five? Mr. Covington was thirty-nine when he was approached by Miss Rutterschmidt. They sought to insure him for eight hundred thousand dollars. You do the math. In thirty years, when Mr. Covington is sixty-nine, Miss Rutterschmidt will be ninety-nine, Miss Golay will be a hundred and one. If this is what the defense will argue to you is just a gamble, putting money out on premiums, hoping that they're just going to collect on someone naturally dying, does this make sense to you?

"What else do you know? When Mr. McDavid began to present problems for them, issues of control, what did they do? Did they act like normal people? No. They brought guns. You heard the evidence that Mr. McDavid invited some people to move into the apartment. The defendants didn't like the fact that there was an outside element being introduced. They wanted the victim isolated.

"Why not let him go? It's because they put too much money into Mr. McDavid, and his life was theirs. They owned his life, is the way that they saw it. They had put over sixty-four thousand dollars in premiums and rent on a man that they did not know for two years, and they weren't going to let him go, because he was worth three-point-seventy-four million dollars.

"They collected two million dollars on his policies, and were seeking more from insurance policies who refused to pay."

The prosecutor reminded jurors that Olga and Helen had invested heavily on the lives of their victims. "They picked up complete strangers, men they did not love or care for, destitute men who were worth millions if dead."

Truc Do projected photos of the mangled bodies of the homeless men on the screen and pointed out their grisly injuries, which were not typical of hit-and-run accidents. While Sandra Salman and Stella Vados wept openly in court at the photos, Olga and Helen just stared ahead and showed no emotion. "This was an intentional running over, not a hit-and-run," Truc Do emphasized. "They should be convicted even if they were not at the scene.

"The crime is complete, and they are guilty if you find that they agreed to conspire, agreed to enter into this, that they intended to kill and commit one overt act. If they conspired, it doesn't matter who actually ran over [the victims]. They are guilty.

"And there is no dispute in this case that this Mercury Sable station wagon was used on June twenty-first, 2005, to run over Mr. McDavid. You know that, because Mr. McDavid's DNA was found on the undercarriage, his blood on the undercarriage. There's no question about it, because it's one in ten quadrillion that someone else's would match.

"You also know that on the undercarriage, the criminalist found clumps of hair along with his blood.

"The fuel line had been broken when the car went over Mr. McDavid's body, and it was repaired. Officer Kolter from CHP told you that the repair was quick and dirty, within almost weeks after the murder, that the car was dumped, a quick and dirty repair.

"There's no dispute that that car is the murder weapon."

The prosecutor went through other aspects that dealt with the strength of their case, such as Mario Medina, the car salesman who'd identified Olga and another woman similar in age coming into his lot on January 20, 2004, to buy the Mercury Sable. "There was no question about test-driving it to see if it was okay. They knew what they wanted," she said.

Truc Do reminded jurors that there was corroborating evidence. That Medina had recalled that the woman who came in had spoken with an accent and she'd given him an actual driver's license that belonged to Hilary Adler. When Olga had been arrested in May and her apartment was searched, detectives had found copies of Hilary Adler's driver's license in her home.

In Helen's Mercedes SUV, detectives found a day planner with the original evidence, the prosecutor told jurors. It was a Post-it note dated January 4 that contained a partial license plate and a partial VIN with the make and model and the name of Hilary Adler. "That certainly ties her to the murder weapon," the prosecutor said.

"Let's look at the charge of murder. When you deliberate on the charge of murder, whether it's with Mr. McDavid or with Mr. Vados, you can be guilty of murder as a conspirator. You can be guilty as an aider and abettor. You can be guilty as an actual killer, which means that once you've gone through the steps and deliberate on the charge of conspiracy, if you believe that these defendants conspired to commit murder for profit, then it doesn't matter who actually ran over Mr. McDavid.

"They're guilty as conspirators just as if they were behind the wheel themselves.

"Another thing—you don't even have to agree unanimously as to how the defendants are guilty of murder. Let's say you go back to the jury room and six of you decide that Miss Golay is definitely behind the wheel. And the other six of you think that she's just a conspirator. That's okay, because the law on this particular area tells you that you don't have to be unanimous. It doesn't matter what the breakdown is . . . as long as you believe that it's guilty of murder as a conspirator, guilty of murder as an aider and abettor, or guilty as an actual killer.

"As an aider and abettor and a co-conspirator, these women are guilty of murder whether or not you conclude they were ever present at the crime scene," Truc Do emphasized.

The prosecutor then got into forensics, and went over the coroner's testimony regarding McDavid's "crush or compression injuries . . . but not one single bone broken of the legs. And this is what Dr. Pena described as *bumper-height injuries*. There were no bumper-height injuries. And Mr. McDavid was five-feet-eleven."

The prosecutor took the jury back to when they viewed the murder weapon. "I watched you get on your hands and knees and your belly, and look underneath that Sable. You looked to the undercarriage. And I was wondering if you all imagined what it would have been like for Mr. McDavid, who was alive at the time that he was run over, to be under all that weight, under that hot metal.

"A number of you stood in front of the Mercury Sable, and if you did, you will understand what Dr. Pena meant when he said *bumper-height injuries*. If you are a victim of a hit-and-run, and you are standing or walking, and a car hits you, you are going to have injuries at bumper height. But not a broken bone to the legs, not a single laceration."

Truc Do had the surveillance video played for the jury of the murder weapon going through the alley, approaching the location where McDavid's body had been found later that night. The video shows the car slowing down and coming to a stop, and then it darkens out for four minutes and twenty-nine seconds. "What's going on in those four minutes and twenty-nine seconds?" the prosecutor asks the jury. "It's murder. It is not an accident. It is not a hit-and-run.

"What you just saw after the car darked out for four minutes and twenty-nine seconds is that it went in reverse. It backed up and then it went forward and out of sight. That is not a hit-and-run. Who strikes a person by accident, reverses, and then goes forward just to run them over in getting out of the area?

"This surveillance video tells you that it was murder in the dark. And that if it's murder of Mr. McDavid, a man whose death resulted in two-point-two million dollars to these women, that was the intent from the get-go."

The prosecutor then went over the cell phone records of Helen the night of June 21, 2005. Aside from the calls made to AAA for a tow truck for the Mercury Sable, which she made at 11:54 p.m. from the Chevron gas station, Helen made two other calls on her cell phone.

Holding a copy of Exhibit 264 in her hand, Do reminded the jurors that on the morning of June 22, Helen had made two cell phone calls that went to voicemail. The first was timed at 12:07 a.m., and the second was made at 12:37 a.m.

"The very next phone call that Helen Golay makes after calling Triple A is to Olga Rutterschmidt at one o'clock in the morning. Miss Golay is on her cell phone and the next call that you have on her phone records is at one-oh-two a.m. from Miss Rutterschmidt, calling her back.

"That's the first person that Miss Golay calls, moments after the murder. At one-oh-two in the morning, they're both mobile, cell to cell. That puts both of them at the crime scene. That puts Miss Golay certainly at the crime scene, and Miss Rutterschmidt is complicit."

Turning to the murder of Vados in November 1999, the prosecutor explained that because of his age, the only kind of policy available for him that would pay off would have been accidental death or dismemberment. When Vados was hit in 1999, Helen and Olga had collected $829,500.

The prosecutor brought up that when Vados' body had been found in 1999, while it was suspicious to law enforcement, they didn't have the evidence until they they had found McDavid's body in 2005.

"As Detective Willmon had testified, his death remained

shelved as a suspicious circumstance accident or hit-and-run until McDavid's body was found. Vados' case was re-investigated, and it was determined that his injuries and death were similar to that of McDavid's."

Finally, after speaking for almost two hours, Do's voice started getting raspy: "This is the summary of the case. You've got two women, two victims who are not connected by anything else other than the fact the women insured their lives, making them worth more to them dead than alive. And they collected two-point-eight million dollars on these men.

"When you consider the charge of murder and conspiracy on Mr. Vados, you do not need to decide whether either one of these women were present at the crime scene. You only need to use your common sense that Mr. Vados was not a coincidence. He was not an accident, but the victim of the same plot that took Mr. McDavid's life.

"Despite the overwhelming evidence, Mr. Diamond told you in his opening statement that his client didn't do it, but the daughter did it. And I'm not sure which direction he's going to go, whether it's the daughter did it alone or the daughter did it with Olga. And I'm actually going to leave the majority of the rebuttal on Mr. Diamond's defense for argument to Mr. Grace, because I'm not exactly sure which direction he's going to go.

"You've heard evidence or statements by Mr. Diamond that the insurance companies conspired. You heard statements by Mr. Diamond that Kecia Golay did it. The only thing I want to tell you about that argument is that it does not matter. If you believe that Kecia Golay is somehow in the mix, it does not change what is certain about Golay and what is certain about Rutterschmidt, and that is that they collected two-point-eight million dollars. And the only evidence you've seen in this case connects to those two women."

The prosecutor said she anticipated that Olga's lawyer was going to argue that she didn't know murder was part of the plan, that it was simply a conspiracy to commit insurance fraud between her and Helen, and she worked for Helen. And that all Olga did was buy signature stamps and join in the fraudulent applications, but didn't know that murder was part of the plan.

"What if I told you that Olga Rutterschmidt had a receipt itemizing the cost of the murder plot? You have that evidence. When they searched Olga Rutterschmidt's house, they found a number of items, one of which is Exhibit One-thirteen," the prosecutor told jurors.

"In her writing are notes reading 'Helen paid out,' and the costs are itemized. On the top of the note, she has calculated four hundred twenty-four by six, office, for a total of two thousand, five hundred forty-four dollars. The office space was the rent they paid in the building where Mr. Covington was housed. That was four hundred twenty-five dollars and they had rented the space for six months, and Helen paid out.

"Olga also itemized what she called *insurances* and how much she believed Helen paid out in premiums. And then Olga itemized sixteen hundred dollars for motels for McDavid after he and his friends were evicted from the apartment they had rented for him. Olga also itemized seventeen hundred dollars for security and the six thousand dollars that was paid for the murder weapon."

Truc Do told the jury that Olga was as much an accomplice as Helen, pointing out that she had collected a total of $901,143.

"The bottom line is that they saw these men as profit. They did not see them as human beings. They did not see them as men. They did not see them as men suffering homelessness issues. They saw them as profit. And that's what this case is about. And when Mr. Sklar and Mr. Diamond tries to argue to you that it's just an investment scheme, as morbid as it sounds, or that it's insurance fraud and that's all it is, don't believe it."

And with those words, Truc Do thanked the jury and sat down.

It was a powerful summation. The courtroom was suddenly quiet. Finally, the judge suggested that the jury "stand up and stretch" while he asked the lawyers to approach the bench for a sidebar conference.

After briefly conferring with counsel, the judge recessed the case until Friday, April 11, at 1:30 p.m., in order to have a cohesive argument from the defense in the case.

Chapter 18

The Defense Speaks—Closing Arguments

At 1:38 p.m. on Friday, April 11, it was time for Michael Sklar, the public defender representing Olga Rutterschmidt, to take the floor. With the brilliant closing by prosecutor Truc Do still fresh in their minds, Sklar knew he had a hard act to follow.

Judge Wesley was delayed on the freeway, and, with the approval of counsel on both sides of the aisle, Steven R. Van Sicklen, the supervising judge at the courthouse, sat in until Wesley could reach the courtroom.

Sklar's closing remarks were very erudite to say the least. He sounded like a professor at law school. For more than an hour, Sklar, a talented public defender, skillfully dazzled jurors. There is an old adage amongst trial lawyers: When the facts are against you, you argue the law and when the law is against you, you argue the facts. Sklar was very calm and compassionate as he spoke about his aging client.

He began by reminding jurors that a defendant in a criminal matter is presumed to be innocent. "It's the foundation of our criminal justice system, and that presumption places upon the prosecution the burden of proving Miss Olga Rutterschmidt guilty—and it's their burden to prove Miss Rutterschmidt guilty beyond a reasonable doubt.

"At the conclusion of the People's case, the defense on

behalf of Miss Rutterschmidt rested, and we rested, based upon our belief that the People's case in its entirety failed to prove beyond a reasonable doubt that Olga Rutterschmidt is guilty of these crimes.

"I didn't do an opening statement because again, we determined that the prosecution has failed to meet their burden, and therefore I didn't need to do an opening statement.

"This is my closing argument as to the interpretation of the facts as it applies to the law, and why I believe that the prosecution has failed to prove the case beyond a reasonable doubt against Miss Rutterschmidt."

Sklar then spent the next twenty or thirty minutes carefully going over and explaining the legal terms, such as the difference between a circumstantial evidence case as opposed to a direct evidence case, and the distinction made by the law between a circumstantial evidence case and a direct evidence case.

The public defender then dealt with the three theories of law that can lead to the liability for murder: that Olga was either the perpetrator of the crime, or, if not, she was an aider and abettor to the crime, or was a conspirator with regards to the crime.

"What it tells you is that even the prosecution doesn't know Olga Rutterschmidt's participation in this incident," Sklar said, trying to make the ambivalence clear.

The lawyer then bounced around and tried to show jurors that Olga had come from poor beginnings. That she'd lived through a world war that had severely affected her native Hungary. That she'd lived through the Depression and, when she came to the United States, lived in rent-controlled, low-income housing.

Sklar spoke of Olga's marriage to Endre, who, by 1976, was out of the picture. The lawyer put into very plain words the fact that she was not employed and, at the time of her arrest, drove an old late-model Honda, and lived on government assistance.

"Let's talk for a minute about Miss Rutterschmidt. She

was not savvy, and was not real bright. Her neighbor of thirty years, Douglas Crapeau, who testified in the case, said that he felt there was something wrong with her."

The lawyer recalled the testimony of Joel Coen, the attorney Olga had used to file litigation lawsuits over insurance policies. "He told you that in the short time he dealt with her, he felt there was something wrong with Olga Rutterschmidt. Things just didn't seem to sink in. He tried to explain things to her, but they just didn't seem to sink in."

Sklar then pointed out that even Detective Kilcoyne had told jurors that in his conversation with Olga, he had to tell her things twenty times and she still didn't seem to understand them. "In fact, on the jailhouse tape, the detective kept repeating to her, 'Olga, Olga, I told you that twenty times already.'

"When you think about it in terms of Olga Rutterschmidt's savvy, her mentality, and you think about the conversation that occurred, you have real insight into Olga Rutterschmidt's lack of savvy."

Olga's lawyer gave jurors an example of how "totally ludicrous" his client could be by saying that somehow she had gotten her hands on a movie script written by somebody else. "I think it was called *Timed Out*. But she tells Helen Golay, 'I typed Kenneth McDavid's name on it, and now we can get thirty million dollars for it.' Somehow, in her mind, you can get ahold of a paper script, type somebody's name on it, and then somehow make demands where somebody will pay thirty million dollars for your script, because you've typed somebody else's name on it.

"The importance of that is, it shows the savvy of Olga Rutterschmidt. I think the only reasonable inference is that Olga Rutterschmidt is not bright. What shall I say? She's simple-minded. She's simple-minded," he repeated.

Having set up the scenario that Olga was a poor soul to be pitied and that jurors should feel compassion for her because she was misunderstood, Sklar went on to tell the panel that Olga had become obsessed with Helen, who was smart and rich, owned real estate and fancy cars, and lived in Santa Monica.

"It's not about money; it's about being with Helen Golay. It's about being a part of this whole thing that she thinks is so smart, this wealthy Santa Monica thing," he told jurors.

"Once she started talking about this woman, she just didn't stop." The lawyer reminded jurors about the testimony of Olga's neighbor, Douglas Crapeau: "She was obsessed with Helen. In fact, she starts claiming she's working for Helen Golay to locate real estate for purchase, as if Helen Golay has retained Olga Rutterschmidt to find her real estate for her.

"As if Olga Rutterschmidt is somehow qualified to be Helen Golay's real estate broker. Ludicrous! Why is Olga Rutterschmidt saying that?

"Either Olga just so desperately wants to be a part of Helen Golay's life that she manufactures those statements, or quite possibly Helen Golay has already begun her manipulation of Olga Rutterschmidt."

The spin Sklar was suggesting to the jurors was that Olga's obsession with Helen was "unwavering, regardless of what happens." But after Vados' death, Olga had apparently concluded that Helen was ripping her off, and called the insurance company, telling them that Helen was cheating them, and that they shouldn't pay those policies.

Sklar then decided to push co-defendant Helen Golay's buttons by placing the blame on her for coming up with the scam to fraudulently insure Olga's friend, Vados.

"At the beginning, when Helen Golay first came up with this plan to insure Mr. Vados, I wonder if she ever really intended to kill him originally. She didn't start making these major financial investments until after Mr. Vados' death. And that's when Helen's operation and the funding of it started getting a lot bigger.

"Maybe she didn't even intend to kill him. And it's quite possible that Mr. Vados really did die in a hit-and-run accident. Maybe it was an accident. Maybe it was a third party. But that particular incident is substantially different than the incident regarding Mr. McDavid, to the extent that Mr. McDavid was drugged."

Sklar's reasoning to jurors was that Helen's plan hadn't then risen to the level of duplicity that it attained later on.

"As a result of the death of Mr. Vados, I believe the evidence is clear that Helen Golay became emboldened. She was determined to have a larger organization. And she was going to now start funding this out of pocket. And she convinced Olga that she was going to provide housing for homeless people in consideration for life insurance policies, convincing Olga that these policies secure reimbursement if the individuals died.

"It appears that's when Olga started working more full-time for Helen. Why do we know this? Why do we know Olga believes this? Because when Olga was speaking to Mr. Covington, she told him she works for people, or a boss, who gets housing for homeless for insurance policies. It's not unreasonable for Olga to believe this, because at this point, Helen is already housing Mr. McDavid and is paying for his housing in consideration for these insurance policies.

"I want to make this clear: This scheme now is fully financed by Helen Golay. She's paying insurance premiums. She's paying rent. She's paying business rent. She's paying for hotels. The importance of that is, the prosecution paid a lot of importance to a note found at Olga's residence entitled [sic] 'Helen's costs.' And it's got a list of costs that are supposed to be reimbursed to Helen out of the proceeds of insurance policies on Mr. McDavid's death.

"And the only place Olga could get that information from is Helen Golay."

The public defender had been talking almost an hour and, concerned that the jury might be tuning out, told them he was getting to the end of his argument in an effort to keep them on their toes.

"Let's talk about the Sable. To a certain extent, the Sable is a red herring. It doesn't mean anything if it was purchased by Olga or if it was purchased by Helen. It just doesn't really matter. We know Olga did not use it on the night that McDavid was killed. But where was the vehicle stored? When it's purchased, it's stored at Helen Golay's residence. It's stored there the whole time, as evidenced by Helen's neighbor Meilisa Thompson.

"Who was driving it the night of Mr. McDavid's death? Helen Golay was driving it, not Olga Rutterschmidt. Where was it towed on the night of the death? It was towed to Helen Golay's residence. Obviously it was fixed. Who had it [the Sable] when it was going to be abandoned after it was fixed? Helen Golay. It was in her possession and then abandoned in Hollywood.

"The People have made a big point about the fact that this place in Hollywood is near my client's residence in Hollywood. But who is it that had possession of that vehicle? Helen Golay. It's just another area where Helen Golay did not advise Olga Rutterschmidt of the full plan."

Sklar next attacked the surreptitiously taped statement. "The problem is that it actually shows Olga Rutterschmidt lacks knowledge of any plan of Helen Golay to kill. The tape itself shows that Olga did not participate in the murders. She did not aid and abet Helen Golay in the murders, and she did not conspire with Helen Golay to commit the murders.

"The tape shows that Olga Rutterschmidt did not know about Mr. McDavid's murder, and did not know about Mr. Vados' murder as of May eighteenth, 2006, eleven months after McDavid's death."

Sklar pointed out that on the day Olga and Helen were arrested, on the way to the federal courthouse to be arraigned, the two women made a quick stop at the Los Anglees Police Department, where they were put in a room together with a hidden video camera and audio recorders.

Sklar insists the stop was made "pursuant to a common investigative technique." Translation? Put them in a room together and see if they'll talk. And talk the two women did.

"In fact, Olga wouldn't stop talking. She just doesn't

stop talking. And she talked and talked and talked. And Helen Golay, she was scared. She was saying right from the beginning, *Shut up, shut up, don't talk to me. You keep talking, I'm going to be moved to another room.* She was worried because she knew what was going on. And Olga Rutterschmidt kept talking. And what did she talk about? She talked about insurance fraud. That's all she talked about."

The public defender reminded jurors that what Detective Kilcoyne did was to come into the room where Helen and Olga were being held and talking, and he mentioned something about some facts that needed to get down "about this murder," hoping to prompt the women to talk about murder.

Kilcoyne testified that the purpose for that was to let the women start talking about the murder. "So what happens after Kilcoyne says the word *murder*? He leaves the room and again Olga starts to talk away, and talks and talks and talks, and what does she talk about? She talks about insurance fraud.

"In order to convict my client of these crimes, you can't find merely she should have known. You must find that she knew. That she was either the perpetrator, and committed the act, or that she knew of the intention of Helen Golay, and either conspired with her or aided and abetted that.

"I can't tell you how a person could be that stupid. I can only tell you that Olga was that stupid. She was. We know she didn't know."

In the end, Sklar urged the jurors to find his client innocent, saying that the prosecution had not proven their case beyond a reasonable doubt. "That's why, at the conclusion of the prosecution case, on behalf of Miss Rutterschmidt, we rested, based upon our belief that they had not proven beyond a reasonable doubt that Olga Rutterschmidt was either the principal, aided and abetted Helen Golay with knowledge, or conspired with Helen Golay."

Judge Wesley arrived at his courtroom as Sklar was finishing his closing arguments, and took his seat at the bench.

After a fifteen-minute recess, it was time for Roger Jon Diamond to present his closing arguments.

He started off by reiterating his theory that Kecia Golay, Helen's 44-year-old daughter, had run down and murdered Kenneth McDavid in cold blood.

"But it has been living hell for Helen, going through this torture, being arrested for this particular offense, although technically she was not arrested for this offense for which she now stands trial. She was arrested for mail fraud by the federal government.

"What is this case all about? This case is about the insurance industry retaliating against Helen Golay because she, along with Olga Rutterschmidt, together came up with the insurance fraud schemes to defraud a number of insurance companies."

Diamond took a moment in his closing comments to lash out at Michael Sklar for taking a swing at Helen Golay by placing the blame for the murder at her doorstep.

"But Mr. Sklar has made a strategic mistake with respect to attempting to blame Helen Golay. To some extent, what he's seeking to do, and it's apparent, to try to get you to compromise, to say, *Well, we'll find Rutterschmidt not guilty and Golay guilty, and that way we'll be able to show the world that we are a fair jury.*

"Mr. Sklar is not a witness in this case. Neither is Mr. Grace, nor Miss Do, nor am I. So we, as lawyers, can only argue based upon the evidence that's presented to you in court.

"So Mr. Sklar, for strategic purposes, is suggesting that it was Miss Golay who actually drove the vehicle on the night of June twenty-first, 2005, and ran over Mr. McDavid. He said that, but he does not know. He was not there. So the question is, who was driving the vehicle that night? A vehicle, by the way, which Miss Rutterschmidt purchased on January twentieth, 2004.

"I'm not trying in any way to blame Miss Rutterschmidt for this particular case. I'm simply responding to a desperate attempt by Mr. Sklar to invite you to compromise and vote for guilty on one and not guilty on the other," he said, pointing out that it was Olga's job to find old, sick, homeless people and insure them, because homeless men don't live long lives.

The lawyer also accused Olga of recruiting younger men like Jimmy Covington, suggesting that she was planning to go out on her own and backstab her partner by insuring these men and then killing them, and not sharing the policy proceeds with Helen.

Diamond rationalized that Helen Golay was 77 years old and was not capable physically of doing what was attributed to her, not just by the prosecutor, but also by Sklar. "She not only is not capable of doing what has been contended that she did that evening, but she was not there," Diamond said.

The defense lawyer then took jurors through the history of the relationship between Helen and Olga with respect to the scam they'd run. "They're both involved with respect to the insurance case. No one is more at fault than the other. They had a scam going with respect to recovering on insurance policies by insuring people who would be expected not to live a long time.

"Mr. Vados was seventy-three years old at the time he died. And at the time, the insurance taken out on his life was for three policies for life, five for accidental death. And then Mr. Vados, unfortunately, died. And it is apparent that he died because he fell in an alley. He was an alcoholic."

Though a prosecution expert witness had testified that Vados' injuries couldn't have been inflicted by a car collision, Diamond explained that there was a possibility they could have, "because there was a heavy rainstorm that evening, and a lot of evidence was washed away.

"And so when he died, they [the police] made a claim around November seventh or eighth, 1999. That was unfortunate for Mr. Vados. He was killed in the alley. They made the claims, and what happens? One insurance company, Monumental Insurance Company, files what is called an *interpleader action* against Olga Rutterschmidt, against Helen Golay and against Kecia Golay."

According to a legal dictionary, an *interpleader* is a procedure when two parties are involved in a lawsuit over the right to collect a debt from a third party who admits the money is owed, but does not know which person to pay. The debtor deposits the debt with the court—interpleads— and asks to be dismissed from the lawsuit, then lets the claimants fight over the payment in court.

"Once that action was filed against Kecia Golay, she became aware of what was going on. That introduced her to the insurance scheme that her mother and Olga Rutter- schmidt were engaged in with respect to this particular technique for recovering money based upon the death of another human being.

"After that case is settled and Kecia is introduced to this concept of making money from the deaths of people who die in a certain way, and there's a lot of insurance on them, she then apparently calls and arranges for the purchase of a vehicle. The call was made on Kecia Golay's phone to Mexi- car to purchase the car.

"The central issue in this case is, who caused Mr. Mc- David's death? What evidence do we have? We have the auto club records. We have the surveillance video showing the Sable Mercury entering the alley. The whole case for the prosecution depends upon who was driving the vehicle.

"Who was in the vehicle? That's the number-one case for you to decide. The identity of the perpetrator."

Diamond offered the jury panel one reason why the driver could not be Helen—she wouldn't have called 411 information for the AAA number to get tow service; she would have used the 800 number on her membership card to call them directly.

And then the lawyer criticized the AAA auto club by accusing them of being behind the prosecution of his client "because the auto club got burned in this case. I gotta tell you, Triple A is not happy with Helen Golay. They feel they got hoodwinked.

"The auto club got burned to the extent of eight hundred thousand dollars. We have a copy of the check that the auto club issued to Helen Golay . . . eight hundred and ten thousand dollars [the $10,000 was for interest that they had to also pay]. The date of the check is October eleventh, 2005. The auto club is behind part of this prosecution in this case.

"But why was it important for the auto club to claim it was Helen Golay? That's their way of getting out of having to pay or being able to recover eight hundred and ten thousand dollars that they've paid on the auto club claim. The auto club got burned in this case, and they're going to teach these ladies a lesson. So what they do is send a representative to court to create the impression that Helen Golay made the call, because it's in the interests of the auto club not to accuse Kecia Golay, whose telephone was used to make the call, of driving the vehicle and causing this particular problem to Mr. McDavid.

"The auto club does not benefit if it's determined that Kecia Golay is the one who killed Ken McDavid. Because since Kecia was not the named beneficiary on the Triple A auto insurance policy, anything that Kecia would have done would not have jeopardized or would not have allowed Triple A to try to recover any money that was paid on the policy. So it's in the interest [of the auto club] to blame Helen Golay and nobody else.

"I submit to you that there was never a plan by Helen Golay and Olga Rutterschmidt to kill anybody. No plan to kill Ken McDavid, as there was no plan to kill Paul Vados."

The lawyer reminded jurors that Kecia was aware of insurance scams going on. "She knows what's going on, and she's not totally a stranger to these ladies, obviously—Helen is her mother. But she also knows Olga.

"But she doesn't know about the sophistication with respect to the two-year contestability clause. She just is anxious. She jumps the gun and she kills Mr. McDavid before many of these policies were in existence for over two years.

"If it were Helen who was involved in some scheme to kill, Helen certainly would not have any interest in making it difficult to collect on policies by killing Mr. McDavid before two years elapsed on many of these policies. It doesn't make any sense. What else ties in Kecia?

"So what happens on the night of June twenty-first, 2005? It's Kecia driving the vehicle, generally aware of an insurance scam going on, wanting to accelerate the process for whatever reason. Maybe she thought she could help her mother and Olga recover money in a different way, rather than waiting patiently for a homeless person simply to meet his death in some other way, say, by natural causes or being mugged in an alley.

"So what happens? The unexpected occurs; namely, the fuel hose is dislodged after Kecia runs over this person. It's a terrible situation. The fuel hose dislodges and the car is able to coast down the sloping alley to the Chevron station, where Kecia makes the call to Triple A."

Walking over to his client, who was wiping tears from her eyes, Diamond placed his hand on Helen's shoulder as he addressed the jury.

"This is an unbelievable nightmare that Helen Golay has been in. It's been horrible for her. It's unfortunate that two men are dead. She didn't do it. But she did involve herself in insurance fraud. And she should be punished for that, whatever the punishment is. But this is a travesty of justice. She has been falsely accused of the worst possible crime ever, murdering another human being."

And then Diamond walked over to where Michael Sklar was seated at the defense table and pointed a finger at him, accusing the public defender of "being a joint prosecutor" in an attempt "to curry favor."

Diamond was absolutely infuriated with the public defender. He attacked Sklar's accusation of Helen as a "desperate attempt. He doesn't have our evidence. We didn't prepare this case together, because lawyers have an individual duty to their respective clients."

Before concluding his closing argument on Friday, Diamond kept beating the drum over and over that Kecia was a suspect in the case, and reminded the jury that even the handwriting expert who'd testified said that he only took handwriting exemplars from suspects—and yes, a handwriting exemplar was taken from Kecia.

Because of the lateness of the day, the judge suggested that Diamond conclude his closing argument Monday morning before Deputy District Attorney Bobby Grace started his rebuttal of the case.

And so, on Monday, April 14, Diamond was back at it again, finishing his closing argument by shifting the blame in McDavid's death. Did Diamond's eleventh-hour turnaround in his defense strategy mean that he thought what he had told jurors the previous week was not going to work? Taking another approach, the lawyer reminded the jury that "Maybe Olga had different plans, maybe Olga had her own scheme, unknown to Helen Golay, to have these people killed.

"What we have here is a classic whodunit," Diamond told the jury, likening it to *Arsenic and Old Lace*. "You don't have a case frequently where two little old ladies are charged with such an atrocious crime. I would be the last one to say it's not suspicious. But you need more than suspicion to convict Helen Golay of murder.

"We'll concede it's pretty sleazy, what's going on with the insurance. These two little old ladies embarked upon a cockamamie insurance fraud scheme. But it's insurance fraud. It certainly isn't murder."

Diamond also discounted Sklar's earlier remarks that Olga was stupid. "Not so," says Diamond, shaking his head. "She was intelligent and intimately involved in the scheme."

He appealed to the jury to find Helen Golay not guilty because it was her daughter Kecia who'd murdered Kenneth McDavid.

"Please acquit Helen Golay of these terrible charges," Diamond pleaded.

After concluding his closing arguments, with the jury not in the courtroom, Diamond filed motions requesting that Helen be granted a separate trial as a result of Sklar's "antagonistic defense."

According to Diamond, Sklar's remarks in his closing argument "undermined my client's chance for a fair trial."

Judge Wesley, who often lost patience dealing with Diamond's many motions during the trial, cut him off this time, saying that the motion was denied. The judge reminded him that it was not "timely," and the lawyer should have made such a request before the start of the trial.

"If you want to blame Rutterschmidt for everything, you're welcome to do it, that's why we have two lawyers," the judge told Diamond.

That said, it was now time for Bobby Grace to have the last word in the case against Olga Rutterschmidt and Helen Golay.

Chapter 19

The Last Word

Monday, April 14, 2008. It was finally time for Deputy District Attorney Bobby Grace to get up and attack claims made by the two defense lawyers, and to answer any outstanding questions that might be lingering in the minds of jurors caused by their rhetoric.

Grace started off taking a shot at both defense lawyers, accusing them of arguing that Olga did it, that Helen did it, and that Kecia did it—in the process, presenting conflicting facts to the jury. He then said that the first person he would focus on was Helen.

"What does she have to say? *My daughter did it with Olga.* Then Helen throws a lot of stuff on the wall by saying the police and the DA are puppets of the insurance companies.

"The next thing they throw up is that old, sick, homeless people die earlier than other people. Then they again throw up that Kecia did it and that Kecia bought the car with Olga and that it was Kecia at the gas station. Finally, the death of Paul Vados was actually an accident."

Grace urged the jurors that, during deliberations, they "follow the money, follow the money" to find the motive for killing the men.

"Who got paid when Paul Vados was killed? Who got paid when Kenneth McDavid was killed?" Grace asked, pointing to Olga and Helen seated at the defense table.

"This is no coincidence, and this certainly wasn't an accident. This was all by the design of these defendants.

"The defendants weren't expecting Paul Vados to die naturally, as contended by Mr. Diamond. Maybe he forgot about the fact that defendant Rutterschmidt and defendant Golay had accidental death and disability coverage on Paul Vados. He could not die naturally. He had to die by accident, and in a way that both of these defendants could get paid. He had to die by a way that fit in the schedule of the insurance companies. They just don't pay you 'cause you died naturally when you have accidental death and disability coverage.

"That brings us to 'Kecia did it.' This is where Mr. Diamond's argument falls apart. Everything he said to you regarding Kecia Golay was pure speculation, conjecture, and—what my mother used to tell me—*if I could have, would have, should have.* He wishes it so. He wants to conjure up something that's so, but there's no evidence to support that Kecia Golay had anything to do with this, and I'm going to show you why.

"Kecia could not profit from Kenneth McDavid's death. Who could? Helen, to the tune of two-point-two million dollars for both Mr. Vados' death and Mr. McDavid's death. Kecia could only profit by killing her mother.

"There's absolutely no evidence that Kecia ever met Kenneth McDavid. None. Mr. Diamond cannot point to one scintilla—and that means any little bit—of evidence that would suggest that.

"What Kecia did was to commit an ID theft," Grace said. "She took the identification of Hilary Adler. But then what happens to that identification? Both counsel[s] completely ignore what happened to the ID of Hilary Adler. Based upon the evidence, that ID was used to purchase the murder weapon, because we know for a fact that Kenneth McDavid's DNA was on the bottom of that car that was used to murder Kenneth McDavid."

Grace then reminded the jury that the car salesman testified that *two* ladies had come to buy this car. "The only person that was seen around the Mercury Sable after it was purchased was the defendant, Helen Golay. And that Helen's neighbor, Meilisa Thompson, showed them photographs of red paint on the wheel of the car that was parked in the alley adjacent to Helen's house.

"The stolen information was in the possession of the defendants. Remember, what did defendant Olga Rutterschmidt have? She had the stolen ID on May eighteenth, 2006, when she was arrested and her apartment was searched. She had the information that was necessary to buy the murder weapon. She bought the murder weapon.

"And on that same date, police found the partial VIN number and partial license plate of the murder weapon in Helen Golay's notebook in her black Mercedes SUV that was parked at her Santa Monica house. The only reason she would have that information is because she used the murder weapon to kill Kenneth McDavid."

Grace took the jurors back to the gas station the night of June 21, 2005, and reminded them that the tow truck driver said it was an elderly woman above 40 at the gas station. "Mr. Diamond is trying to say that Kecia Golay was involved. But again, this is some more of his wishing and conjuring up evidence that's not there," he said.

Next Grace tore into the argument that the murder of Vados was actually an accident, and that Helen and Olga had lucked into the money they'd collected from his murder. "Who sinks money into paying premiums on policies for a seventy-three-year-old man, hoping he dies by accident? A considerable amount of money was being paid by defendant Golay in the quote, unquote that the victim Paul Vados dies by an accident that's covered by the insurance policy schedule. In other words, you don't get paid just because somebody died. It has to be a certain type of accident.

"What the defendants hit upon, and what their plan was, to have him killed, murdered by a car and make it look like an accident. This was a murder, not a hit-and-run."

Grace pointed out the similarities to what had happened with McDavid, which both defense lawyers conceded was murder. He cited the testimony of the coroner that the injuries sustained by both McDavid and Vados were similar. "The same crime scene, an alley, dark, alone, the victim's position in the middle of the roadway. There was no glass fragments, no car parts and— Use your common sense. There were no skid marks.

"Why is that important? Because both individuals were purposely run over. The individuals that ran them over didn't stop; they ran them over, crushing their bodies. That's why there are no car parts. That's why there are no glass fragments. And who got paid? Helen Golay and Olga Rutterschmidt in both cases."

Shifting gears, Grace ripped apart Olga's defense that Helen did it and that Olga didn't know murder was part of the plan. Grace attacked her lawyer for saying Olga was poor and stupid, and therefore would never have been involved in a murder because she didn't have the smarts to pull something like that off.

The prosecutor pointed out that if she was that stupid and mentally imbalanced and had no job, how come "she was able to collect almost one million dollars in six years of this murder plot? And she didn't put in a dime of her own money. Who fronted all the money? The defendant, Helen Golay. Who else could get almost a million dollars and not put up any of your money? And her attorney gets up here and calls her stupid? This is a terrible travesty. She's been totally mischaracterized.

"Olga Rutterschmidt is not dumb. She was very aware of the fact that she had been cheated on some of the policies regarding Kenneth McDavid, and she expressed her displeasure about that."

Grace replayed for the jurors the surreptitious videotaped conversation between Helen and Olga after their arrest. In it, Olga berates Helen for being too greedy and taking out too many "insurances" on the men. The prosecutor urged the panel to listen carefully or to follow the transcript so that they could pick up the subtle remarks that Olga makes, which would help them understand the complicated relationship between the two women.

"It was a relationship built of greed, which bred distrust and deception. Mr. Sklar argued that a big part of that was that the defendant, Helen Golay, had tried to cut Olga Rutterschmidt out of profits by applying for policies where there was no split with Olga. But in fact, Olga had deceived Helen Golay, trying to apply for $545,000 in policies on her own.

"They are both crooks, and when you both are crooks, neither one can trust the other. This was all about the money. Each of them had their own independent desire for money. And they were on equal footing.

"Do not be fooled. This was a murder. A murder plot, plain and simple. Not shenanigans, not insurance finagling. This is murder."

Another area that Grace highlighted was that up to a month before they were arrested, both Helen and Olga had tried to scope out more potential victims by stopping by at the Hollywood church.

"Mr. Sklar tried to argue that Olga Rutterschmidt was obsessed with Helen Golay, that she wanted to be with her. To do everything to be like her. She was obsessed about Helen Golay making more money than her. This is why the tape is so great, because you can go right to it and you can see all the references that the defendant, Olga Rutterschmidt, makes about the money, and the fact that Helen Golay had had all these extra policies."

Grace raised a significant point that may have hit home for jurors when he talked about "blood money. When you kill people for money and there's several people involved, that blood gets on everybody's hands.

"You can bet that Helen Golay is not going to pay fifty percent of the proceeds to Olga for not doing work. She would have to put in work. And you know that Helen is cheap, because you saw on the tape, she was complaining and warning Olga about the attorney fees that they might have to pay if Olga cut loose one of her attorneys, that they had already filed suit. This is a woman who keeps track of her money.

"These men were sacrificed at the whim of these two defendants. And let's get something straight: Mr. Diamond, in his argument, tried to refer to the defendants as *little old ladies*.

"And when you were being *voir dire*d to determine whether you could be fair and impartial jurors in this case, you made a promise, you promised Miss Do and I, and the defense attorneys, that you would not convict these defendants based on their age or the way that they looked.

"Similarly, you said you would not use those facts to have sympathy for these defendants, and Miss Do and I are going to hold you to that promise."

Wrapping up his rebuttal, Grace reminded the jury that what the two defendants had done was "by far the worst of the worst. They didn't need the money. They weren't poor and destitute. They went out of their way to target men who had nothing. The only qualifications to get on their murder list were that these men needed help. They needed help and they got, not help, but a noose by these two defendants so that they could get paid.

"They targeted men who are invisible in our society, and they did that for a purpose. They knew that the insurance companies, and possibly the police, would overlook these men because they didn't have money. Apparently they did not have families that came looking for them. They were targeted because of their circumstances, because of where they stood in life. And the defendants spent from before 1997 up through 2006 plotting murders for profit in secrecy. This was a conspiracy. By its very nature, it's secret.

"And in that secrecy, in that darkness, these defendants thought that they would never be brought to justice, because things were clouded. But their undoing was their greediness, their deceit, their duplicity, and their lies.

"Because of these defendants' greed, they got caught. And that greediness was able to shine a light so that their guilt could be exposed. And in that light, these victims can be seen for the human beings that they were."

Chapter 20

Deliberations and Verdict

It was late Monday afternoon by the time Deputy District Attorney Bobby Grace had finished his rebuttal in the murder-for-profit case. Although there was less than an hour remaining before court would recess for the night, Judge Wesley nonetheless handed the case over to the nine-man, three-woman panel, after nearly two days of closing argument from attorneys, to give them a head start in the deliberation process.

Before closing arguments, the judge had instructed the jury that their decision would be based on the evidence in the case and that he would be giving them instructions on the law. To make understanding the law easier, each juror was given a booklet that the judge and the lawyers had prepared days earlier in an effort to simplify any questions that might arise during deliberations.

Because it was a lengthy trial, the judge consulted with the defense lawyers and the two prosecutors, and it was decided that the alternate jurors would not be dismissed, but would be taken to a separate room from the deliberating jury to await the outcome of the case.

Judge Wesley also took time before sending out the jury to give them some hands-on instruction, such as defining *reasonable doubt.* A reasonable doubt is just that: The proof must be so conclusive and complete that all logical dispute of it is removed from the mind of the ordinary person. The legal dictionary defines *reasonable doubt* as "a doubt based upon reason and common sense"—the kind of doubt that would make a reasonable person hesitate to act.

The judge also explained the elements needed to convict the women of murder, and put into plain words what constituted conspiracy, giving examples on how to define *aiding and abetting*, and what that term means as related to the case.

The judge also reminded the jurors that they must not consider in their deliberations the fact that Helen and Olga did not testify as evidence of their guilt.

For five weeks, ever since testimony in the case had begun back in March, the jury had been keeping an ongoing daily diary, writing down, in school composition books, elements of the proceedings that they considered vital to the case. Those notebooks and the 277 exhibits the prosecution had presented during the trial, plus the dozen or so defense exhibits, were also sent into the deliberation room for the jury to consider.

Because of the lateness of the day, the judge only let the jury deliberate for an hour, then ordered them to be back in court on Tuesday, April 15, at 9 a.m., to resume their deliberations.

The panel was fast at work all morning debating the merits of the case. It wasn't until the afternoon that they buzzed the court twice, signaling that they had a question.

The courtroom was virtually empty except for the families of Paul Vados and Kenneth McDavid, who were keeping a vigil.

Once the lawyers and the court reporter were assembled, both Helen and Olga, looking nervous and exhausted, were escorted by a sheriff's deputy out of a nearby holding cell to seats next to their lawyers. They tried not to react, but both of them looked bewildered, not knowing which way to stare. Olga appeared disheveled. Usually she wore a plastic barrette that held her hair neatly in place, but a closer look showed that she had instead used a broken hair roller that she'd twisted to tame her long tresses—unsuccessfully.

The judge showed the lawyers the note and then read it in open court. The panel wanted to know what would happen if they were not unanimous on one of the criminal counts.

The interpretation of the note took courtroom observers by surprise. The defendants appeared worried. Olga reached over to ask her lawyer a question. Helen just stared at the ceiling. Did that mean the panel was close to rendering a verdict—so soon?

After consulting with the lawyers, the judge referred the jurors to an instruction he had given them earlier that they should try to reach agreement on a lesser charge. The only lesser charge possible in the case was second-degree murder, rather than first-degree.

Because of the way their note was worded, suggesting they were close to a conclusion, the judge decided to ask the panel if they had reached any verdict. They indicated that they had reached some partial verdicts and said they had placed them in a sealed envelope.

The judge ordered that the verdicts be placed in his chamber safe until they could be read in open court on Wednesday, April 16.

That day, Judge Wesley was seated at the bench and the panel were all in the jury box. No one could have predicted that the jury would reach a verdict so soon after the start of deliberations. The tension inside the courtroom was mind-boggling. It was almost scary, the room deathly silent. The quiet scene was similar to when the eye of a hurricane passes over and the atmosphere is eerily still. The only sound was from the judge as he tore open the envelope and read the five verdicts on the sheet that had been prepared for the deliberating jurors.

Helen was convicted on two counts each of first-degree murder and conspiracy for taking out millions of dollars in life insurance policies on Kenneth McDavid and Paul Vados. She looked down and bit her lip, then buried her face in her hands. It seemed for a moment that she was trying not to cry, but then she became teary-eyed.

The reading of the verdicts seemed anticlimactic. "She's very upset that jurors agreed with the prosecution that it was Helen who called the auto club for a tow. But she's confident in the appellate process," Roger Diamond told reporters later, during a brief recess. "One of the major issues in the appeal will be whether jurors should have been allowed to see a DVD of a surreptitious recorded videotape in jail between the two women shortly after they were taken into custody."

Diamond appeared shocked at the guilty verdicts of his client. But that didn't stop him from lashing out at Olga's lawyer, public defender Michael Sklar, for suggesting in his closing argument that Helen had driven the car that ran over McDavid without Olga having any knowledge of the murder plot.

"You might say that the ladies did not do very well today," Diamond admitted.

Olga, on the other hand, was confused, and didn't understand her conviction: She was found guilty on one count of conspiracy to murder McDavid for financial gain.

Relatives of Vados were satisfied with the verdicts. "Their plots were pure evil. We have no pity for these women," Stella Vados said.

Because the jury had not finished their deliberations as they pertained to Olga, the judge sent them back for further discussion. It soon became obvious to veteran courtroom observers that the jury was struggling on reaching a verdict on the second conspiracy count as it related to Vados, and on either of the murder counts against Olga for Vados and McDavid.

Olga had been stoic as Helen's verdict was read. At first, she simply put her chin in her hand, and then she glanced around the courtroom as if looking to see if there were any familiar faces in the audience. But neither Olga nor Helen ever had any close friends or relatives attend the trial.

What made the scene so surreal was that two years earlier, the girls were virtually on top of the world: eating dinner out every night; going to an occasional movie.

Helen, at least, had always looked glamorous, visiting her hairdresser two or three times a week to get her bleached-blonde hair teased into elaborate updos, and always wearing tight-fitting dresses more appropriate for the body of a Paris Hilton. Both women now looked frail and haggard, facing life in prison without any possibility of parole.

A short while after the jury resumed deliberations, they buzzed twice, indicating that they had a question, and back they came into the courtroom. This time the panel wanted testimony of three witnesses re-read to them, and also asked that they be given a laptop so they could review all the DVDs that were in evidence, including the videotaped conversation between Helen and Olga after their arrest.

The read-backs the jury wanted were those of Olga's long-time neighbor, Douglas Crapeau, who said that at Olga's urging, he'd brought a gun to McDavid's apartment; Patrick Lamay, who'd been thrown out of McDavid's apartment on orders of Olga; and Maria Zamarripa, the on-site manager of the building where Vados had lived, who'd testified that she believed Olga's crying, after learning Vados had died, had been sincere.

The video needed to be viewed again to ascertain one important point: that neither woman discusses or brings up *murder*, even though Detective Kilcoyne, at one point while they are being taped, mentions murder to them.

On Thursday, April 17, at the request of the jury, the judge ordered the attorneys to return to court to make additional arguments so that the panel could decide the remaining counts in the case: the conspiracy count involving only Vados, and the charge that Olga had murdered McDavid and Vados.

In the second round of closing arguments, prosecutor Truc Do said that "there is not a single example in this case that any of us can point to in which Miss Rutterschmidt has ever spoken the truth about the victims, She lied to Norma Ceja, Zamarripa's daughter, when she said, 'I'm Mr. Vados' daughter.' She lied to all the insurance companies that you've seen in this case when she said, 'I'm Mr. Vados' cousin. I'm

Mr. McDavid's cousin.' She has never spoken the truth when it came to her relationship with the victims in this case.

"You are asked to believe that this woman cared for Mr. Vados based on nothing more than what comes from her, no other source of evidence. Mr. Sklar wants you to believe that Olga Rutterschmidt grieved and mourned the death of Mr. Vados. That she was hurt when he became missing. That she was hurt when he showed up dead.

"What did Miss Rutterschmidt do in between the time she was worrying and crying for Mr. Vados? She lied about the circumstances of Mr. Vados' disappearance to a police officer. On November seventeenth, 1999, Miss Rutterschmidt went into a police station and filed a false missing persons report, claiming she was Mr. Vados' cousin and claiming that he had gone missing on November fifth, 1999. That's what she was doing between the time she was worrying and crying for Mr. Vados."

When Olga's public defender Michael Sklar had argued that his client could not have plotted the murder of Vados, the prosecutor urged jurors to ask themselves, "Why would she file a missing persons report, lying about the circumstances in which this man disappeared?"

Truc Do also pointed out to the jury that when Maria Zamarripa had told Olga that Vados was missing, Olga told her he had died in an accident.

"She not only lied to the police. She lied with Helen Golay, the woman that you have convicted of murdering Paul Vados for profit. And they are both there at the police station, lying together about the circumstances in which Mr. Vados had disappeared."

The prosecutor said that Sklar would argue to jurors that Olga was simply the employee of Helen, and that she got duped. "Golay is not the mastermind behind this. They are both fifty-fifty beneficiaries. They are both fifty-fifty partners in this entire scheme, which is a plot to murder for profit.

"She was not being duped by Helen Golay," the prosecutor argued. "She's very much in the thick of the plot with Miss Golay.

"She is very much the mastermind behind this, as is Miss Golay." Do noted that Olga is heard on the surveillance tape talking to Helen about starting a new business with a "similar setup.

"And what was she talking about? She's talking about setting up additional businesses, much in the same way as she urged Miss Golay, after Mr. Vados had only been in the ground for seven months, to embark upon another insurance fraud scheme. And this is what she said:

" 'See, the way I wanted it, it would be no problem. You fucked up this.

" 'I wanted a new business for two million dollars . . . It's all fucked up now. I had a business ready to set up . . . That's what I had in mind, see? It's all fucked up now. I had a business, ready to set up.'

"This doesn't show that she's being duped. This doesn't show that she is just the employee following Miss Golay. She is very much the mastermind behind Miss Golay.

"She is talking on that tape about murder and collecting life insurance policies. She's got two dead bodies, and has collected millions of dollars, and is talking about a new business with the same setup.

"When you hesitate to believe that she's capable of doing something as evil as plotting to murder someone that she had a relationship with, think of Mr. McDavid," Truc Do said.

The prosecutor urged jurors not to believe the defense when they brought up that Olga had paid rent and provided food for Vados and McDavid because she cared for them. "It was all a ruse, as were her tears when Vados died. Is she capable of feigning grief and hurt? Of course she is."

Portraying Olga as "a cold-hearted killer" who'd bought the car and held on to it for eighteen months, the prosecutor said, "so each day that she looked into Mr. McDavid's eyes, a human being . . . somebody she had conversations with, visits with—and she looked this man in the eye and knew she was going to kill him to collect three-point-seven million dollars . . . She not only knew she was going to kill him, but she knew exactly how.

"So if you question if Miss Rutterschmidt is capable of murdering someone . . . she was up close and personal. What kind of a person is capable of living with murder in their heart for seven hundred and twelve days?" the prosecutor asked.

The public defender's response was delayed more than two hours because a juror did not feel well and did not return to court after a morning break. Judge Wesley said he hoped to continue the re-arguments later in the day.

At about 2 p.m. the jury buzzed once, indicating that they were ready to resume hearing arguments.

Michael Sklar told jurors that "there are people on the panel that must have this nagging feeling, 'I think she did it.' There are people that must have this nagging feeling, 'I'm not sure it's been proven.'"

Sklar suggested that jurors would be able to hold their heads high if they found there wasn't enough evidence against Olga. "That's justice, and you should own that.

"The question really is, Has the state proved beyond a reasonable doubt each and every element of the crimes charged? This is not about speculation. It's not about guessing. . . . It's not about passion and prejudice.

"If one or more of you decide that you need to further deliberate on a count that was read before we discussed this conspiracy [in re-arguments], you have a right to ask your foreperson to send a note to the judge to say that 'I want to reconsider the verdict that was read on my behalf in court,'" Sklar said near the end of his argument.

The re-argument concluded at 3:30 p.m. The panel was sent back to the jury room to continue their deliberations.

Within a short time, those who were still sitting in the almost-empty courtroom could hear loud muffled shouts coming from behind the oak door where the sitting jury was presumably fast at work.

The noise was unexpectedly punctuated by the sound of two buzzes, signifying that the jurors had a note for the judge.

It took almost thirty minutes for the bailiff to find the prosecutors and defense lawyers, who had scattered throughout the courthouse at the conclusion of the re-argument. When the note came out, Stella Vados and her boyfriend, and Sandra Salman, her brother Robert, and their lawyer, Gloria Allred, were the lone holdouts in the courtroom spectator section.

When everyone was finally assembled, Judge Wesley informed the lawyers that the note read that they were deadlocked on two counts, but had made a decision on the third. With that, the judge buzzed the jurors, giving them the go-ahead to enter the courtroom. When they were seated, the judge asked the foreman to read the verdict.

After hearing the new round of arguments, the foreman said, the panel had convicted Olga of the first-degree murder of McDavid, but was deadlocked on the remaining murder charge related to Vados, and on conspiracy.

As the Thursday murder verdict was read, Olga turned to her lawyer and opened her mouth in an expression of disbelief, and began weeping.

Without giving the judge a clue as to which way they were leaning, the foreman said they were at an impasse, 11–1 on the charge that Olga had murdered Vados, and 10–2 on conspiracy to murder him for financial gain.

Before ordering the panel back on Monday, April 21, to resume deliberations, Judge Wesley had to replace a member of the regular jury who could no longer serve, as a result of his having made prior travel plans weeks earlier.

The replacement of the new juror with an alternate meant that the reconstituted panel had to start all over on its talks regarding Olga's two outstanding counts.

But it took the new jury about an hour to announce that they had reached a verdict, convicting Olga of first-degree murder for financial gain in the death of Paul Vados, and of conspiracy. As it was being read in open court, Olga began scribbling on a yellow legal pad, but otherwise showed no outward emotion.

After the verdict, a jubilant Bobby Grace told reporters that the prosecution had been able to show that the women were fueled by greed. "It's clear that money was a driving force behind these women. We were able to use that motive as a big foundation for our case, and that was important. They spent a lot of their time worrying about money, trying to get money."

Truc Do put it this way about the two women she had prosecuted: "They didn't need it, but they wanted it. The motive was definitely greed."

The reporters covering the trial wanted to speak with the jury, but Judge Wesley sent out word to the waiting press corps that the jurors had indicated they did not wish to speak with reporters and left the downtown criminal court building without commenting.

But Bobby Grace did speak with the panel after the verdicts were published in the courtroom, and offered details of their deliberations. "They seemed to be a cohesive group," he said. "They were pretty convinced of the McDavid murder right away. Two jurors said they had more trouble deciding whether Olga was guilty of Vados' murder.

"In fact, they felt that in some ways, she was smarter than Helen Golay, because it was Golay that fronted all the money to house the men for two years, and that Rutterschmidt didn't put up any money, but collected nearly one million dollars."

After the jurors said they were hopelessly deadlocked, the judge had asked them to try again, and gave them a three-day weekend. That appeared to do the trick, Grace said.

"I think it just took the weekend for those one or two jurors to realize that the evidence as to the Vados counts was not any different than the McDavid murder," Truc Do added.

The prosecutor thought that perhaps jurors were a tad

slower to convict Olga because there was some evidence that she had a "caretaking relationship" with the victim.

The jury also told Bobby Grace that they were impressed with the evidence showing that Helen had called for a tow truck not far from where McDavid's body was found in the alley. They also told Grace that they didn't put too much credence in Sklar's contention that Olga was stupid. "They felt Olga was just as big a part of the whole scheme as Helen," Grace said.

Before the women were taken back to the holding cell, Diamond asked Judge Wesley if Helen could be sent to the California Institution for Women in Chino, 35 miles east of Los Angeles, so that her 8-year-old granddaughter Sophie could visit her with her mother, Kecia.

The judge explained that such decisions were up to the Department of Corrections and Rehabilitation, and that he had no authority to make such a request.

After the verdict was announced, Sklar said he would begin working on an appeal for a new trial for Olga, but would not have any other comment about the case.

For the Los Angeles County District Attorney's Office, the conviction of both Helen and Olga was a clean sweep across the board. In a statement, District Attorney Steve Cooley said, "Justice has now been served in the murders of two homeless men. The final chapter will be when the defendants are sent to prison for the rest of their lives for the killings that were spawned out of greed."

Los Angeles Detective Rosemary Sanchez, who, with Dennis Kilcoyne, had investigated the case from practically day one, told reporters that the crucial piece of evidence was the discovery that Helen had called AAA asking for service for a disabled 1999 Mercury Sable station wagon about 1,000 feet from McDavid's body the night he was run over.

Kilcoyne agreed with prosecutors that the girls did not need the money. He said Helen was well off and that authorities had seized somewhere in the neighborhood of $800,000 to $900,000 from Olga's bank account that had not been spent. "These women are clearly evil, evil people," he said outside court. "To prey on the homeless and disadvantaged and weak, it's no different than picking on children."

Patrick Dixon, head of the district attorney's Major Crime Division, said the verdict resulted from "a lot of hard work" and "inter-agency cooperation" of the Los Angeles Police Department's Robbery-Homicide Division, the FBI, and the California Department of Justice and Department of Insurance.

Sentencing day for Helen was scheduled for June 24, but was delayed until July 15 when Olga was set to learn her fate. Prosecutors had asked the court for the delay to spare the families of the victims the trauma of having to deliver their impact statements twice to the judge.

By the time Tuesday, July 15, rolled around, the ninth-floor courtroom where the trial had been held was packed with police officers, detectives, deputy district attorneys and such distinguished reporters as Linda Deutsch of the Associated Press. Seated in the audience were the families of Vados and McDavid, ready to give their victims' impact statements to the judge.

As usual, all eyes focused on the door where Olga and Helen were waiting in holding cells to make their grand entrance. A hush fell in the room as the door opened and a sheriff's deputy brought out the two guests of honor and led them to the defense table. Both were wearing bright orange prison jumpsuits, only this time they had some added jewelry wrapped around their waists—chains that were hooked to their wrists, and handcuffs. The stringent security was a real-life reminder to the two women that they were convicted killers.

Judge Wesley got right to the business at hand and meted out the punishment for the Black Widows by sentencing them to two life prison terms without the possibility of parole.

"The men needed only food, water, and shelter," he told both women. "They needed a helping hand. They thought they were getting that helping hand from Ms. Golay and you, Mrs. Rutterschmidt. Instead, these unfortunate men were sacrificed on your altars of greed."

It seemed that the judge was gunning for Olga, because he next addressed his remarks to her, hitting her right between the eyes.

"During this trial, Mrs. Rutterschmidt, you recognized something in Ms. Golay that you had not recognized of yourself when you pointed your finger at her and said, 'You're greedy.'"

The judge, of course, was referring to the secretly videotaped conversation between the two women in which Olga repeatedly accuses Helen of greed for having gotten additional life insurance policies, which Olga says led to their arrest.

The judge said he'd researched the meaning of the word *greed* and found definitions including "A selfish desire for money, with no intention of using it, just the desire to have it."

Judge Wesley said he condemned them for the killings and then brought out that, although there was no possibility of parole, a probation pre-sentence report on the women indicated that "they have no conscience and are a serious threat to the community."

The two women sat in silence and appeared defiant as the judge handed down their sentences and made his remarks.

It was then time for the families of Vados and McDavid to speak. For weeks during the trial, they'd heard testimony on how their loved ones were murdered, and their bodies crushed. They'd seen pictures of victims lying in the alley, in their own blood. The families sobbed and waited, knowing that they would finally have their say, and let the judge and the world know their feelings about Helen Golay and Olga Rutterschmidt.

"My brother, Ken McDavid, did not deserve to die the way he did," Sandra Salman told the judge. "I never thought I would be sitting in a criminal court watching a trial in which my own brother was the victim, murdered by two elderly women in their seventies." Choking up as she described the devastation the death of her brother had caused her family, her lawyer, Gloria Allred, placed an arm around Sandra's shoulder.

"These two women conspired to take my brother's life purely for monetary gain, and they deserve to spend the rest of their lives in prison. . . . it makes me very sad to see how low these women have sunk in this country, where human life is equated with personal profit. These women have killed two men that we know of, and their only regret is that they were caught.

"I am glad this nightmare is finally coming to an end," Salman said, but added that it had been cruel of Helen and Olga not to tell her the whereabouts of her brother's remains, so that they could be taken to his family plot.

Stella Vados described what had happened to her father as "inhumane. I want to know why my father's life had to end like this. He didn't deserve that. No one does. The defendants were greedy and selfish, and that is why they committed murder."

Gloria Allred told the judge that she hoped the case would turn the spotlight on the homeless, and pointed out that they "are an extremely vulnerable population," and that it was "our duty to assist and protect them."

As for the life sentences handed down by the judge, Allred said, "This is tantamount to the death penalty. They will die in prison. I think that's a just sentence."

Outside the courtroom, Roger Diamond said he would appeal Helen's conviction. "She's clear-thinking, and she's very upset, obviously, that she's been convicted. She believes she's innocent. She's very concerned about the future."

Before court adjourned, the judge denied him a motion for a new trial. Diamond is also alleging misconduct by Sklar.

Truc Do was satisfied with the stiff sentences given Helen and Olga. "The defendants orchestrated the most evil and deliberate murders that I and my co-prosecutor, Bobby Grace, have seen in our careers as prosecutors.

"Life without parole was quite a lenient sentence," she said. "I think that age was a factor in terms of this office's decision to not seek the death penalty, which they were clearly eligible for."

Nine days after they were sentenced, Helen and Olga were awakened during the middle of the night and bused to the maximum-security facility in Chowchilla, 260 miles north of Los Angeles. Chowchilla is the largest women's prison facility in the United States, with a capacity, as of September 2007, of 4,230 prisoners.

Helen and Olga have made friends at their new home. The girls can exchange their stories in the prison yard during recreation hour at Chowchilla with such infamous inmates as Betty Broderick, the 61-year-old former San Diego socialite convicted of the November 5, 1989, murder of her former husband, Dan, and his second wife, Linda; 79-year-old serial killer Dorothea Puente, who ran a boarding house in Sacramento and cashed the Social Security checks of her elderly and mentally disabled boarders, killing those who complained; and Susan Atkins, at 60, the youngest of their new colleagues, who, with Charles Manson and others, killed nine people, including actress Sharon Tate, the wife of director Roman Polanski.

A convicted defendant is entitled under American law to appeal his conviction in an effort to overturn the jury's finding of guilt. As of going to press, neither Helen Golay's nor Olga Rutterschmidt's appeal has yet been resolved.